D1557412

ROMAN GOVERNMENT'S RESPONSE TO CRISIS

A.D. 235–337

RAMSAY MacMULLEN

NEW HAVEN AND LONDON, YALE UNIVERSITY PRESS, 1976

CONTENTS

ILLUSTRATIONS

PREFACE

On the earlier edge of the least-known stretch of Roman imperial history, one feels first its chilly shadow like a traveler approaching the Alps toward the close of an autumn day. No more than a setting sun shines on the Antonines; Severan times grow darker yet; and at their end, with the murder of the young Alexander in 235, blackness settles down. The historian thereafter pursues his way through what he feels to be a complex mass of many vast events almost hidden from him by the obscurity of his sources. He emerges into a gradually clearing light, but into a different country—as if he had entered the depths of Monte Bianco and discovered an exit from Mont Blanc.

Before and After differ, that much he can see. The connecting, explanatory links he can hardly join into a sequence of cause and effect. He is accustomed to begin his study of a period with the political narrative. That means the story of great persons, for example, emperors. Three cover more than two thirds of the century on which the following pages focus: Gallienus, Diocletian, Constantine. Surely history can be made out of their reigns. But no one who has tried to write a biography of Constantine can say at the end of his efforts, "Now I know this man." Diocletian's image must be seen distorted through the fires of burning churches and polemical tracts. As for Gallienus, the fullest "contemporary" account reaches us in the works of six men, the Scriptores Historiae Augustae, who after many decades of scholarly debate resolve themselves into a single mischievous and nameless figure writing some generations later than the period pretended. He (or they) cannot be trusted an inch; so there can never be a "Life," at best only a "Life and Times" of Gallienus. Lesser rulers with their commanders, governors, and courtiers are correspondingly less reported, though there are plenty of them. Indeed, it can be only arbitrarily determined which among some scores of them are to be called "real" as opposed to would-be emperors, and whether Achilleus is Domitianus, Uranius is Sampsigeramus, or (in short) what on earth is going on. The dizzy tumble of reigns, plots, droughts, raids, wars, deaths, and plagues across an era that must have been fateful and dramatic in the highest degree remains for us incorrigibly confused.

There is, however, a level of events lying just beneath the political narrative, a level of developing, heavily pressing problems and responses to those problems. Here continuity may be found, for they were long-lasting. Here, too, a much more richly documented and intelligible setting for emperors may be found within the circle of their advisers and higher officials, whether at the center or on mission to the provinces. What they thought and did to meet the dangers of a dark time is what I try here to describe.

During the later stages of my work, I was fortunate enough to be based in Oxford. I must acknowledge the support of the National Endowment for the Humanities that made this possible; and, although this is not the place to acknowledge also all the cordiality and courtesy offered me by many persons in and out of the university during my stay, I must certainly record my obligations to the various collections I worked in—especially my thanks to the Librarian of the Ashmolean Library and his marvelously expert and helpful assistants.

Finally, I am in debt to Professor P. A. Brunt, Dr. A. J. Graham, Dr. C. E. King, Dr. H. Chadwick, and Professors N. Lewis and O. M. Pearl for their generous sharing of knowledge on specific points indicated in the notes below, and most of all to Professor F. G. B. Millar, for providing corrections and improvements to the entire manuscript. It is pleasant to recall everything that makes this book, its faults aside, the work of a transatlantic fraternity.

Christmas 1975   R. MacM.

1

THE PERCEPTION
OF DECLINE

If the half century after 235 is approached in the manner
of its contemporary historians and through the most
salient and accessible facts, its chief features can be arranged in a comprehensible line. First, foreign wars. Alexander Severus' unsuccessful handling of these prepared his
death. These too prevented his successors from gaining a
firm seat in the throne they scrambled up to. Such recurrent failure to restore political stability generated civil
strife as much as it attracted invasion. Augusti (convenient
title, claimed by pretenders as by the more legitimate
figures in purple) had therefore to arm themselves on two
fronts. They needed money in unprecedented quantities,
and laws and men somehow to produce it. Armies, bureau-
cracies, and taxes all grew suddenly, simultaneously. At
the same time, the economy in the areas closest to the
scenes of wars became less able to meet the demands
placed on it, because it was pillaged and fought over; and

that combined mint master and paymaster, the desperate emperor of whatever reign, accordingly stretched his supplies of silver over a larger and larger bulk of more and worse coinage. Inflation set in, to a degree unprecedented. With this (as with a super-added plague, divinely appropriate to cap the whole structure of catastrophe), even folk inside the least disturbed areas like Campania or southern Gaul had to reckon, and adapt their lives to it. Those who could not adapt to inflation were the losers, most of all the saving classes, the people with money out on loan, the small-town well-to-do on whom so much of imperial success had rested for so long. They joined the rural poor in a readiness for desperate experiment. If the incumbent emperor was only an enemy, try another; if Rome had failed, try independence. Like ice floes gently and not very far detached from the parent body by great forces, two parts of the empire split off for a decade or so: one enormous section of the East, another even bigger in the West. All that Augustus had compacted, that Hadrian had decorated, or Marcus Aurelius labored to preserve, groaned, cracked apart, decayed, ceased to function, or was seen as inimical.

The study of every aspect of this period needs the nourishment of evidence that simply does not exist. One scholar complains of a dearth of data concerning the senatorial order, another concerning internal trade taxes, another concerning Samian pottery, and a fourth concerning city elites [1]—a random poll of frustration, but significant, since it touches subjects that should have left abundant traces of themselves. Even testimonies to what we know must have happened are rare (though a little less so than narrative accounts that tell us what to look for): people swept away by raiding armies and laments for "our brothers' and sisters' captivity";[2] thanks that a local patriot "at his own cost to the present site transferred Fortuna Victrix, along with statues of Victories, from a deserted, untended location";[3] or the horrified report from some besieged city, "Such things have gone on as never were since time began: now it's cannibalism and not war."[4] No triumphs, then, no worshipers, but much fighting.

A fuller catalogue can be drawn from an astrologer whose handbook of the art in some chronologically vague way sums up the turn of the third century.[5] A person of that time who presented his horoscope for analysis evidently expected to find in his life, again and again, "the burden of poverty, so he will hardly have supplies of daily nourishment," "the loss of all he owns," "the undermining of his finances and great enemies and frequent tumults on the part of the populace," "children put out to die," "often made captive and from free birth dragged down to slavery," "soldiering laborious and lingering forever in barren regions," "frequent moving about of residence, always in foreign regions," "a condition like servitude, so as to be always under another's power," "fetters, jails, imprisonment," "exile and conviction," "the flogging of condemned men," "entanglement in great debts," and so forth, with crushing repetition.

Added to the more familiar bulk of evidence from archaeological and historical records, such glimpses of variform suffering lead us to expect from its contemporaries proofs of an awareness of general decline. They cannot have lived through the worst decades of the third century without realizing that their world was collapsing about them. That at least is what we would expect. To meet our expectation, we have indeed a number of passages from literature in several genres that seem to fit very well. Whether they really do fit, on closer inspection, is another question.

A good point to begin with is the reign of Septimius Severus. There is no room or reason here to attempt an assessment of its overall tone. The senate "voted that his age should be called, and in all written records likewise inscribed as, 'The Golden' "[6]—but that may be dismissed as optimism, or conventional flattery. Tertullian praised the universal ease of communication, trade, travel; the opening up of new land for agriculture, growth of cities, increase in population; though from that came pressure on the food supply, strife, shortages, famines, deaths, and so on in natural cycles.[7] He saw too the end of the world, and wanted none of it.[8] His view is more balanced than that of Hippolytus, his contemporary, whose writings form part of a corpus of far more luridly apocalyptic vision.[9] The diversity of their viewpoints supports the very obvious proposition that different groups judged the reign according to its effects upon themselves. If pagans saw Christianity's "damned vices twining daily across the whole world,"[10] and dealt with moral decline by persecution, the persecuted cursed the age for the opposite reason and expressed their reaction in terms and images drawn from their own special beliefs. Attacks by the wicked on the faithful were, they thought, a prelude to the last act in the divine drama. But whether Christians or senators or prophets or any shade of opinion in between should be trusted to characterize Severus' reign is nevertheless very doubtful.

Moral decline as a sign of approaching universal collapse was widely acknowleged. Mankind would become "confused, deceitful, faithless, guileful, jealous, plotting, treacherous, spiteful, quarrelsome, fickle," in the prediction of eastern astrologers; [11] in Christian tradition, there would be strife, greed, sin, fraud, theft; [12] and the end of the cycle of ages, from gold down to iron, Romans had seen since the Republic as periodically upon them, notified by the corruption of old-fashioned virtues.[13] There was no era in the Empire, no matter how flourishing, in which someone did not arise to argue from general vice (as he saw it) to the certainty of general downfall.

More specifically eastern, but not only Christian, was another dire inference drawn from wars. The end would come in bloody chaos, every man and state against every other. While this was a prominent feature in the Sibylline oracles (to which the Roman state had official recourse),[14] the same picture also derived, with much extraneous coloring, from Scripture.[15] "Nation shall rise up against nation," says Origen, "and kingdom against kingdom, and there will be famine and plagues and earthquakes in places. *Haec enim omnia initia sunt dolorum. . . .* For just the way a body sickens before death. . . , such is the organism of the world when its corruption sets in." [16] The vision recalls Tertullian's, in following out the consequences of terrestrial decay, through the loss of nature's generative powers, to dwindling harvests, and so to bitter fighting over whatever sustenance remains.

But the organic metaphor, traced out here in the 240s, also parallels that of Dionysius of Alexandria, who in 260 or a little later writes of the diseases, plagues, and depopulation that people can and should notice around them: "though the human race upon earth is thus ever diminishing and consuming away before their eyes, they do not tremble, as its total disappearance draws nearer and nearer." [17] Cyprian speaks of plagues, drought, and thin harvests, in 252 or 253, as do Victorinus about 300 and Arnobius and Lactantius a decade later.[18] Earthquakes are seen as another sign.[19] Vital forces ebbed, creation grew old. Such was the universal law, to age, to decay, and pass away.[20] By the same law would Rome's long life and empire come to an end. The organic metaphor slipped into an anthropomorphic, which itself had a long tradition. Most often, the phase of Rome's maturity was attributed to Augustus,[21] but many writers from the Republic on to the fifth century offered variations and embroidery on that theme.

Rapidly surveyed, the ways of visualizing decline appear to have developed from three traditions—Greek, Persian, Jewish—but to have gradually intermingled or overlapped. They circulated orally, becoming from time to time fixed in a written form that has survived (the Sibylline oracles come first to mind).[22] They could be set in motion by a civil war, invasion, or natural disaster, and any one such event drew up to the surface of popular consciousness an accompaniment of many happenings quite unconnected or, from a sense of appropriateness, invented out of whole cloth. As a body of ideas from which to derive an historical account, the pictorialization of decline, in whichever of its several forms, must obviously be used very cautiously; as a means of understanding a stormy period—"decline" in the modern sense, or the imminent collapse of civilization—it is still more deceitful. For the close joining of man-made and natural afflictions into a single explanatory vision was the product of a fundamentally unhistorical approach. It may be called superstitious, religious, literary, or deterministic, no matter what, so long as the essential fact is clear, that very large phenomena were attributed to forces beyond human comprehension. No difference was discerned between political instability and plague: both fell upon the empire according to some cosmic or divine order. Just as *popularia verba* blamed all ills indifferently on Christians, so Christians blamed wars on *daemones;* or both groups in bewilderment blamed a vague, uncaused senescence in nature.[23] Lacking the tools for analysis that could distinguish among types of causes, people turned instead to set scenes of drama or myth made out of its own traditional elements.

The tendency of a writer to judge a period according to its effects on his particular community—the point made at the beginning of the chapter—or in terms of traditional dramatic myths can be illustrated by Cyprian. Just in the decade in which the ultimate disaster was forecast from signs of depopulation, he finds "the globe crammed, the world filled" with the human race, every home crowded with children.[24] But here he is preaching against worldly distractions. The determinant of his views was pastoral needs. When he turns to the afflictions of the Church, he likens them to features of familiar prophecy and adds other conventional elements, such as the falling off of population. In a different context, different thoughts (or facts) enter in. In Decius' reign, under the scourge of persecution, he and his fellows depict their times in the darkest colors, and the emperor himself in apocalyptic form as "the great dragon, precursor of Antichrist," [25] while, with the passing away of the worst of cruelty and division within the Church, the whole empire emerges in brighter tints, and the conventional catalogue of famine, earthquake, war, plague, and vice is put aside.[26] "His contemporary Dionysius of Alexandria emphasized under Valerian the decay of the Empire brought about by wars, revolts, plagues and manpower shortage, but after the seventh year of Gallienus' reign was over and the persecution of the Church ended, he became astonishingly optimistic." [27] The pattern is plain enough: it was no appreciation of Rome's total agony that drew forth a litany of laments—real though they were, some of them. Rather, it was the agony of Christians that caused them to see everything around them as the scene of the world's end, an end likewise embracing and punishing their pagan oppressors. The truth about depopulation or seismic activity in the 250s is no more to be sought in Cyprian than an historical understanding of the times he lived in.

Another writer, Commodian, reflects in his work, without question, a period of crisis. There is no denying the tone of his Apologetic Poem, a large part of which contains prophetic visions: "The beginning shall be our seventh persecution—behold, even now it shakes the door and is forced into being." Apollyon at the head of a Gothic invasion will come, spreading slaughter, hastening to the capital, trampling down the pride of the senators. Nero raised from Hell will appear too, in the East, "at the very end of time." The earth shall grow parched, famine set in, and plague spread abroad. Successive scenes of disturbance and horror will follow upon each other, miracles and bloodshed.[28]

It is easy to point out the closest parallels between all this and the genre (if it should be called that) of the Sibylline oracles; so no particular phraseology or historical element in the verses can be expected to tell us very much about the era in which it was written. Besides, the tradition on which it draws had an unextinguished life to the end of the third century and afterward, too, a tradition by which both Jews and Christians worked out through an ecstasy of revenge their hatred of the Roman state.[29] Here again, the very passions of the *Carmen apologeticum* may be literary and inherited rather than responsive to specific contemporary scenes.

But the main problem in using the text lies in deciding just what it is contemporary with. The continuator of Jerome's *Famous Men* in the 470s describes Commodian as coming after Lactantius.[30] Though the statement could be in error, internal evidence is very ambiguous. Scholars have proposed with some plausibility dates ranging across nearly two hundred years. That being the case, it really seems impossible to use the text to prove anything at all, however likely it may be, *a priori,* that some such work should have been composed for and during the Church's trials of the third century.

Because of the vastly greater chance of survival enjoyed by Christian writings, linked with the likelihood that they would, from 250 onward for generations, reflect the darkest general perception of the empire, they do not constitute a fair witness. The history of crisis cannot properly be left to Hippolytus, Tertullian, Origen, Cyprian, the anonymous *Liber Clementis, De laude martyrii,* and Sibyllines, Victorinus, Lactantius, and Arnobius. In the far broader stream of pagan literature, on the other hand, the sense of decline, rather than shocked comment on some specific misfortune that had befallen Rome, is not easily found. Dio, a senator when senators were at a discount, sees an age of iron, but one not irreversibly decadent; Herodian, laying out his story of the years from Marcus Aurelius to the present, believes his readers will find it a source of delight.[31] The spirit of the age up to the 230s can hardly be inferred from these two writers. In the 240s we encounter a longer piece of commentary on the times, longer, that is, in its concentration on a single short span of years: an anonymous oration to (probably) the emperor Philip.[32] He is congratulated that "the whole earth is at peace, land and sea crown their leader, Greeks and barbarians are in accord," the empire is firm, safe in harbor, all fears put to rest. The description is of course next to impossible to fit into real circumstances. Under Philip there were great wars almost incessantly in the north and northeast, titles

won in 245 or 246 (Germanicus Maximus) and in 247 or
248 (Carpicus Maximus), thereafter more heavy invasions,
scattered revolts (Pacatianus and Iotapianus), and a rebellion begun in 248 and successful the next year (Decius)—all
surely sufficient to fill a short reign.[33] The comments of
the orator on the ill condition of Rome before Philip de-
serve no more credit than his paean to the present peace,
the latter so bizarre that it might seem enough to relegate
the speech to the category of a school exercise. But not
even that exit is a safe one: a parallel exists in the likewise
anonymous essay, *On the Sublime*. Despite its reference to
"the peaceful condition of the civilized world," it has been
attributed to Gallienus' reign.[34] All that can be truly
learned from the courtly effusions of these two writers is
that a public statement quite at odds with reality as we see
it could be calmly made and calmly accepted by its contemporaries. Such obliviousness is, however, a significant
fact in itself.

Finally, two papyri, in which an appreciation of decline
has been detected. The first gives us Alexander Severus,
wishing to remit the crown-gold tribute "so my subjects
may not be required to make a payment beyond their
means," but confessing "the present insufficiency of public funds." It is "my resolution to combat decay not by
winkling out taxes, but by moderation alone . . . to
make the empire greater." [35] Not much, here: no more
than an open acknowledgment of having too little in the
imperial pocket, just as was made to Philip's face by our
anonymous orator, or earlier by Tiberius, Vespasian, Domitian, and Hadrian themselves to a public audience.[36] A

later papyrus of mid-century [37] recalls, through a city senator's speech, "when affairs were in a state of prosperity," and another party to the hearing adds a reference to a measure taken by Septimius Severus "when the cities were still prosperous." The presiding official says, "the argument from change away from prosperity applies just as much to villages as to cities"; [38] and the parts of the text that interest us conclude with a pious affirmation that the divine emperor will restore the situation. Both papyri reveal an awareness of deterioration: the first revives the memory of Trajan and Marcus Aurelius, "my ancestors," says Alexander Severus, whom he would like to imitate; the second recalls better times of fifty years earlier and makes clear the agreement among all the speakers that there had been a falling away from a happier period of larger cities and more wealth.

Some choice, some need for action, some suffering or misfortune started in people's minds trains of thought, ranging more widely across time and space. Millenary myth gave shape to present experiences and projected them into a future of cosmic collapse; or they were referred into the past, into eras variously chosen but, by agreement, better. We will return to this easy nostalgia later. Whether prophecy or retrospection (and of the latter, we encounter surprisingly little) constituted a sense of decline is hard to say, for that would seem to require a special realization that the third century was different from others. In fact, none of the responses to crisis is new in kind. What alone is new is at most a greater frequency of traditional responses, inevitable in the circumstances. At-

tacks on cherished institutions—property, Church, or political stability—crowded upon each other in actual fact,
without, however, leaving in our sources any distinct
"spirit of the times."

The historian of course does not welcome so negative a
conclusion. It stands to reason, he would say, that when a
civilization comes near to breaking apart it must undergo
some consequent change in its unconscious, even if not
in its conscious, self. Put a little more concretely, its citizens must be expected to suffer from despair, gloomy concern, escape into fantasy or frenetic diversions, guilt, intro-
version, reliance upon a dogmatic structure of salvation,
or the like. Necessarily, phenomena of this sort lie along
heights almost beyond the reach of proof or refutation.
How difficult the search for them may be, a glance at some
of the most often accepted findings will show.

In the empire's decline, it would be commonly agreed,
faith in cool reason and free inquiry increasingly yielded
to revelation. What was put forth as intuited or imparted
from a superhuman source won far more respect than
what satisfied everyday powers of thought. The latter had
to be tested and perhaps modified in combat with experience and criticism. It turned outward to its audience
and developed in the fresh air. Revelation came from looking inward, from mystical communications. The seer
looked not toward other minds but toward union with the
divine, toward one supreme Truth beyond challenge or
correction; and even as he fixed his gaze on an infinitely
remote horizon, he could still say, "All things are within."
Apollonius, Justin, Marcus Aurelius, Maximus of Tyre,

Numenius, and so up to Plotinus and his successors, demonstrate the development in thought with increasing strength.[39]

Their relation with the sensory world was unhappy. Men are seen in the final act of repudiation, like Peregrinus mounting his own funeral pyre, or like the young around Epictetus from whom he reports expressions of a death wish. The body torments people, making them appear sick souls, like Aelius Aristides, or forcing them to punish it with acts of hardship (Marcus Aurelius) or violent asceticism (Origen); for it is their prison, and life an exile from the soul's true home. It is "an exile in the midst of a hostile world that man cannot recognize as his own: misfortune, misery, abomination; wrenching and agony." [40] The Christian declares to his interrogators what his civic status is: he is a citizen of Jerusalem, he longs for its coming. Similarly, the Gnostic, holding to a faith the most characteristic of the age: he roots his loyalties in beings and places at war with terrestrial life. Gnosticism had already touched Christianity in the first century. In the second it comes to its full power in a quite chaotic growth of related beliefs—heresies all, as they came at last to be judged. Marcion and Valentinus are two of the principal prophets, both canonized by transformation into "-isms." They typify a black and white dualism that unfolds in both religion and philosophy after them.[41]

It is said that distressed times, sufferings, fears, and uncertainties provide a climate favorable to more intense religious and philosophic developments and thus explain important aspects of the third century [42]—not that those aspects had no earlier roots, of course, but they would never have attained anything near their actual dimensions had it not been for the nourishment of material conditions. Put crudely: asceticism, dualism, mysticism, and a number of related phenomena show us the spirit of third-century man responding to surrounding crisis.

But this line of interpretation, though the facts underlying it are clear, raises real doubts. First, as much of the evidence must be combed out as can be explained in a way that fits other circumstances, in order to keep under control the exuberance of the historian's craft; for any practitioner worth his salt could accommodate Aelius Aristides' hypochondria equally well to the first century—"ingrown preciosity suitable to an age of only imaginary ills"—as to the third—"a sensitive soul made sick by over-spreading barbarity." The successes of Mithraism likewise have been credited to features—promises of salvation, closeness of community—that could just as well suit any era at all, or to features—soldierly grades of worshipers, cosmic redemption through a bloody duel—better fitted to conditions that prevailed in Mithraism's waning than at its high point. We have too many explanations. Clio, learning an indiscriminate embrace over the course of her long life, is no longer an honest woman.

Second, chronology. The inward turning of resentment against the outer world can be discovered in a letter of 146; [43] the *Poimandres,* Maximus of Tyre, and Numenius belong to the second century; Aristides and Peregrinus are figures of the 150s and 160s. The corpus of Gnostic writings had by then already grown to maturity, and "the wave of pessimism that swept over the West" (not just the western part of the Roman empire) and carried Valentinus to prominence must be dated to the second quarter of the second century.[44] Marcion by then had developed the views for which the Church expelled him, and had begun his preaching in Rome. Christianity there responded to the two heresiarchs with obvious enthusiasm. Puzzling questions follow. What was there about the capital under Hadrian that required the doctoring of Marcion and Valentinus? What was it about their homes in Pontus and Egypt that produced their somewhat similar outlook on life? And what force can be ascribed to material conditions in shaping the third-century spirit, if altogether different conditions in the warmth of the earlier second century proved so congenial to just the same growths? The evidence of religious and philosophic movements resembles that of Commodian: if it works at any point over a stretch of two hundred years, it works nowhere, usefully.

The search for some awareness of decline is thus satisfied neither by direct statements of Cyprian and others in the group discussed with him nor by indirect implications of gnosticism and allied currents of thought. We must try a third corpus of material in which that awareness has been detected: the portraits of contemporaries (plates 1 and 2). Some scores, most of them in stone and clearly or probably having the emperor as their subject, have been often arranged in a rough sequence from 235 to 337, showing several changes of style. The first, "impressionistic," sets in rather sharply in the 230s, followed by "Gallienic" in the 250s and "Tetrarchic" from the 270s. The labels are of course crude but convenient.

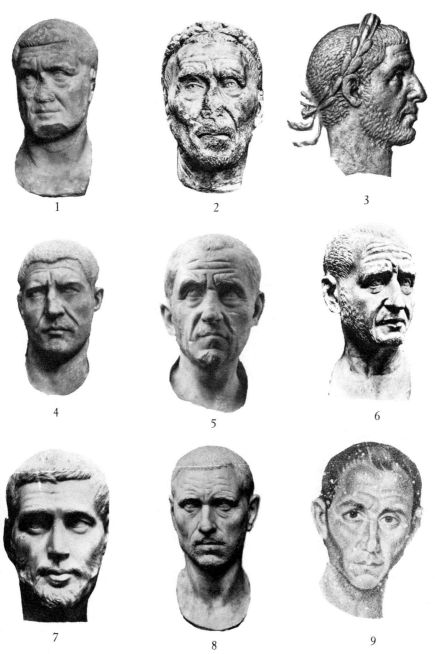

Plate I. Roman Portraits, "Impressionistic."

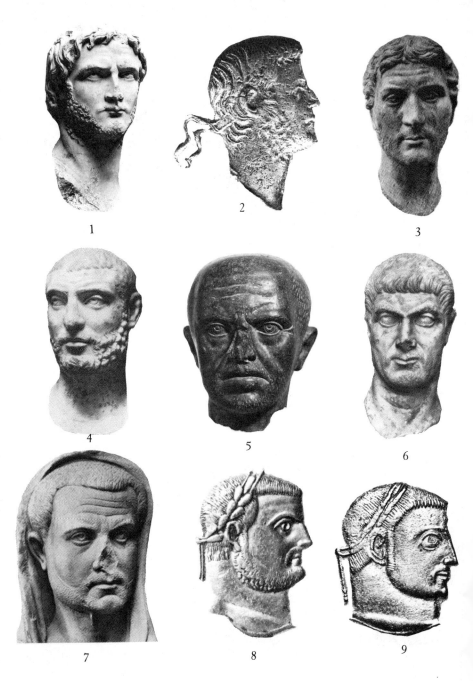

Plate II. Roman Portraits, "Gallienic" and "Tetrarchic."

"Impressionistic" points to a transient quality in facial expression, the catching of a fleeting mood or moment. Typical is Philip on a coin of 244, his mouth turned down in a delicately rendered, almost ironic line, his gaze intent and alert, his forehead wrinkled over lifted eyebrows. In the round, he is depicted in much the same way.[45] What is especially obvious to the most superficial student of the group to which these examples belong is the tension dominant among them, a tension verging on alarm, at least uneasiness. It shows first at the outset of Maximinus' reign, prevailing across the reigns of his successors in a number of well-known studies of both private and imperial subjects.[46] Commentators agree in stressing the anxious, nervous tautness of these faces, the asymmetry of glance or of the eyebrows, one raised higher than the other or drawn more sharply to a frown of perplexity. The turn of the head catches a quick motion of concern, the mouth slants down with distress, with wry self-awareness or sadness. Little anticipates this fashion even as late as Alexander Severus' reign. Its flourishing comes with surprising swiftness. And it is surprisingly ill-suited to the propaganda needs of the ephemeral figures on the throne, who seem to have chosen the best sculptors of the day to spread abroad the image of a worried man caught off balance. Hence (and because private individuals favored the same vogue of representation) it is supposed that the conditions of the time had penetrated insensibly to art, revealing in plastic form "the revaluation of values forced upon men by a grim and turbulent age, in which all stability and certainty seem to have gone from earth." [47]

There are, however, serious difficulties here. Perhaps

the least of them is the occasional piece of sculpture that experts argue about because in some respects but not in all it seems to belong to the impressionistic stream.[48] It is, after all, not hard to understand how different regions and workshops might turn out works that departed from the prevalent styles around them, both before and long after the impressionistic period. But impressionism was, it seems clear, by no means a novelty; rather, a revival. For that fact, explanation may be sought (not very persuasively) in the wish to recall to the public the happier milieu of early centuries; but regardless of the explanation, we are faced with the task of explaining also the psychological connection between art and historical setting in Flavian and Republican times.[49] Were people in those earlier ages equally shaken by calamities and decay around them, by anxiety and tensions that forced themselves into an outward expression in portrait busts? While such a recurrence of periods of despair is possible, and would rescue the connection between a worried face and a worried time, it seems more likely that Roman artists for esthetic reasons noticed, admired, imitated and popularized the style of a remote past, quite without reference to political events around them.

And this way of viewing a new fashion in sculpture can more easily accommodate the gradual disappearance of impressionism for a while, at the very moment when events took a turn for the worse. "Gallienic" came in, marked by certain differences in technique that need not concern us, and, more important, by different qualities of expression: a masterful calm and symmetry combined with an intensity of gaze, aslant and penetrating or raised slightly upward such as we see also in some of the emperor's coin issues.[50] Art historians find an antecedent to this style in Antonine sculpture and, yet more striking, in the classical feeling of Augustan sculpture. That has suggested ties with the favor shown by Gallienus to the Hellenic tradition, to Athens, to Plato: a classicizing "renaissance," as it is often called. The interpretation, even if it could be better supported, does not bear on our inquiry into the question: Whether contemporary art echoes the sounds of strife and chaos that filled the 260s.[51] More to the point is the attribution to Gallienus of a conscious and deliberate attempt in his official likenesses to recover a long lost serenity.[52] For that, however, court control over the artist would have to be assumed to a degree for which there is no direct evidence and which fits very ill with the number of similar busts produced both earlier and later than Gallienus. As with impressionism, we have parallels too many and too close between sculpture of the 260s and quite other periods. A head found at Athens illustrates the difficulty. Its upward-tilted eyes, the cold but subtle surface, the long hair and fixed expression seem to belong equally well with the 260s, the 230s, or the mid-second century,[53] depending on who is the supposed subject and what local artistic tradition may have been at work. The "Gallienic renaissance," so attractively knit together with the emperor's Hellenizing, his neoplatonizing, and his need to withdraw the spirit of his rule from turmoil into a haven of retrospective tranquillity, seems to melt away under careful study.

Overlapping with the Gallienic period, the equally mis-
named "Tetrarchic" (or primitive, or expressionistic) provides from the 270s works of a quite new mood.[54] Most
familiar are a number of portraits in porphyry, accurately
repeated in coins and, less accurately, repeated also in one
detail or another—treatment of the subject's hair or eyes, or
general blockiness of concept, and so forth—by a wider
corpus of sculpture. In contrast to the often brutal confidence of the essential Tetrarchic, however, the same
period picks up from the impressionistic some of the
latter's "inner, painful and incurable imbalance," reflecting "a fragmentation and splitting of the soul."[55] Under
Constantine still other fashions emerged, not really relevant to questions of decline; for by the second decade of
the fourth century, the empire might be fairly considered,
in the medical phrase, out of danger.

To let the glance pass thus rapidly over sixty or seventy
years of Roman portrait sculpture is no very satisfactory
exercise for historians, still less so for the proper student of
art. The latter can hardly be blamed as an interpreter; but
he nevertheless proves the less useful to historians as he is
the more scrupulous. Under his close analysis, supposed
harmonies between the mood and the portraiture of an
age, between politics and esthetics, seem to break down.
The edges of sharp change dissolve, similarities criss-cross
the map of style, and attributions to this or that reign or
tradition are shaken loose. Subtleties and exceptions are
identified. The loser is logic. For the derivation of impressionistic anxiety from the chaos around it, so plausible at
first sight, cannot stand up against the discovery of the

same traits in heads carved in Marius', Caesar's, Titus', or Constantine's day; nor can neoplatonic calm, taught by Gallienus, explain very much if the same look appears on faces of the 250s. If we knew as much of the chiefs of ateliers employed by the emperors as we do about Benvenuto Cellini, we might find that they, like Cellini and his rivals, stimulated each other to experiment, fastened upon quite capriciously determined vogues among the patron class, studied the past for inspiration to set new vogues, and tried all the while to extend and refine their own genius. To the extent of their success, in no matter what whirl of general collapse, they counted their commissions and pronounced it, after all, a tolerable world.

In a later chapter, something will be said of the movement of news around the empire; but whether or not the worst penetrated to every corner, it is not easily imagined that, in some Athenian workshop, the chisel following the lines of a face at the same time followed the headlines. The craft had its rules, its inheritance of skills, its momentum unresponsive, indeed oblivious, to things like budget deficits or invasions. The same man who deplored these at the street corner with a friend put them clear out of his mind when he got down to business with his apprentices.

Not that such indifference at first persuades. It lacks, in W. S. Gilbert's phrase, "artistic verisimilitude." It does not make sense. The fragments of the past seem rather to invite, almost to implore, arrangement into patterns expressive of some comprehensible, esthetically satisfactory truth. Historians respond. One of the most famous, Jacob

Burckhardt, looks at portrait busts of the third and earlier fourth century and finds that "most of the figures of this period show in part a natural ugliness and in part something diseased." Even in Constantine's visage lurks "something cunning; yet panegyrists and Church writers are at one in the exclamations of delight at his beauty. This is not mere flattery but evidence of a low standard of comparison." The empire, through plagues, rebellions, external wars, neglect of agriculture, anxiety, and misery, has fallen into "senescence." "The genuine antique life" has gone, along with freedom and beauty. Transition to decline across the whole period of our study thus forms itself into a coherent portrait, through Burckhardt's genius.[56] In the same way we have seen literary passages from Cyprian, philosophies and religions, or sculpture interpreted to fit their times. The interpretation is truly artistic, in the great tradition of Procrustes.

What is at fault here is the belief that common experiences—inflation, barbarian raids, political instability—will be seen in the same way by every group or person they touch, thus giving a common character to the age. Rorschach's inkblots provide the simplest reminder that such is not the case. Common experiences must pass through different modes of perception, which will screen out or alter different parts, according to the degree of interest or the associations aroused in different people's minds. It is no cause for surprise, then, that the ills that afflicted the empire were not understood as one interconnected whole or that they cannot now be arranged as such by valid historical interpretation. Rather, they were confronted as if they were separate experiences by pagans, Christians, artists and philosophers, the rulers and the ruled. It is with Romans in these latter two roles that we are most concerned.

2

PROPAGANDA

What Romans of the third century thought about the past affected the way in which they thought about the particular stretch of the present they were enduring. Their views were in some points peculiar. The Constantinian astrologer quoted in the preceding chapter refers to a number of great figures Greek and Roman as far down as Pompey; but he skips then to Plotinus (died 270). That suggests that he did not carry in his head any real knowledge of the flow of events to more recent times. Lack of a surviving narrative account of Plotinus' own generation and a bit beyond is only too well known.[1] It is likely, however, that works on the third century now lost were then received with little analytical understanding, certainly with less enjoyment than works on more hallowed periods. Their readers, when they turned to composition of their own in other genres than history, very rarely mention emperors later than Trajan (with allowance made for Marcus

Aurelius in special connections). In the fourth century, a panegyrist with a taste for erudition will serve up a jumble of names —Nerva, Titus, Antoninus Pius, Augustus, Hadrian, Trajan—with no indication of their context, interrelations, or order at all.[2] Vegetius and Jerome, discussing matters that seem to require the drawing of parallels to their own times from the 200s A.D., go back instead to the 200s B.C. They are not ignorant. They have their books. History is spread out before their eyes, but they see only events and persons floating loose in a timeless past, without caused links between them—a gallery of isolated portraits and anecdotes made classical by remoteness.

It had always been thus. To pick up the tale of nostalgia in Trajan's day, the younger Pliny may be instanced: "I am one," he declares, "that admires the ancients." [3] But Marcus Aurelius is described as "a devotee of antiquity," Gordian praised as a man "who has restored and enlarged over his own world the ancient peace of life"; Plotinus calls himself the bearer of truths from ancient, godlike men; a noble of the 320s is praised for "his edifying actions, of an old-time honor"; and so it goes on into the fourth century—an unbroken tradition of love and yearning for the days of yore.[4] There, most clearly, could be found an uncaused, unexplained excellence in morals, wisdom, and every other facet of life.

And if one were to reach back even further, one might find the Golden Age. More in compliment than seriousness, we may suppose, its return was discerned in Caligula's, Nero's, and Septimius Severus' day and again in Macrobius', not periods that should be given very high

marks for happiness.[5] Only the familiarity of the image
led to its misapplication. But in the later third century
that image came forward with a certain appropriateness
and with much force. Its favorite scenes appear with a
new frequency in mosaics of that period, Christian and
pagan: prodigal nature yielding her harvest without a
struggle, the farmer and shepherd—typical figures of the
dream—pursuing their lives without toil or intrusion. All
is peace.[6] In written form, it runs through the biographies
of Probus, ascribing to him promises of a new age.[7] An
orator of 298 attributes its presence to the joint rule of
Diocletian and Maximian,[8] and a little later Lactantius
dwells on it at length. Its chief characteristic, like that of
the notalgia touched on just above, is moral. It hardly
needs historical causation, only an abrupt and blessed turning to virtue.[9] For no described or necessary reason, suddenly there will be no wars, no strife, no swords or soldiers,
no avarice or plotting or litigation or even place for any
laws, for all men will spontaneously wish to live justly and
benevolently.[10] It is, in sum, the mirror image of the onset
of the word's decline and, in its origins, equally beyond
the sphere of ordinary mortals' control. Longed for, far
away in time yet always imminent, the Golden Age gathers into one idyll everything that the empire had perhaps
earned by the termination of its crisis.

Over the separate elements of this happiness the emperor was believed to preside. Its enemies he stamped
down by his personal exertions, marching, living, and
fighting like a common soldier at the side of his men.[11]
His civilian subjects he raised up in gleaming cities,

through his munificent building programs.[12] All such physical amenities were in his gift, aspects of a divinely favored age or reign, of the *felicitas saeculi,* a phrase recalling the reign of Saturn over the Golden Age.

Nature herself—good weather, calm seas, rich harvests —throughout the realm obeyed the emperor's *felicitas,*[13] so that his fleets could navigate in safety and his people never suffer from want. Sometimes it was his *pietas* that drew upon himself and them all blessings,[14] sometimes his *iustitia.*[15] Whatever his virtues, single or in sum, they insured a catalogue of rewards far beyond anything other mortals could command: beyond valor, victory, beyond marketplaces and aqueducts, goods to trade and rain to moisten the fields in abundance. Hence the cornucopia that appeared so often on imperial coins of all reigns; hence the bizarre borrowing of Demeter's corn-crown by Gallienus, and the personifications of the seasons dancing joyfully about the palace, in mosaic pictures.[16]

Virtue could engender its very self in others, too, thereby assuring even further happiness. It was an obligation on the good ruler to see to that, by direct attack on vice. In the same way that cities financed programs of moral improvement, believing that morals could be taught in schools,[17] and higher (which is to say rhetorical) education was credited with the power to elevate the ideals and improve the manners of older students through its vivid exampla,[18] so the government was expected somehow to make its subjects better people. That notion had had its comical consequences in the sumptuary laws of the Republic; yet they were still debated seriously by the senate and extended by the emperor in the earlier Principate. In the third century Dio puts into Maecenas' mouth the recommendation that the ruler "review and oversee families, estates, and morals of both senators and equestrians, of men as of their wives and children, and himself correct what does not call for punishment but may, if neglected, become the cause of great evils"; the Historia Augusta attributes to its more commended subjects—Alexander Severus, Aurelian, Tacitus—active roles as censors in the Republican sense;[19] and emperors continued in the early fourth century to enjoy the praise of panegyrists for their "new laws established to control *mores* and destroy vice." [20]

But moral education could not stop with laws. It must employ every means to reach every sort of person. The emperor's armies he commanded by simple fiat. Their quintessential virtue was not to be legislated into existence: it was simple *disciplina,* and that, it was his special responsibility to maintain by strict and strenuous leadership in old Roman style. So we see Constantine wearing that Republican decoration, the *corona civica,* in his coin portraits, harking back to military practices half forgotten, and receiving compliments on his descent from Claudius II, "the first to reform a lost *disciplina.*" [21] To his civilian subjects, on the other hand, the emperor could not use the word so appropriately. He must teach them rather through exhortation, remonstrance, and stern warning. Though the substance of what he had to say was traditional, the tone was new. Anyone who compares imperial edicts of the earlier Principate with those of the third century and later must be struck by the rising note of moral didac-

ticism. Not sufficient is the definition of a wrong; its re-
pellent nature must be made clear to all. It is, for example,
not the infraction but the motive, not the crime but the
cunning, *calliditas,* of fraudulent persons that needs correction,[22] or, in Diocletian's famous edict on prices, greed
for money:

> Our country's good fortune—which may be thanked along
> with the immortal gods in recalling Our wars waged suc-
> cessfully, the world's condition being now calm and
> settled into the deepest bosom of tranquillity, and en-
> dowed with the benefits of peace for which We have
> labored with the sweat of Our brow—should, as the
> better part of the state and Rome's standing and majesty
> alike require, be well and truly set out and fittingly embel-
> lished so that We, who by the benign favor of the divine
> powers suppressed the past storming attacks of the bar-
> barian tribes through the slaughter of their peoples, may
> erect defenses around a peace established for eternity with
> the necessary safeguards of justice. For if, where unre-
> strained and furious greed rages—a greed without respect
> for mankind and hastening to its own increase and aug-
> mentation not only each year but each month or day, even
> each hour and moment—some restraining plan may be
> applied, or if Our common fortune can sustain with
> unshaken spirit these orgiastic outrages by which it is in
> this fashion daily more injured, perhaps some room might
> be left for prevarication or silence, since a general restraint
> on one's feelings might soften a detestable cruelty and
> wretched plight. But because it is the single desire of an
> untamed madness to show no regard for Our common
> needs, and it is almost an item of faith, of an avarice

spreading and surging with recurrent fevers among the
wicked and licentious, that it should desist by force not
free will from tearing at everyone's fortunes, while those
whom the ultimate of poverty has dragged down to a
realization of their lamentable state can no longer ignore
it, We as We look out, We parents of the human race,
must interpose justice as judge of things, so as to confer
what Humanity itself had long hoped for but could not
secure, by the remedies of Our foresight, an amelioration
for the common benefit of all.[23]

The text, or rather, these few opening sentences, serves
very well to illustrate the explanatory, pulpit tone that
emerges toward the end of the crisis in its better documented decades. The origin of the tone has something to do
with the infusion of rhetoric into law, a matter we will return to in a later chapter; it has something to do with official style as it developed in the Greek-speaking provinces
and with their rising influence on the court. But that alone
will not provide a full explanation. For the Dominate also
loudly advertises what is not a specially eastern idea but is
certainly characteristic of exhortation, "the public good." [24]
We must imagine a government confronting the gravest
and most perplexing confusion of problems which it has
neither the historical sense to arrange in a chain of causes
and effects nor the individual analytical skills to divide
into the man-made and the natural. Plagues and defeats,
undifferentiated, are equally ascribed to the fault of a bad
ruler, just as good harvests and victories are equally to the
credit of a good one. It is as a single, indivisible whole, not
a collection of interests, aspirations, regions, and vulner-
abilities, that the empire is thought to approach its deterio-

ration into an age of iron or rise into the perfection of gold. If it is to rise, that must be through goodness pure and simple (using both words in both their senses)—not through those secondary or tertiary factors that the modern observer detects underneath the tendencies of the time. Government in its almost childish view appeals against inflation by excoriating greed; against the impossible costs of the military, by blaming war in the abstract; and against the inadequate trickle of the tax yield, by calling for the taxpayer's zeal and loyalty. "It tries to cover all its acts with moral principles and divine approval"; [25] for the crisis is one of people's wickedness that must and can be reformed through the redirection of their desires.

In addition to his strident sermonizing, the personal qualities of the emperor are to be offered to his subjects for their instruction. On "the good ruler" there are not only many, many surviving speeches but tracts on how to write them—a task probably easier than the reading of them. A brief reminder of such familiar works, one bearing on Aurelian, is quite enough. A speaker puts the question, "What makes bad emperors? it is asked. Now first, my friend, is a loose life, *licentia;* next, material wealth, *rerum copia;* further, vicious friendships." [26] But if the emperor can possess or attain virtue, so the argument will proceed, then his subjects will follow by themselves. As a model to others, he will be imitated; he shows in his conduct what he will or will not tolerate; and still further, he surrounds himself with good men, good because he has sought them out or shaped them. From the center outward thus radiate all qualities needed for an age of gold.

It hardly seems an exaggeration when, as the emperor

enters his audience chamber, petitioners shout, "The gods preserve you for us! Your salvation is our salvation! In truth we speak, on oath we speak!" [27] They could not indicate a more complete trust. But there is nothing new here, no desperate, abject dependence growing out of experiences of the crisis; for with variations according to time and place, claims of the ruler to hold the fate of his world in his hands with some more than mortal authority had been freely made and freely acknowledged. The very least arrogant or blasphemous reached back to Augustus' relationship to Caesar. If he was less than a god, then he was at least descended from divinized predecessors. In that tradition, Septimius Severus invents links to Pertinax and even to Commodus, last of the real Antonines; Constantine derives a probably fictitious descent from Claudius Gothicus; and, in between, the rootless Gallus tries to insert his family into that of Decius. [28]

Or if less than the gods, then he might still be accepted as their appointee, in touch with them and thereby able to draw down their favor upon all his doings and his subjects. "Aurelian under attack by a mutiny declared that the soldiers were deceived if they thought the fate of rulers rested in their hands, for he said god bestowed the purple —holding it out with his right hand—absolutely, as well as marked the length of the reign"; and on another occasion, he challenged his barbarian enemies to a test of strength, with the boast that "the aid of the divine will be with us." [29] Protecting deities may on coins loom next to the emperor's tiny figure, or he may be shown with his eyes lifted upward to a source of far-off but favoring

omnipotence.[30] A great number of inscriptions, literary
texts, and works of art of many kinds emphasize the beneficent ties betwen the powers above and their chosen
agent on earth.

But in the third century, at the very beginning of the
crisis, the ruler as a midget next to Jupiter Savior appears
for the last time. Thereafter the emperor's own image
swells to fill the field of vision—for example, in scenes of
his divine munificence,[31] or when he depicts himself in
the company of a favoring god who must stand, no bigger
now than himself that sits on a throne.[32] Some decades
later, Aurelian puts forward more prominently and consciously than any predecessor the claim to be a living
god,[33] and an increasingly insistent and divinizing vocabulary of self-praise marks the emperors' titles as the third
century goes along. While most individual elements may
be traced back to this or that antecedent in some earlier
reign, cumulatively these adjectives of adoration provide
a higher and higher platform to stand on, one very nearly
touching the heavens.[34] Restoring, saving, directing, re-
pairing, or extending the globe of his power, as *restitutor
orbis* and so forth (or the globe of specifically Roman
power, which he frees as *liberator orbis Romani, conservator rei publicae, restitutor libertatis et rei publicae*); bringing peace eternal and public safety; bestowing freedom
once again, or security—in all these guises the ruler rises
to Olympus. By no name is he more clearly borne aloft
than "Restitutor." From mid-century on, it enjoys a dominant popularity.[35]

The eminence of the emperor recalls a scene in the early

300s at Nicomedia, when a new pair of Tetrarchs mounted
to power. "There was a high place about three miles outside the city at whose summit Galerius himself had assumed the purple, and there a column had been erected
bearing a statue of Jove." [36] The setting suggests the intent
of the rulers to give the greatest possible advertisement to
some one favored deity—in this case, of Diocletian's choos-
ing. In calling himself and every good aspect of his reign
"Jovian," by every route of communication that could
reach his subjects, he may surely be credited with conscious policy. Two characteristics have been detected in
that, and much discussed: the drift toward monotheism,
and to the past.

The first relates to our subject only tangentially; for it
is beyond proof or disproof whether concentration on one
divine figure arose from the realization of its usefulness in
unifying a riven realm, or from many centuries of spontaneous syncretism in the empire, or from the challenge of
Christianity, or from the tilt of influence eastward to lands
of solar cult, or, lastly, from an intolerant pressure for con-
formity to whatever the *dominus et deus* on the throne
demanded of his people. All these propositions have been
defended. Their defenders would perhaps agree among
themselves only in hearing a louder voice, a more strident
tone, in which religious convictions—sometimes very old
ones—were expressed over the two or three generations
after 250. Whether that in turn is no more than an aspect
of the louder didacticism that can be heard in imperial
laws and pronouncements, or whether it rises in the strife
of beliefs, pagan against Christian, or whether it expresses

despair in merely human solutions to cosmic crisis, are
questions drawing us into a further area of dispute. Surely
the religious history of the third century is the most difficult to understand.

One point on which there is singularly little evidence is
particularly essential, too: we must be sure that the shouting of religious slogans by imperial propagandists was
actually listened to, and actually moved people. From
analogies in other eras better known, it is perfectly fair to
support either side of conjecture on that question. Acclamations might be mechanical, votes of thanks mere
convention, and the very Tyche of the emperor a quite
meaningless concept.[37] But in fact there are—if no demon-
strably sincere assertions by ordinary citizens, "We hear
and we believe"—at least indirect signs of true religious
feelings generated by the emperors' communications. Inscriptions and the dedication of altars sometimes point
unmistakably to the emotional involvement of worshipers
in the imperial cult.[38] It might develop its own hymns,
mysteries, initiates, and elaborate meetings presided over
by "sebastophants," or attach itself to another mystery
cult like that of Cybele or Dionysos, or enjoy the celebration of its anniversaries and vows in the bosom of one of
the empire's thousands of crafts associations.[39] Italy and
Africa as well as the more predictable eastern provinces
supply just such testimony.

If the very personification of the humdrum, Vespasian,
could be received as a healer of the blind in Alexandria,[40]
there is the less reason for surprise that the Severi, father
and son, should have appeared to a citizen of Numidia in

a beneficent vision and, through the touch of the imperial tribunal, restored the sight of another citizen of the capital.[41] It was thanks to Trajan and Serapis that dwellers in Upper Egypt struck water, and the new well was proclaimed on coins as providentially revealed; thanks to Hermes-Thot and Marcus Aurelius' piety that an irresistible rainstorm lashed the faces of Rome's enemies in battle (and other coins duly declared that too, with the legend, *Religio Augusti*).[42] So Marcus erected a temple in the capital to Hermes, just as Aurelian did, to the Sun-god of Emesa, who had turned the tide in his favor.[43] It is impossible not to see in these various acts and incidents a genuine belief in the emperor's special role, touched on earlier in its various aspects: the role of favorite of the gods, instrument by which they touch the fortunes of his realm, and actual possessor of divine powers himself. The very forces of nature, as we saw earlier, obeyed him, or obeyed the gods acting through him. Unchallenged stories went about, and unfeigned thanks requited his *pietas*. He in his turn clearly recognized the value here to be exploited, and in coins or sculptured reliefs or public ceremonies largely lost to us he fostered the image of his powers as truly superhuman.

Vespasian, Marcus Aurelius, Aurelian, and Constantine were also among those emperors who enjoyed a special audience with a god in the privacy of his temple.[44] The last three emperors, along with others of the third and fourth centuries, also witnessed epiphanies on their behalf in the heat of battle.[45] If such a favor were granted to them, it seems likely that they themselves originated—at the very least, they spread—the reports that Sol, Jupiter, or Apollo had through them brought victory to Rome's cause. It was again divine aid that helped in the lavish amplification of Byzantium, to become Constantinople.[46] Bringing water to parched fields, controlling the winds and rains of heaven, driving back hostile armies, and beautifying the empire's cities, in all of these roles the ruler thus fulfilled the hopes of his subjects for a Golden Age. Those that believed in him were not disappointed; his worship was not empty; and if we can credit the evidence discussed above, that man-made and natural forces were inextricably confused in people's minds, we can credit likewise a general faith in the control over both types of force by His Divine Majesty. Advertisement of his miraculous acts would not be doubted, especially in the later Empire. For more by coincidence than cause— though the interpretation need not be argued here—that was a time in which miracles found increasingly ready acceptance. Oracular sayings circulated more widely, prophets spoke more often in the marketplace, magical feats were more credulously studied and imitated, and the restraints of common reason became a little less common decade by decade even among the more highly educated.[47] With the private aspects of this mood we are not concerned, though no doubt the man who hexed his neighbor's cows would be the more likely to swallow some grander exhibition of the same sort by his emperor. The public and historic aspects, however, return us to the time of crisis. It worked upon minds well stocked with images and myths of supernatural change, minds jostled by actual events that brought those images and myths to the surface.

Even as far south as Ephesus a Gothic raid penetrated by sea and in 263 besieged certain refugees in the sanctuary of Apollo outside the city. Had they not had the god's help, it would have gone ill with them; but he opened a spring for them, giving them water to hold out against "Ares in barbarian guise." The inscription telling the story has survived.[48] It serves as transition from miracles advertised, to outer enemies on the move, from the Golden Age with the monarch and the gods securing it, to a different attachment, the Roman empire itself.

Whatever might be thought of plague, inflation, and other invisible threats, the human forces attacking from without were real enough. They struck at a collection of provinces assembled by accident of conquest, a forced unity having at first less sense of membership than of subjection. To feel that one belonged to the empire, rather than to a separate, once hostile, heritage, was unnatural. For the great majority of inhabitants, local loyalties—to tribe, village, city—never ceased to count first; but if the Greeks of the eastern provinces were speaking of "our" empire by the mid-second century,[49] it is likely that western provincials with a less proud heritage shared the same attachment. At the outset of the crisis, the death of an African citizen in a civil war "for his love of Rome," *pro amore Romano,* may be taken as a sign of a patriotism transcending one's place of birth, embracing the whole of the empire; in mid-crisis, eastern provincials receive imperial thanks "for their oneness with the Romans"; toward the end of the crisis, Egyptians are heard shouting at a public as-

sembly, "Roman power for Romans, forever." [50] In the
midst of these testimonies, at some undiscoverable point,
the words "Romania" and, in opposition, "barbaria" developed in Latin of the streets and worked their way upward
into literature.[51] They allow a glimpse into the popular
mind, where evidently a polarization between "we" and
"they" divided as never before the dwellers on the inside
from those without. A glimpse through language is a
thousand times more significant, because less self-conscious
and contorted, than the occasional literary texts we can
use; but nevertheless, these latter, too, echo an execration
of the outer forces, a hatred of *barbaria* that grows equally
with the threat to the *pax Romana*.[52] Panegyrists from
Gaul from the 280s on display before the emperors the
same triumphant ferocity that emperors themselves por-
tray on their coins, from the 240s on, with greater frequency, in scenes of barbarians beaten, speared, dragged
by the hair, or trampled beneath the hooves of an imperial
war-horse. Animosity advertised brought closer together
all who feared Rome's enemies.

Descendants of colonists sent out long ago to Antioch
in Pisidia, perhaps conscious of the Gothic and Persian
threat, in the 250s issued coins of a nostalgically patriotic
type: the goddess Roma with a barbarian kneeling at her
feet.[53] A generation later, on the opposite edge of the empire, Carausius offered "Rome's renascence" as the slogan
of his rebellion.[54] From a less surprising source, the emperor and his own mints, issued a rising paean to Eternal
Rome and the goddess Roma.[55] Veneration of the city's
ageless Vesta seems to have taken on new meaning from

the mid-third century; similarly, of the old "Genius populi Romani" on Aurelian's coins, still more on Diocletian's, and veneration of the wolf and twins on coins of the Tetrarchs.[56] It was Decius in mid-century who revived the all-but-forgotten office of censor; Diocletian at the end who elevated to a special height—even on a column outside his capital in Bithynia—the quintessentially Roman guardian, Jupiter;[57] Decius again who gave a sharper prominence to the term "Roman" itself in his edicts against the Christians; and Valerian, Diocletian, Galerius, and Maximin who imitated him in their own campaigns to arouse a persecuting zeal.[58] If pagans were to be turned against their neighbors, the best way in a period of invasions was to identify those neighbors with the outer enemy.

There is unquestionably a focus on Romanness in all this, produced or at least favored by the sharp challenge of external attack. The closest approximation to one rallying point for all inhabitants of the empire, the nearest thing to unity, lay in the ancient capital and its traditions. And external challenge must certainly have reminded people that they had more in common with each other under the aegis of Jupiter or Jove, than with the nations beyond their frontiers. To that extent, crisis defined more clearly than for many, many generations the center of imperial civilization. But the definition is perhaps best understood in a chronological sense. Physically, the city of Rome was after all the center of nothing in the third century. Power resided far away, in Aquileia, Milan, Trier, and especially in the string of military and civil headquarters stretching from Carnuntum down the Danube and across the Hellespont to Nicomedia. Outside Nicomedia rose the column surmounted by Jupiter. It was an odd place on the map for Rome to revive. But Diocletian there was thinking of history, not geography. His choice of the site was no odder than Carausius' of London. From both points, it was equally easy to reach what both men wanted, a greater, surer past.

The wish was expressed by everyone in his own way. While Pisidian Antioch, in a sea of Greek-speakers, struggled to remember Latin and the origin of its Roman citizen colonists, the truly Greek cities around it were introducing into their local coinage their own third-century changes. They were recalling their founders: Alexander, Heracles, Dionysos. If we follow their gaze, we find it fixed on a point remote in time rather than space. Similar reassertions of inheritance, linguistic, religious, artistic, or historical crop up elsewhere through the thin topsoil of Roman rule in the course of the third century.[59] In the shap of return or revival, they as much as *Roma* can be accepted for what they all were, manifestations of uneasiness in the present and search for something better.

Senators as such (perhaps descended from a Syrian or Punic noble) were bound to assert their special derivation from the halcyon days of the Republic, and to be therefore the most consciously antiquarian; emperors as such (Pannonian or Italian, it made little difference) celebrated a more recent apogee, under Trajan, perhaps. Hence that name taken by Decius, and his special coin issue laying out in all their magic his heroic predecessors, the *divi* of the throne he sat on.[60] For their part, provincials had their own traditions, offered not in defiance of Rome but in retreat from a world no longer safe or satisfying. "Retreat," "return," "revival"—all with the same telltale syllable that marked imperial propaganda: *renovator, restitutor,* and the like terms the emperor took to himself. His subjects gave thanks to him as *reparator, conservator patriae . . . , recuperata republica.*[61]

There is another aspect of propaganda that does not fit well with the idea of aggressive old-Romanness universally imposed but does fit under the notion of various groups tolerant of each other's retrospection: namely, propaganda favoring local departures from Roman custom. A good test can be made in Diocletian's reign. Therein, it is generally agreed, appeared a marked conservatism, nowhere more plain than in his religious policies. Yet among the gods enjoying his favor were the Celtic Belenus, the Persian Mithra, and the Syrian baal of Doliche,[62] and at the shrine of Apollo in Miletus he erected a statue of the god, perhaps in gratitude for support afforded by the oracle to the persecutions.[63] He seems, then, to have been no fanatic for Jupiter but rather a typical adherent of paganism—no different from a fellow Tetrarch who congratulated Tyre on its powerful protector-baal, or from predecessors who put on imperial coins the names and portraits of city and regional deities.[64] It is something between courtesy and piety that directs these and other emperors to the god most worshiped in whatever place they visit; for they hope (if they act from conscious policy) that he may thereby increase support for their regime.

As the second century went along, all the many local
gods of the empire were arranged into a comprehensible
order. It was accepted in the third century by individuals
of every stamp. It assigned to each people as a guardian
the deity they worshiped; it attributed to that deity their
welfare and very survival; and, in a view from which
Christians naturally departed, it respected each cult, however strange, by reason of long lineage. What Tacitus says
of the Jews could thus be applied to all cults in the Roman
world, *antiquitate defenduntur*.[65] A Christian raged in
vain against the inflexible veneration accorded by pagans
to their own past. "They take refuge in the judgment of
the ancient forebears who, they allege, were wise, and
made test, and knew what was best." [66] On exactly the
same grounds, a pagan raged against the first Christian
emperor because he was a "changer," *novator*—not (and
precisely here lay the heart of the problem in the third
century) a *renovator*.[67] It was in that little "re-" that so
many claims to leadership and gratitude were made,
claims that embraced an infinite choice of loyalties by tol-
erating any and every regional tradition. Whatever was
long approved was right.

Though the Great Persecution lies to the side of our
subject, it illustrates certain themes dominant toward the
close of the crisis. Diocletian is in command, enjoying real
support as "father of the Age of Gold." [68] He stands for
peace achieved, reverence for each people's guardian gods,
a return to the purity of older ways and worships. Against
him and his successors in the eastern provinces stand re-
bellious subjects scornful of traditions, looking not to the

values of the past but to a future black with the clouds of further convulsions and final judgment. A war of beliefs was inevitable. The Tetrarchs fought for men's minds with many devices. They made use of familiar emotive terms as weapons—"our forefathers," "the times of yore," "piety," "divine favor" and "blessedness," "the public good" and "discipline"; they made use of staged public demonstrations, polemical tracts and forged "proofs" of the persecutors' arguments, stridently worded announcements and edicts given maximum publicity, open trials and "confessions," symbolic pictures on coins like political cartoons, and enforced teaching of the accepted doctrine to schoolchildren.[69] Nothing was neglected that could ensure the triumph of truth.

But all these means of controlling opinion, these so admirably modern devices, were not invented by the Tetrarchs. They happen only to be more fully reported than is usual because the persecuted, along with their memories and records—may it ever be so!—happened to survive. Other sources make plain that government throughout the crisis as before and after paid attention to propaganda.

A host of generally accepted values could be played upon like a piano, and the notes arranged with artistic effect into whole tunes or symphonies quite intelligible to the student today, and presumably so also to the original listeners—who must have heard, then, and understood. But did they respond? To that absolutely central question it is hard to give a straightforward answer. Very likely the most familiar notes, sounding as *providentia, abundantia, fides militum, aeternitas, novum saeculum, felicitas, pietas, victoria, pax,* and so forth, aroused little feeling, at least in normal times. By the same token, emergencies should have sharpened popular sensitivities. Yet we can advance a short way beyond such conjectures, first, through supposing that the government was a better judge than we of the effectiveness of its propaganda, second, by seeing what clear attempts it made to reach its audience with timely messages.

Imperial portrait busts, for example, were hurriedly produced and distributed at the outset of each reign for the only possible purpose of familiarizing people with the idea that the new occupant belonged on the throne and that he was, by possession, therefore legitimate.[70] It is hard to demonstrate a subordination of artistic style to propaganda in imperial sculpture, but in both the third and fourth centuries, texts make explicit the concern of rulers at least to show their face in replica as widely as possible, by means of statues or in big, colorful cartoons depicting their prowess in hunting, their victorious battles, their tumultuous receptions by welcoming crowds;[71] and, however subjective our reactions may be, when we glance over the series of styles—the "impressionistic," "Gallienic," "Tetrarchic," and at last Constantine's —we cannot help but feel a growing appropriateness, a more and more conscious psychologically effective relation between the stone portraits of the emperors and the tremendous powers to which they laid claim. Certainly they thought enough about their public image to doctor it. They manufactured false exploits to seem more soldierly, false titles to seem longer and firmer fixtures on the throne.[72] Reaching out to specific points of support, their coinage addressed flattery and greetings to key army units —EXERCITUS ILLURICIANI—or key regions—PANNONIAE.[73]

Evidence of this kind should be enough to convince the most skeptical that, in the judgment of each regime, popular adherence to its claims and programs really could be strengthened by advertisement. It would be captious to doubt that judgment. On the other hand, it goes beyond our evidence to attribute to the Roman public as delicate, alert, and learned an ear for the overtones of propaganda as modern scholarship has developed. The notes struck on the keyboard are most likely to have constituted a sort of background music, half heard the majority of the time and capable of stimulating more active response only through unusal emphases and messages. Even these latter had only partial success. The recalling of truly Roman traditions, often from remote antiquity, is less likely to have produced the sense underlying the word "Romania" than the barbarian presence on each citizen's doorstep; for each citizen defending his own territory showed no preference at all for an old-fashioned, an Italian, a senatorial leadership. Each territory, if it did not go so far as to place a crown upon some local hero, still maintained—rather, increasingly asserted—its separate cultural inheritance. No force of persuasion, then, succeeded in creating a Roman patriotism.

Moreover, a second theme, necessarily sounded very often because so deeply felt—the theme of return to the embrace of the past—was really no more than tautological. Life had been better, once (as historians today would say, comparing the third with the first century). It had been better "once upon a time," as contemporaries of the crisis would have phrased it, more dreamingly. No one then or now could deny a downward turn in the empire's fortunes. But recall of the past suggested nothing constructive. It was a retreat, pure and simple.

Only a third theme, that of the emperor's all-saving role, may have been sounded to much effect. No one of course can say for sure whether it merely echoed or whether it roused popular feelings. In fact, however, propaganda was controlled by the throne. It was the most obvious lesson of the third century to make that institution more secure against an endless series of pretenders and to gain for it a more oracular eminence, from which its occupants could exercise command over the crisis. And it is a fact of history that what emerged from the crisis was the Dominate. Surely it is not too much to claim for all the trumpeting of miracles, the sonorities of obeisance, or the summons to abject belief, a real part in strengthening the monarchy. Surely the exertions and sacrifices demanded of its subjects by the state were less grudgingly offered to a Presence so enormous as Aurelian's, Diocletian's, Constantine's—at least while the crisis lasted.

3

INTELLIGENCE

The mind of a government, including its officials all together, in whatever period, is rarely studied. It appears an
unattractively ordinary subject, no matter how important.
And intellectual historians or historians of ideas, who
should take up the task, may share a belief not unknown
among academics generally, that only an intellectual can
have an idea. The task, however, must be faced. Inadequacies in the record must be somehow filled in. And we have
already glimpsed the dreams, values, and perceptions of the
third and early fourth century shared, in fact most easily
detected, within the very class from which officials were
drawn. We can go on to add now at least an outline, first,
of government officials' mental equipment as it fitted
them for their jobs, and second, of the kind and amount
of information on which their administrative programs
had to be based.

Foremost and best known to us among officials were "rich men . . . boasting and claiming they knew everything, armed with faith in letters"—faith, that is, in all kinds of literary and rhetorical skills.[1] The respect granted their art and their prominence in both central and municipal government is attested even in the ill-documented crisis. The less distinguished among them could rise as secretaries;[2] those of a middle rank attained municipal magistracies and commemoration on their cities' coins;[3] while the aristocrats of the profession made their way to the summits of the imperial bureaucracy, especially in law. The connection between their usefulness there and their original training could be easily perceived by anyone properly educated as late as the eighteenth century: for there is "nothing so likely to improve you in that most material qualification for a lawyer, as translating Greek and Latin orations into English."[4] A precisely similar justification in Roman times (with omission of English) surrounded higher education in rhetoric. Even its most fustian, silly, and mechanical elements—its rote and drill, its turning of Cicero into Demosthenes and vice versa, its preoccupation with words over substance, its clashing casuistry over fantastic trivia, its memorizing of set texts and whole dictionaries of quotations and exempla, its mastery of bombast —all were considered somehow valuable. Very often in family lines of men who had gained success and who used their money for their sons' education, or sometimes by the desperate scramble upward of newcomers through the costly training process, a stream of literati and rhetoricians flowed into government.

Beyond the blunt fact of their being employed at all, a better proof exists of the high value set on them. The state offered support to what we may call secondary schooling as preliminary to higher education. For the latter itself, the state provided scholarships and teachers' salaries more generous yet, even in a time of financial troubles.[5] True, the salaries were paid not directly but through tax exemptions or payment authorization to the cities; scholarships took the same form; but backhanded subsidies of this sort were quite usual. It is true also that more abstract studies lumped under the term "philosophy" fell out of favor, and science likewise, as we will see. Their expendability only threw rhetoric into higher relief. Finally, it is true that the flourishing state of rhetoric in the second century appears not to have carried through the bleak 200s; but its reappearance in the 300s testifies to the success of government in the interval, in saving so essential and (as it was thought) so practical an aspect of culture.

When we turn to the point really in question, the usefulness of their education to the elite of government, doubts are bound to arise. On the face of it, there seems no reason why men with such training and mental habits should not have been intelligent, thoughtful, orderly analysts of their times. Yet, after all, an education in texts and talking is not the same as an education in history, and it was history, happening all around them, that they were required to understand. In the third century, the sensible Dio Cassius barely suffices to balance the triviality of Marius Maximus—both consuls, both historians.[6] After these, we must skip to the jejune and moralizing Aurelius

Victor, Festus, and Eutropius, much later, to gain any sense of how government officials (as these all were) perceived the flow of events. They are not a trio to inspire much respect.[7]

Schoolboy diligence in word choice and syntax often survived into adult years. Great noblemen loitering in the palace could be overheard discussing the nicest points of philology [8] with a mixture of preciosity and pedantry that carried right up from the second to the fourth century and drew court figures into the judging of generals and emperors upon the basis of their command of literature. When these hypereducated magistrates and bureau chiefs gave expression to their thoughts, it was in a manner no better matched to their responsibilities than their judgment of human qualities. Their style will be discussed in the next chapter. It should be said here, however, that documents of their drafting have puzzled many a modern student and can hardly have been much more easily understood by their contemporaries.[9] When we consider officials' formal education, which is to say, oratorical and literary, its effects seem to have been positively harmful within just the realm of its supremacy, the humanities.

Turning to other disciplines, we must judge how advanced they were by looking at the failures they could tolerate. We can hear that chaplain and professor in the court of Constantine, Lactantius, in his capacity as sociologist. He wonders whether there are cities in heaven. "If there are two sexes among the gods, sexual intercourse will follow; and if so, they must consider houses a necessity, for they are not so lacking in virtue and modesty as to indulge in this freely and openly. . . . If they have houses, it follows that they have cities." [10] His approach to the question carries the ethical and bookish along an extraordinary path; but his was a voice listened to by the emperor.

The intrusion of literature into alien fields had long been allowed. In a medical treatise, irregular heartbeats may be explained in terms of trochees, spondees, and iambs by a writer who went on to a lengthy work on botany, in hexameters.[11] Columella uses dozens of quotations from the *Georgics* to beautify his book on agriculture, until finally, toward its end, he bursts into song himself—some hundreds of lines on topics that Vergil had wisely neglected. A writer on surveying techniques from time to time inserts into his pages snippets of Vergil or of Lucan (misquoted),[12] and a high government servant employs his leisure in decorating a map with marginal poems in the style of Sappho.[13] None of these little items positively convicts Roman education of defrauding the civilization that supported it. Equally inappropriate or absurd applications of verse in polite society of the eighteenth century could be picked out, and misused so as to deny the very existence of scientific knowledge in that age. Still, the Roman examples seem to suggest that intellectual fashion contaminated technical studies with skills and learning derived from, and properly belonging only to, philology and oratory.

The state of geographical knowledge presents special puzzles. In the late third century maps of the world existed for students in schools, showing cities and peoples as well as natural features,[14] but we have no idea of the accuracy of anything of this sort—probably not of a very high level, since from the same period the Peutinger map, in surviving copies, wildly distorts what it presents,[15] and the Diocletianic edition of the Antonine itinerary is no better.[16] A little earlier, the work of the Ravenna cosmographer cites as authority a number of purely fictional predecessors, with a freedom recalling the worst habits of the Augustan History; [17] and a little later the anonymous *Expositio totius mundi,* of Constantius II's reign, incorporates from some recent predecessor a mythologizing picture of the East, and independently makes really extravagant errors about the north and west of the empire.[18] The fact that at least one of these overviews of the empire, the Antonine itinerary, probably met military and administrative needs [19] should not inspire confidence—quite the reverse. While there is no doubt that maps were consulted for military planning, the planners can have had no clear idea of what they were doing.[20] Ammianus, a professional soldier and an intelligent officer, places the river Durance on the wrong side of the Alps, though he had probably seen it himself; Commodus' advisers urged the completion of the Danube campaigns so as to "set the boundaries of empire at the north sea"—advice betraying a radically wrong conception of the world.[21]

At the very outset of the Principate, Agrippa had drawn up an atlas of the world with a commentary based on the best information available at the time. Augustus put it on display in Rome.[22] We hear of various later cartographic expeditions and efforts up through Hadrian's reign.[23] We

can seldom guess how scientific they were. But when
the elder Pliny gives distances, citing such efforts, everything else known of Roman maps suggests that he had in
front of him little more than illustrated travel reports,
really route-pictures just like the surviving ones; and his
mileages are subject to major error.[24] As to the commen-
taries to maps, on which he also draws for surprising detail, they have nothing to do with cartographic representation. We will return to them below. The sum of the matter confirms what was said earlier about technical skills
among the aristocracy of government, that they were not
cultivated in any scientific fashion, indeed, were barely
tolerated for specific needs of administration. That was a
good Roman way of looking at them—at a price. The
price to be paid lay in the lack of a means of seeing clearly
in the mind's eye the larger implications of geography. The
best intellects, surely because of a defect in their training,
turned from that to verbal description.

Arrangements for transport of tribute or army supplies,
or the visualizing of short-range, tactical problems, the
Romans could of course handle perfectly well. A wealth
of practical knowledge accumulated as much in their
living memories as in their records. The process owed
much to habits of appointing the right man to the right
job. Though a "state mayor," as he may be called—*logistes,
curator civitatis* or *reipublicae*—was as a rule not native to
the city he ran, there are many exceptions who knew local
problems firsthand.[25] Discrimination—for skills, however,
rather than for local knowledge—shows also in appointment of *praefecti civitatum*.[26] Moving up the scale of re-

sponsibility, equestrian officials were more often than not
stationed near their homes,[27] and special linguistic, accounting, regional, or military aptitude was acknowledged
in the appointment of Latin-speakers to the western provinces, for example, or former tax farmers to government
tax-collecting posts.[28] In this way, administration made use
of accumulated practical experience; and the principles
that we can see in operation in these various field appointments were at work, too, in the emperor's central bureaus,
progressively subdivided. The history of this latter development is well known.

Provincial government, looked at more carefully, seems
to have undergone a steady rationalization over the course
of the Principate.[29] The danger was recognized, however,
of going too far—of entrusting power to people where
their private interests or following might be too strong.
From Marcus Aurelius' reign onward, therefore, no one
was made a governor in his home province,[30] nor was he,
in the third century, to seat native provincials on his ad-
visory council.[31] On the other hand, his council does seem
to have embodied an *ad hoc* competence in the business
before it—legal, for instance, or military—and to have
represented a close familiarity with the region.[32]

As to the governor himself, it is obviously very difficult
to guess his fitness from the list of prior offices he may
have held. Many scores of careers known from earlier
centuries have been minutely studied without really coming to life; but in any case relatively little evidence that
would yield even blurred impressions has reached us from
our period. In consequence, it is perhaps best to offer only

three conclusions: first (as has been suggested above), that suitability of candidates was considered, in assigning them to a frontier of pacified, an eastern or western, command; second, that they had around them a useful variety of advisers; third, that they may have had to lean on the council and aides for much help, through their own incompetence. That last possibility arises from conjecture, based on the size of the pool of talent from which legates had to be drawn.

To the extent that it depended on agents of senatorial rank, government was committed to candidates chosen quite young and in ludicrously small numbers. By sheer necessity, the great majority of quaestors thus had to be elevated to praetorships (with posts that fitted promotion) and the great majority of these in turn elevated to consulships (with further higher appointments thereafter).[33] One of every two possible candidates for a legion would receive that command; three of every four consuls would rule a province. It stands to reason that a system could have produced better men in their fifties and sixties if they had not in effect been chosen in their twenties, and a better quality could have been assured had the choice lain among more competitors.

Around the turn of the second to the third century, a particularly large increase was made in the number of procuratorships.[34] These involved in broad responsibilities equestrians drawn from an adequate pool. In succeeding decades an occasional equestrian is found where there had traditionally been only senatorial governors; and in the 260s a change was introduced by which, first, praetorships were no longer the precondition for formerly senatorial governorships and, second, senatorial rank normally barred a person from legionary commands.[35] While these changes are not clear-cut or complete in every particular, their general scope is well known; and it is not hard to see their general results, too. They opened high military posts to long-term soldiers, and civil posts to a candidate class—the equestrian—that was many times larger than the senatorial. They may thus be taken, in sum, as a slowly defined criticism of the emperor's earlier dependence on the senate to fill top field commands. The common sense of staffing, clearly enough visible in the matching of tasks and talents at all periods, in the period of crisis gained ground against the prescriptive right of the aristocracy to fill the highest echelons of government if and to the extent they wanted. Progress, however, never attained or even closely approached its logical end: promotion solely by merit. Or rather, merit continued to be defined in a manner that included many qualities having nothing to do with effectiveness in office.

Mastery in literature, as we have seen, never lost its prestige. But however unsuitable its artificiality and prejudices to the daily duties of the elite, at least it guaranteed their literacy. What of their "numeracy"—to use that jargon term? A great deal of their work could be done well only if they could handle numbers. It is instructive to observe their mistakes. In so elementary a matter as the total of imperial victory acclamations (on which at least modern students depend for chronology), inconsistencies crept in;[36] for the dating of documents, no universal official calendar ever suppressed the many different ways of reckoning the beginning and length of each year—a failure that led to all sort of confusion.[37] Competent scribes might disagree on how to write small figures, and large ones produced serious confusions or inconsistencies in wills, official inscriptions, or tax records. Such errors are perceptibly more common in the third century than in the second,[38] and in anything more complicated than simple addition and subtraction. In the absence of a decimal system, fractions gave particular trouble. That is apparent in Egyptian land surveys and in a treatise addressed to Marcus Aurelius, who had apparently often complained of his ignorance in this skill. The writer of the treatise confesses his own ignorance as to how certain details are handled at Rome, implying regional differences in notation.[39] Given the low esteem enjoyed by mathematics, its neglect is not surprising. The ruling classes, with their own fixed ideas of what constituted the right subjects of study for gentlemen, neither encouraged nor received much education in it.[40] Presumably they left it to slaves, whose training for the central government and attendance on governors is well attested.[41] But it seems reasonable to suppose that officials having the ultimate responsibility for tax yields, salary totals, army expenses, and the like could not think through their problems very well. They were handicapped by quite rudimentary skills in calculation. Once again, the focus of intellectual training on literature is to blame.

Literacy and "numeracy" in the empire at large are impossible to estimate in absolute terms, but in relative, they both declined during the third century. No one would deny this. It was characteristic of the values of the ruling elite that they should always have maintained support of liberal studies while allowing more basic education for the masses to deteriorate.[42] The inevitable consequences followed. Perhaps no generalization can be ventured on the basis of an illiterate village secretary (!) under Commodus, illuminating though the one case may be, or on the basis of Diocletian's law permitting illiterates to be city decurions; but a study of inscriptions of all the Latin-speaking provinces shows a significant vagueness in people's knowledge of age.[43] They say on epitaphs and the like, "So-and-so, about 30 years old," rounding off their guess. Such approximations produce a disproportion of age-at-death figures in multiples of five; more still, in multiples of ten. That factor of disproportion is higher not only as one gets away from Italy to more backward regions, not only as one moves from the center of a city into its suburbs and then into the countryside, but also as one passes in time from the earlier to the late Principate. And in the latter period, cities gradually sink toward the level of rural areas. Knowledge or ignorance of age may fairly be taken as an indication of people's general accessibility to control, that is, of their knowing and being known to the operations of government.

From the Greek-speaking East, only Egypt allows a similar statistical approach. Results from that province, however, confirm the picture seen in the West. The total number of surviving papyri and ostraca begins to drop off under Septimius Severus. More significantly, it is not private documents like letters, leases, sales, contracts, and wills that become rarer—not till after 300—but public documents dealing with taxation, appeal, or meetings of officials.[44]

Putting together the two kinds of evidence, epigraphic and papyrological, from East and West, we are at least safe in saying that government commanded less frequent and exact knowledge and communication over its subjects in the period of crisis than earlier, that they put less in writing and kept worse records—precisely as one would expect, of course. For common sense unassisted would draw such consequences from the political chaos of the 200s, the increasing poverty which would affect schools, and the decline of urban life. As fewer people could write and count, this lack of skills would cause a matching decline in the quality of information available to governors and central officials. No matter whether these men were well equipped for their jobs intellectually, no matter how suited they were by experience, they could only act on the basis of what they knew; and the substructure of inventory that they relied on to form their policies grew weaker in just the decades of their greatest need.

About many aspects of life that can be called political in a very broad sense—about what people were thinking, what programs of change they were likely to tolerate, what degree of loyalty they felt to their governor or their emperor—government received news of a sort that fits better in the following chapter. But a specially important sort dealt with the empire's wealth. The number of its people underlay calculations for recruiting and for levying poll taxes; the amount of land in cultivation and its harvest each year underlay the levying of tribute to support Roman *plebs,* frontier forces, palace staff, and provincial headquarters. In appreciation of the need to know just where he stood for all these purposes, Augustus gathered information systematically from every region he ruled, and what he found out, his successors for many generations could more easily refine and keep up to date. The fullness of the overall results surprises. It allowed him to list (evidently in brief form, "all written in his own hand") the number of citizens and allies in the armed forces, client kingdoms and provinces, and the direct and indirect tax yield; to say how many Roman citizens of a certain property rating lived in a given region (Cyrene); and (on the assumption, generally agreed on by scholars, that the elder Pliny drew on Agrippa's map and commentary) to run down the alphabetized names of counties, cities, towns, and tribes in a province, each with its total population.[45] Many inscriptions record the activity of his agents in the field, *a censibus* or *ad census accipiendos.*[46] Their work stretched out over years and years and was faithfully renewed in later reigns, apparently on an ad hoc basis. There is, perhaps only by chance, a larger than usual number of relevant inscriptions dated to Hadrian and again to Septimius Severus. The former seems also to have introduced a fifteen-year cycle of population recount,[47] and the latter made a special tally of equestrians.[48] The two measures indicate how formidable a machinery the emperors controlled. All the categories of evaluation developed by Augustus survived, or were further improved up into the early third century. Severus' staff, for example, could have told him (with what accuracy is another question) how many resident aliens there were in Rome studying law, how many Roman citizens in the empire, how many veterans honorably discharged, how many persons over the age of a hundred, or the total population of a province.[49]

Along with demographic information, almost as a part of it, went a knowledge of wealth. This sometimes included a house in the city, slaves, possibly cash in hand, one's total value.[50] But so complete an assessment is attested only in narrow or special contexts. For the empire at large and in all periods, only real property can be assumed to have been subject to compulsory declaration. That meant surveying.

In a strict sense, every square mile (just like every individual and every slave and chest of gold coins) was known to someone in the empire. For the present and for the Roman government's purposes, however, all that counts is knowledge available for use in handy form. The whole story of centuriation can thus be left aside, except as it yielded the basis—grid or *forma*—by which hitherto unregistered lands were first measured out.[51] In half the empire the work had been done already by pre-Roman administrations. By the next stage, maps defining the bounds and status of lands were compiled in duplicate, one copy for local archives, a second on bronze for the central repository in Rome, there housed—many tons of inscribed metal sheets, we may suppose—in the *tabularium* (*sanctuarium*) *Caesaris*. But more convenient transcripts

on parchment or papyrus were prepared, too, and consulted in cases of dispute.[52] They determined the legal
condition—granted to individuals by benefice, set aside
for a colony, retained in state ownership, held by a provincial city, or whatever—of territory; within which, a last
phase of surveying determined precisely who owned
what.[53] On ownership in turn fell taxation, according to a
fixed format that was at least supposed to prevail. "In the
census *forma,*" write Ulpian, "care must be taken that
plots are entered in the census in the following way: name
of each estate; in what city and village; what are its two
nearest adjoiners; how many acres of arable sown in the
last decade; how many vine-plants in vineyards, how
many acres and trees in olive orchards; how many acres in
meadow mown in the last decade"; and so forth, by instructions showing very careful technique.[54]

The job of bringing ownership maps up to date lay with
local authorities. In their records office, big or small depending on the size of the city, they kept track of property
transfers, aided by the private citizen; for he came to them
to notarize and deposit in safety the deed of sale.[55] Good
land never ran away (though bad might be abandoned).
Any new titleholder would wish his acquisition to be
known. Natural conditions therefore insured that anyone
interested—Cicero in Sicily, Caligula in Gaul—could
quickly find out the disposition of all real estate of value
within a city's territory, at least in normal times. By the
same system, landowners as persons also were caught in
the net of administration. If they did not answer to their
names, their fields stood bond for their appearance, for

their tax payment, or for anything else required of them. In default, it could be confiscated. On the other hand, keeping count of the landless raised difficulties. Since machinery for a full, active census by the central government cost far too much, and since punishment for failure to register oneself worked only if offenders could be caught, there was really no way to apply force. Fraud and neglect on the part of the village official would work their way up to the metropolitan level, and to the governor's, and so to that of the imperial bureaus, quite uncorrected, even though major and obvious inadequacies doubtless would attract attention somewhere along the line.

The alternative was to encourage spontaneous compliance. Into the early third century, the advantages that attended Roman citizenship attracted the registration of an increasing percentage of the population; so did special privileges, mostly immunities. Up to a certain age, and again after a certain age, one was exempt from taxes and liturgies; the large number of one's children might bring reward; attested legitimacy, or local citizenship, might make one's way smoother; qualification for free food might depend on enrollment; and of course it meant a lightening of one's taxes to report a flight or death in one's household.[56] So as to profit from these various advantages people were even willing to pay to be registered.[57] And periodic remissions of tax arrears drew fugitives back into the net, especially in census years.[58] Nevertheless, only that last device can have done much to reach rural areas, where village officers lacked the resources, sometimes even the literacy, to do a good job, and where squatters on abandoned or never-surveyed land could be detected only by direct inspection.[59]

Viewed over all, the gathering of data on population seems likely to have functioned surprisingly well, so as to produce quite minute statistics in convenient and centralized form, but only in time of prosperity. It required voluntary compliance, such as could be stimulated by the offer of rewards of one kind or another. In the better-run districts, which are also the better-known to us today, easily consulted codices summed up the day-to-day operations of large staffs of clerks in handsomely housed public registries. A parallel and in some ways parasitic gubernatorial staff could thus obtain and forward to the emperor up-to-date figures on the number, age, and wealth of citizens in each province. This harvest of information, however, required a favorable climate. If contact with government should ever seem to citizens more hurtful than helpful, then the system would certainly produce very unsatisfactory results.

Third-century conditions brought decisive changes. In Egypt, to the very edge of the crisis, census material continued to be collected efficiently, and even later, past 250: local officials knew only too well the declining numbers in the cities, especially among the richer classes, or used the census rolls with chilling efficiency in the persecution of Christians;[60] but thereafter, until the Tetrarchy remodeled the whole system, the old machinery for registration of any sort simply came to a halt.[61] It is likely that, in Egypt as elsewhere, liturgists working it at the local level[62] had to be driven themselves; and when the necessary energy and direction from above were no longer applied in politically chaotic times, they let their jobs drop. If so relatively undisturbed a province as Egypt suffered, then we can imagine far worse effects in frontier areas overrun by invasions. Even bronze maps could be destroyed, when war lit the fires.[63]

Whatever the details of deterioration in the supply of essential data to the government, there can be no doubt that the Tetrarchs had much to do. Syria, Palestine, and Arabia provide evidence of a major program of resurvey, including an almost unprecedented attention by the cental authorities to the minutiae of boundaries and land evaluation all the way down to the smallest units of ownership. The process commenced in 297 or a little earlier, in preparation for a new tax structure. After a decade, Galerius redoubled its operations in the area he commanded most directly, Bithynia.[64] In the intervening years work had been going on steadily, at least in the East (the western provinces being hidden from us), very much like Augustus' great inventory. But there is no sign under Diocletian that it touched people as opposed to land. That fact may account for the minor role he assigned to taxes on the propertyless, and their virtual abandonment by Constantine. On the other hand, as we will see below, Diocletian's tax system did take careful account of the individual citizen as a necessary adjunct of productive land; and under Constantine the census rolls were once again in operation.[65] Finally, in Egypt Diocletian is known to have introduced a new census cycle for periodic up-dating, which Constantine changed to make less frequent.[66]

Recurrent, large-scale measures from the 290s on, for a generation, show just how serious the need was felt to be, for an accurate count of resources. The emperor of course was concerned about getting and using money and manpower, not about informaton for its own sake. Ever the pragmatist, in his conversations with his council he surely dealt with specific problems as they arose. Yet solutions cannot have been agreed on without recourse to compendious reports of a statistical kind. Someone must have been asked whether the strength of the realm would support a war with Persia. At that point, all labor given to the gathering of data found its justification. We cannot advance further, to say how well it answered its purpose, in an absolute sense—whether better by a five-year census cycle, for example, or better by a fierceness of inquest that almost punished compliance. Instead of complying, indeed, more people slipped through the administrative net year by year; fewer every year knew how to read or write and became therefore the less useful as registrants or registrars serving the government's purposes. But in a relative sense, Roman government as an intelligence certainly represented from Diocletian on a great improvement over the chaos of ignorance that prevailed during the crisis.

Some idea of the difference between, let us say, the 260s and the 290s can be drawn from comparison of two brief passages belonging to an earlier and a later era. The first describes the calm of the mid-second century, when the emperor "has no need to wear himself out traveling around the whole empire to make sure of each point. It is very easy for him to stay where he is and manage the entire civilized world by letters which arrive almost as soon as they are written, as if they were carried by winged messengers." [67] To be sure, the speed of his communication may have been a little less than winged. Letters traveled not by carrier pigeon, not by horse, but by mule and donkey; sailing ships waited on the season.[68] Still, the picture of the smooth centralizing of facts and news was believable in the empire at its height. After the crisis, recovery was never complete. In the East in the 390s "it was impossible to add to the account anything accurate about affairs in the West; for the great distance of time by sailing-communication rendered reports out of date and valueless by delay. Anyone able, through travel or service, to know state matters there recounted them according to his likes, dislikes, and whims. So if anyone brought together three or four such persons with conflicting stories. there was a great war of words. And traders too lied without exception." [69]

There is the ring of truth to this latter passage. Moreover, being so vivid and specific, it prompts the same way of looking at problems during the crisis. At the center were men who felt responsible for the world's salvation. They must meet the danger of its ruin by great efforts. Specifically, they must determine at some given moment just what troops must be called on, where they were stationed at the time, how long and by what route they must travel to the point of challenge. The emperor and his advisers poring over the Peutinger table and over dispatches known to be four months old can have confronted only clumsily—indeed in this scene they do much to explain—

the empire's vulnerability to simultaneous attack on more than one front. Behind that vulnerability loomed larger difficulties, ill perceived. If reports came in from some border area that there were no supplies to be had, its resources would have to be canvassed in discussions based on memoranda of its former harvests. If these showed a change, then it must be asked why good land had gone out of cultivation. If it was answered that labor to work the fields was lacking, then where had everyone gone? Could the report be trusted, telling of a fifth or a third of the population suddenly lost to sight; and if so, were adjoining areas in a better condition, or were they too distant, or themselves deserted? From whatever resources remained, was it feasible to make good the deficits discovered? And for the future, how could resources be assured? So extended and complex was the unraveling of the empire's power to defend itself, it strained every power of comprehension. The two powers were one: for defense required a planned response. And planning revealed at work the best and worst of the administrative mind.

In communicating with its subjects, government should first have secured broad literacy and then have spoken the people's language. It did neither (though the intent to arouse and instruct is very much in evidence) because it would not betray, but rather placed ever higher value upon, rhetorical display. Physical destruction left cities in need of repair. The emperors instead built palaces and subsidized the training of mosaicists and fresco painters in place of mathematics teachers and surveyors, because the object was, after all, recovery of lost grandeur, and the usefulness of skills in counting could not be understood. In their absence, the ponderous folly of price fixing; in their absence, costly fumbling with the money supply; in their absence and in the absence of other skills of inventory, worst of all, the crisis as a whole took on more than human and natural dimensions. So, while remarkably energetic response was offered to mere symptoms, many of the causes were left to interpretation through myths and moralizing. Men were thought to have grown worse, for no reason but the gods' anger. In a divine and preordained drama was thought to lie the reason for shaken loyalties, food shortages, or the disappearance of whole generations from the census rolls (above, chapter 1). Courage and energy abounded, to face even these; recovery had its heroes, its flashes of discovery and invention; but its results reflected the characteristic strengths and weaknesses of the governing intelligence.

4

LAW

To whatever the state wanted of its citizens in the third and early fourth century, according to whatever central plan or policy, legislation gave expression. In theory, it controlled the governed; in reality, it darkened rather than defined their lives. "Between the idea and the reality, between the motion and the act, falls the shadow."

Its theoretical control arose out of the fundamental aim and origin of law, to supply an alternative to self-help. In offering its arbitration it could indirectly shape every aspect of society: for example, the distribution of wealth contested under such purely civil headings as sale or inheritance. Far more obviously, it asserted its control through criminal and administrative law, that is, through the defining of what contributed to the common good. In a state gripped by dangers, quite a priori we would look for a shift of emphasis from civil to criminal and administrative law, from the realm of Rome's traditional eminence to a realm it had neglected—from a realm in which *utilitas publica* would most often be mentioned in circumscribed, local contexts, or not at all, to one where "the common good" embraced the empire very broadly; in short, from the Digest to the Codes. Exactly that great shift of emphasis confronts us in the compilations surviving to this day. The very books on our shelves tell us of a response to crisis.[1]

But actual as opposed to theoretical control over the crisis was not to be gained merely by writing a different kind of law. Its success depended on the respect commanded by its source. The emperor, for reasons of safety as well as awe, in the period of crisis interposed new corps of special guards between himself and ordinary human beings; hung curtains before the openings to the palace and its inner chambers; and cut himself off still further by a wall of silent and always standing courtiers around himself seated and oracular.[2] Distance on distance, magnificence on magnificence, gold on silver, swords on silk, were piled up to an Olympian height for the exaltation of the ruler. When he deigned to appear to his people, it was like the epiphany of some god. His residence was holy. His mere wish was law.[3] "Rejoice, Romans," he could intone over the very tax payments he demanded, which taxpayers cringingly called "the august." [4] If their obedience faltered, the embodiment of Mercifulness, Tranquillity, Piety, and Kindness reproved them with sonorous sermonizing.[5] Great efforts were made to invest his words with every quality that could insure veneration. A special color of ink, special rhythmic prose patterns, and a dic-

tionary of special words belonged only to his pronouncements. Hence the manner of their reception. "A ruler
sends his edict to a province. What do the provincials do?
They accept it and rise to their feet and uncover their
heads, and read with reverence and awe, with fear
trembling." [6]

Locally, at the level of such scenes, governors echoed on
their master's behalf the same notes that he sounded from
his palace. They devised formulae of honorific salute to
third-century rulers, repeating them verbatim across whole
series of inscriptions ordered for public display, proclaim-
ing the *Indulgentia novi saeculi* and the emperor *Invictus
Restitutor orbis,* who had insured *res prospere gestae.*[7] It
was governors who must compose advertisements of the
emperor's demise or accession: "In a white-horsed chariot,
having just now mounted aloft . . . ," or "Everyone in
crowds offering sacrifices and prayers . . . ," and so forth
—so run the texts.[8] Governors again added respectful but
edifying introductions to imperial edicts for local publication.[9] Imitating palace ceremonial, judges withdrew their
own majesty behind embroidered hangings;[10] and even
to municipal magistrates, imperial decrees secured the
privilege of sitting in public meetings, while others had
to stand.[11] Thus outward signs ornamented and raised up
the whole structure of command.

The emperor, the idealized Alexander Severus or the
real Hadrian or Septimius Severus, drafted no legislation
without consulting a panel of experts.[12] From the second
century in Rome and from the third century in Beirut, we
hear of laws schools, too, at the latter city flourishing more

and more as the center of power moved eastward.[13] With the codifications of Diocletian's reign—Gregorian, Hermogenian, Collatio legum Mosaicarum et Romanorum[14]—a fifth year had to be added to the course of study at Beirut. Its graduates were in great demand, fine careers opened out to them,[15] for their own half of the empire served increasingly as head of legislation and adjudication. That, incidentally, drew a western science into an area where Greek prevailed. In consequence, Latin was both consciously and casually spread by Diocletian and his successors, and painfully learned by young men ambitious to rise in the bureaucracy.[16]

From all periods of the empire comes testimony to the care taken by the emperors that their will should be amply known to their subjects. Claudius, for example, writes, "I wish this edict of mine to be registered by magistrates of the cities, colonies, and municipalities in Italy or outside Italy, and by princes and powers through their own emissaries, and to be displayed not less than thirty days where it can be easily read from the ground"—though perhaps more significant of wide implementation of imperial edicts is the fact that the last phrase could be abbreviated in inscriptions, as being everywhere familiar: $u(t)$ $d(e)$ $p(lano)$ $r(ecte)$ $l(egi)$ $p(ossit)$.[17] There is another kind of test: actual knowledge and use of laws by everyday citizens, evidently benefiting from multiplication and preservation of copies in the provinces.[18] Limiting ourselves just to the third and early fourth century, we can see the proofs of accessibility of law through its citation by appellants, some of whom reach back to a period a hundred years or more earlier. Sometimes the same text survives to this day in more than one place. Diocletian's Edict on Prices, inscribed in stone in many eastern towns and implied in perishable form elsewhere, is the most famous illustration; but much is suggested by a text from Ephesus, in which the governor bids competing plaintiffs to produce for him laws, edicts, *senatusconsulta,* and any relevant parts of Ulpian's treatise *De officio proconsulis.*[19] Obviously he expected parties to this case—granted, it was a major one with a full team of experts—to be able to assemble quite a legal dossier.

Another inscription, where the emperor sitting as judge engages in an argument with the plaintiff, brings us to the matter of his approachability. That could insure his better acquaintance with the problems of the empire, as well as the better administration of justice. Here too, just as he tried to make his will clearly known to his subjects, so he granted them access to himself, not only during better-documented and less disturbed periods but in the third century also.[20] His personal participation, however, is hardly attested in trial scenes beyond the Severi. Ceremonial isolation may account for the fact that thereafter he is to be seen reacting in person only to delegations of complainants [21] whose size imparted both courage and a good deal of massed formality to what they said. Individual members may speak up, but ordinarily the group acclaims or requests as a whole, and the emperor remains very much in command. "The idle utterances of the people are not to be listened to," declares Diocletian in one irritable exchange—irritable perhaps from overwork. In

our sources for his reign, nearly a hundred provincial appeals can be counted, most often arising out of their own
preparatory meetings at home. Diocletian it is who says
elsewhere, "the means of petition are, We think, not to be
granted to everyone unreservedly and indiscriminately." [22]

In fact, from the second century on, government procedures had come to involve an increasing dependence
on central direction. Though this was all too natural,
Trajan and Hadrian and Antoninus Pius were alert to the
ill consequences it might bring with it: they might be
drowned in ink.[23] They had to issue orders on contro-
versial matters referred upward to them by governors, or
replies (*rescripta*) to private parties' appeals (*libelli*) for
reference downward to provincial authorities. The stream
of decisions required of the emperors in person swelled
continually, up to a high under the Severi. There is reason
to estimate at some 1,500 the annual number of libelli
answered by Septimius,[24] and nothing in the logic of constitutional and legal developments seemed likely to relieve
this overwhelming press of business. As it turned out, of
course, a period of chaos followed the death of the last
Severan. Thereafter, evidence for what we have just discussed—publication of laws, the citizen's familiarity with
it, and access to its highest source—is for a time very
scarce or totally lacking. Not before Diocletian's reign
does it reappear.

To give consistency to the law and thus to insure ready
compliance, it was necessary to keep track of it in both
central and provincial archives. The former yielded the
materials for codification under Diocletian or for applica-

tion to particular cases as they came up. Severus can pull out letters of Antoninus Pius and Marcus Aurelius in settling the status of a Moesian city just as Claudius could quote letters on the status of Troy.[25] Storage and retrieval of documents were thus sufficiently systematized to be of some use, just how much we will judge a little later. But provincial archives, attached to various offices, seem to have played at least an equally important role. In Egypt, village and city magistrates recorded their actions, so also district supervisors, the juridicus, and the governor.[26] Records were open to public inspection. Those of the governor, like those of the emperors, must have been voluminous; for he seems to have handled an equally heavy case load. In the early third century, during two and a half days of hearings at Arsinoe, the Egyptian prefect took in 1804 pleas, answers to which were displayed locally for the benefit of anyone interested, and published also in Alexandria.[27] In Alexandria, the satirist Lucian had served as a clerk a generation earlier: "I would," he recalls, "appear to have been responsible for no inconsiderable part of the government of Egypt, entering judgments and putting them in proper order, and writing up what was decided and said along with the verdicts of governors, to be preserved and entrusted to the public archives." [28]

What we know of other provinces fits well with this evidence.[29] From many areas east and west, from 250 on to the toleration edict, Christians' trials preserve for us evidence of the accessibility of court records, and therein the whole routine of arrest, hearings, verdicts, and penalties. Governors are liable to contradiction just like Caracalla or Diocletian; and like Diocletian and Constantine, their administration of justice may on occasion be submitted to the bar of public opinion in open meetings of some freedom. At any rate, Constantine encourages provincials in their assemblies to express their feelings about their governors with cheers or boos, not merely of claques (*clientelae*). Easier said than done, perhaps. Those same records of the persecutions reveal the savagery that might be applied against the "atheists" of Africa or Palestine, no different, as far as that goes, from measures taken to coerce reluctant taxpayers.[30] It was a cruel age, more so than the earlier centuries of the Principate. Comparisons are difficult to draw, but the need for respect of law with which this chapter began seems in the stress of troubled times to have been amply reinforced by brutal punishment aimed at its wretched victims in deliberately advertised and didactic form.[31] Terror was a kind of teaching.

From top to bottom, the external structure of law has a uniform appearance. Allowing for differences in position, master and servant, emperor and governor of the smallest province alike paid regard to the facade, so as to make it properly imposing. For all their conscious isolation, serving to exalt and set them apart, they are also seen in direct touch with their subjects. By meetings with petitioners and by receipt of a great flood of correspondence, they could understand and answer real daily problems; and in framing their answers, they got help from a staff whose literary and specifically legal training were fostered by various kinds of state grants and who had at hand repositories of previous decisions to consult. Lucian, to judge from his writings, had a crisp, easy style and a first-rate intelligence and knew how to work. Ulpian's powers were phenomenal. If these two men were in any way representative of the legal bureaucracy at the central and provincial levels, it could hardly have been improved. And the fruits of their thought received proper treatment: a fair copy in purple ink, if it was an imperial edict; dispatch by state post; duplication for local archives, and public display *"u. d. p. r. l. p."* as the abbreviation went, "so it can be properly read from the ground." Thereafter, enforcement brought to bear moral suasion or thumbscrews, as needed.

The whole picture of the machinery of Roman law is of course perfectly familiar. Sketched out as it has been thus far, it arouses admiration for its logic, its size, its nicely fitted parts. But our concern lies with its actual operation, first, and then with its suitability to the saving of the state in crisis. Were patterns of oppression of one class by another becoming apparent? Patterns of evasion? Were obligations to the state fairly served out? Loopholes and inequities repaired? Such were the questions important to government and important to our inquiry. As we proceed further, it will be seen that the doubts indicated at the outset of this chapter are confirmed by the study of the workings of the machine.

At the height of the empire, the best of rulers were reminded that they must not set themselves above their own decrees (that was apparently something they were prone to do), and a whole province could be dismissed as "ignorant of law." [32] An emissary to eastern cities reports how oblivious they are of their own charters in the sharing of their citizenship,[33] and other communities much nearer Rome showed a kind of casual defiance of officialdom, no matter how often rebuked.[34] Officials themselves did not always prove very responsive to higher authority. They were too long habituated, from Republican times, to a most independent exercise of office. On their tribunals, they were likely to conduct themselves in a quite arbitrary fashion, going so far as to disobey specific directives from above even in capital cases—the instances emerge most clearly through the record of the persecutions [35]—or brandishing threats of hideous severity that reflected not what they could find in the statute books but their irritability and arrogance. It is only fair to add frustration, too. Dependent on informers, with almost no civil policemen and a quite inadequate number of soldiers as substitutes, they had no easy job in bringing to bear the force that in theory they commanded. Hence, their exasperation directed against any evasion or defiance.[36]

The machinery of Roman law, then, looked more formidable than it was. At rest, it inspired respect. In motion, its interconnections proved loose; an autocratic force at its center, though unchallenged, did not closely engage or drive the gears of government; in misalignment, agent parts protested shrilly or barely turned at all. It was thus in Rome; it was thus in a small provincial town. At every point of operation deficiencies appeared quite out of character, it would at first seem, with the schools and libraries and courts of law, and the many officers appointed to put it into effect. But the third century further revealed the unsuitability of the machinery for the handling of complex emergencies.

A bill of particulars may take up where legislation itself ordinarily began, that is, at the local level. Let us imagine something gone wrong. News must travel to the capital. If initiative lay with a private citizen, we must ask whether a system which should have ensured uniformity, control, and a full flow of information to the emperor really did achieve all these benefits. In fact we have, from a slightly later copy in Egypt, a declaration of Alexander Severus also recorded in the Digest: "To the Council of the Bithynian Greeks: I cannot see how anyone can be prevented by the judges from making an appeal, since there is another route toward the same end, and a better one, leading to myself. For to use outrage and violence toward petitioners and surround them with soldiers and, in brief, to wall them off from approach hither, is forbidden to proconsuls and governors." [37] A century later, in the most emphatic way possible, Constantine reiterates "to any person of any position, rank, or dignity whatever . . . , let him approach me. I myself will hear everything, I myself will conduct an investigation"; and in another text, "the petitions of municipalities shall be brought intact and unimpaired," that is with nothing "changed or mutilated," to praetorian prefects.[38] Intimidation, force, censorship, and fraud all thus combined to block the path upward to the source of ultimate justice—only too successfully. For, besides the indirect proof lying in repeated, evidently ineffective, legislation, we have from Egypt a number of petitions to the emperor preserved because they were caught fast in some intermediate office, and there used as scratch paper.[39] No better fate could be assured to personal visits to Rome. One should allow two years for them [40]—a sign of the very sluggish operation of appeal, though setting one in motion in the first instance might develop just as slowly: on a capital charge, it must be lodged within six months of conviction in Italy, twelve months beyond the Alps, eighteen months across the sea.[41] The law's delays have always been proverbial. Constantine in 319 aimed four directives at the problem. Two dealt with a shortage of lawyers, who abandoned cases discouragingly entangled in the bureaucracy; one dealt with bureaus that failed to act before the statute of limitations ran out; and a fourth with bureau chiefs whose deliberate inaction made a nullity of the orders they were supposed to enforce.[42]

On the other hand, where it was an official who took the initiative, his appeal for guidance lay through much overburdened channels of decision. We have seen how congested they were, how heavy a work load was shouldered by the emperor and his staff. They could not in the early second century prevent, and by the late second century they encouraged, the referring of a flood of business from local to central authority. Thence issued advice to the judge.[43] So far as it concerned criminal and administrative law, and in both its development and its authority, it left a good deal to be desired. The *ius coercitionis* of governors, the power arrogated to themselves by such lesser officials as procurators, had not been much changed by the codification of the provincial edict; form and outcome of cases to which the state was a party remained even in the classical period perfectly uncontrolled and unpredictable,[44] and up into the fourth century, as we have seen, it was still possible for the judge of a Christian to release, imprison indefinitely, or execute the accused quite on his own. A treatise like Ulpian's on senatorial governorships, or Modestinus' special attention to municipal obligations, thus represented in the first half of the third century a marked advance.[45] It came very late in the day. Henceforth, demands made upon the civil population for services of all sorts were to increase dramatically, and, correspondingly, litigation to which the state was a party. It was Rome's misfortune that the experts necessary to continue the refining of law in this undeveloped area were succeeded by mere bureaucrats after Alexander Severus.

So far as civil law is concerned, developments are less closely relevant to our subject. Questions regarding gifts, divorce, testaments, contracts, and so forth had been answered by the great jurisconsults over the centuries speaking directly to private inquiry or indirectly through the judicial system. Their monument was *ius,* law as opposed to laws. By 240 their line had come abruptly to an end. Thereafter, inquiry aimed only at the emperor, bureaucratization replaced scholarship, and the day of *lex* set in. Given the nature of the crisis, all this was to be expected. Hostility toward the too intellectual, the discarding of niceties, contempt for the quibbler, all showed themselves in many aspects of later Roman culture. Why not in law? [46] Moreover, to stimulate obedience to a reordering of the economy and society, government sharply increased its propaganda. That affected many institutions, as we have seen. Again: why not law as well? In fact, in the last phases of recovery, Diocletian dissolved into a single office the bureau once dominated by jurists answering libelli and the bureau dominated by rhetorizing stylists issuing commands and pronouncements, *epistulae*. While the resulting contamination was kept within bounds by Diocletian's respect for the inheritance of ius, Constantine gave it free rein. Bombast broke into the most vulnerable intricacies of his legislation.[47] In a law of 316 that explicitly puts jurisconsults out of business, once and for all, after many laborious centuries, he demotes "mere technicalities" to second place beneath moral, or moralizing, considerations; and in 321 he determines to eradicate "the endless haggling of the law experts." [48]

There were the accumulated consequences of the 200s brought to bear upon a particular set of institutions. The Dominate transformed law from a discipline to a means of discipline—which could, one would suppose, serve better to confront the needs and dangers that beset the empire. Yet there was a price to be paid.

At the same time that floods of new rules issued in response to new social and economic difficulties, the skills to rationalize those rules were at a discount; great collections like the Gregorian were being assembled, while their contents were oversimplified and distorted; [49] and periphrases, preaching, self-praise, and highly colored phraseology rendered laws increasingly hard to understand. For proof, the reader need only imagine himself as a semiliterate citizen in the public square of a not very big eastern town, agog before the preface to the Price Edict. The experience is a revelation—not in the way Diocletian meant it. But the same features of style can be seen throughout official

documents of every sort.[50] Scholars commonly identify
them as "vulgar," "vulgarrechtlich." I would attribute
these qualities to the use of less educated servants in the
bureaucracy, even in high positions, matching the rise of
superstition and magic into the leadership levels of religion,
antiintellectualism in philosophy, the gaudy grandilo-
quence of domestic and private architecture, and many
features of the plastic arts. All such developments, in law
as elsewhere, would naturally arise from the disruptions of
the crisis, such as shook out senators from governorships
or brought the barracks into the palace.

A soldier-emperor was after all not likely to have a jurist's way of looking at things. So far as he gave himself to
legislation, the results might be badly framed. If he suffered *damnatio memoriae,* his edicts died with him.
Hence, the two respects in which the third century in
particular must have suffered.[51] Even in better periods,
however, there was no adequate filing system for imperial
directives or decisions, to give them continuity. Against
evidence that they could be and were consulted, more revealing instances must be set, showing their limitations.
Trajan, for example, is found in the absurd situation of
asking his agent in Bithynia (who had just consulted
him) for a copy of an earlier emperor's decree, unavailable
in the capital.[52] Evidently he expected it to be found somewhere in provincial archives. But such a free correspondence as Pliny's and Trajan's could be conducted only in
a world at peace. Once again, the disruptions of the third
century must have accentuated already existing weaknesses in the system of law.

The singularity of cities and provinces in respect to law is most striking. Pliny and Trajan acknowledge the claims of Bithynian cities, papyri speak of "Egypt's law" for decades after the gift of universal citizenship in 212; Papinian yields to Antioch's claims, or to the usury regulations of any district at all; Gaius speaks with the same respect of local leaseholds; and so it goes through the third and fourth centuries.[53] To revert to Trajan's letters: where variety ruled, obviously the emperor could not—at least not with any compass or ease. "I can give no generally applicable decision," he answers to a question Pliny raises; to another question, "there is nothing to be found in the *commentaria* of Our predecessors that applies to all provinces"; and once more, "I have consulted a senate decision bearing on this sort of case, but it deals only with senatorial provinces."[54] He accedes quite matter-of-factly to a patchwork of special jurisdictions, special rights, and degrees of autonomy. He had no choice. To be sure, the eastern half of the empire which is best known to us happens also to have been the most privileged. Allowance must be made for that. As we move toward the west, we see the royal writ running more freely.[55] Whatever the region, nevertheless, laws regulating marriage, let us say, or rates of interest had to be tailor-made to local peculiarities and could be broadened only gingerly to include other places by afterthought and experiment.[56] A related difficulty arose from the exercise of local jurisdiction by makeshift or non-Roman judges, prefects of unincorporated communities, procurators, *defensores civitatum,* ad hoc substitutes for regular judges, marketplace magistrates, commanders of resident troop units, big landowners and squires, and so on through a long list of persons whose fitness, training, and verdicts were really beyond imperial control.[57]

In these rights and arrangements, looked at as one whole nexus, the emperor's predominance of course stands out quite unchallenged. In bringing that predominance to bear, however, he had to accept many restrictions. Perhaps least trammeled but also least relevant to our subject was his reply to some individual appeal; but even here, to avoid possible conflict with some other locus of privilege, he must take care not to suggest that his decision was valid everywhere. In legislation that he originated out of the needs of his own government—the most relevant for us—here too he had to consider the heterogeneity of his realm, through slightly different laws for slightly different provinces. And at the end, he knew very well that his will would be misinterpreted or ignored or never known at all in numberless little towns and rural communities. They did not lack their courts, only they were not in any true sense Roman imperial courts.

Details of the difficulties just sketched generally elude us. On so important a question as the grant of universal citizenship, and despite decades of modern debate, all we can say is that Roman and local law continued their history of mutual interpenetration undisturbed. But even that broad statement serves our purpose in showing the resistance of the empire to uniform restructuring by any grand enactment. Another, more concrete demonstration emerges from the history of taxation. "It is noteworthy that Diocletian could not achieve the implementation of his system except in the region closest to his capital"; [58] no less noteworthy, the many other proofs of tax policy baffled and unfulfilled (in chapter 6, below). They betray in the most vital areas of government and in the sharpest emergency how far apart were the theory and reality of absolutism.

Roman jurists and emperors were not blind to reality. They made place for it not only under the dispensation of specific founding charters at specific historical junctures (for instance, the Lex Pompeia in Bithynia) but under *consuetudo* as well. That term, "custom," explained at an abstract level the toleration of variety. At a lower, more practical level, it saved money; for the price of imposing uniformity has always come high. "Custom grown old is rightly regarded as a substitute for law," and "rights are secured which have been approved by long-standing custom and observed over a number of years, no less than those in written form" [59]—such declarations over the third century carry forward a traditional willingness on government's part to limit the weight of its task, to leave well enough alone, to hold back from too much legislation. It is jurists who speak, not officialdom. Their toleration of a rival to both ius and lex is all the more significant, and survived and was extended somewhat under Constantine.

Granted, it never takes the form of a blank check. Custom is restricted to a supplementary role, filling gaps left in law proper; it must be patient and earn its acceptance through *longi temporis praescriptio,* the claim of time unchallenged over ten, twenty, or forty years; and it is acknowledged principally in administrative areas, not civil, that is, principally in connection with market regulations, municipal elections, public nuisances, liturgies, boundary posting. These were always of least interest to classical jurists, though bound to receive an increasing attention in postclassical times. What we can also observe, however, if we turn from juristic writings to specific executive decisions, is a considerably broader surrender to consuetudo. Trajan once again provides illustration. Faced with "long-standing custom usurped, contrary to law, . . . a compromise recommends itself to me." He will forbid future abuses of the sort being discussed but not correct the past —precisely the decision taken by Nero in a similar case before him and by Septimius Severus after, and with the same scrupulous reference to "usurpation." [60] Domitian yields to "custom shortly developing into law," as Gordian to "primordial custom," [61] and Constantine merely follows their example in his legislation.[62]

But law is not isolated from its times. Just as it reflects some of the broad changes to be seen also in third- and fourth-century sculpture, "vulgar law" and "popular" art making a pair, so it might be expected to reflect the backward glance that can be caught in the religious visions of the crisis. These were touched on in the first two chapters above. A special reverence for the past speaks in Diocletian's legislation; with some admixture of a new spirit that permitted innovation, it speaks in Constantine's legal philosophy as well.[63] Provisions established for no more than ten or twenty years it hallows as "ancient," suggesting how unhistorical was the viewpoint prevailing, how eager to discover some anchorage in tradition. But tradition, long-standing usage, usurpation, status quo, consuetudo, *mos,* whatever the name given to it, of course constituted an enemy to change just when change was most needed, and respect for it constituted an admission that the Dominate itself could not have its way with its subjects. They had *their* ways.

Which returns our discussion to the machinery of law seen at the local level. Having begun, some pages back, with the appeals and requests for guidance that carried thence to the capital; having described there the tardy shift of attention from civil to criminal and administrative law, and the collapse of classical jurisprudence; having shown the weakness of administrative law forced into accommodation with the variety and intractability of custom, we must see what happened when word came down from Rome to the governor's office.

That word was likely to be long. At least under Diocletian and his successors, as we have seen, polysyllables and periphrases were freely used even in legal documents. Administrative documents much earlier had anticipated that development. The humblest clerk, the shoddiest soldier collecting taxes, did his best to dignify his acts with the style affected by the chancery. Private citizens followed suit, referring, for example, to expenses as "the extraordinaries." [64] Such circumlocutions were intended to impart something special. That was their more obvious purpose in official communications. They might equally blur or hide the truth. Their rapid spread in the third and later centuries accompanied and smoothed the way for corruption.

Officials have always sold their services. They demand payment either directly, as bribes from citizens, or indirectly, as salaries from taxes that citizens pay. In an economic sense, a corrupt government may be more efficient than an honest. Not in a political sense, however; for its agents may offer their obedience to other paymasters. By way of illustration, the three years 319–321 offer a group of directives against collusive delays by bureaus that should enforce the law; against "perverse and inflamed governors" who impose illegal penalties; against "the neglectfulness of governors who defer obedience to imperial commands"; against "a person who had been corrupted by a bribe and has given an unjust decision"; and against "the fraudulent statements of officials." [65] A particular fury of frustration seizes Constantine at the prevalence of judicial verdicts put up for sale:

> The chamber curtain of the judge shall not be venal; entrance shall not be gained by purchase, the private council chamber shall not be infamous on account of the bids. The appearance of the governor shall not be at a price; the ears of the judge shall be open equally to the poorest as to the rich. There shall be no despoiling on the occasion of escorting persons inside.[66]

It was by no means a new problem that emerges from this passionate rebuke. Minor tips and presents had long oiled the contacts of petitioners with those more powerful than themselves: in Roman army camps, in the anterooms of the great, in municipal records offices. Not before the third century, however, does a wealth of testimony to the practice gather round the provincial governor himself.[67] His role as the executive link in the machinery of law needs no explaining, nor do the consequences of his corruptibility. That the statutes he posted up in Ephesus or Carthage might be obscurely worded, or the curtains and ceremonies around him forbidding, counted as nothing beside the fact that he might be bought. That more than any other barrier divided the emperor's will from fulfillment among his subjects.

Cyprian knows the system as a contemporary; "There is nothing to be afraid about in the laws. What is for sale is not feared." [68] As much might be inferred from the stridency and repetitiveness of legislation. Emperors had to shout to be heard—and were still ignored. Nor would we have before us in our sources so many rebukes to government servants for doing too little or too much if they had not really been too often derelict. But add yet one more fact: that Constantine decreed a certain limit to the "rake-off" army commanders could demand from civil officials delivering their supplies.[69] With that, set against all his raging at corruption, he confesses outright his lack of control over the grand machinery of autocracy. Between his will and his subjects "falls the shadow."

Deterioration of government, thus demonstrated (if always out of reach of exact measurement), set in because of the crisis itself. That conclusion emerges from two sets of figures. The first, the number of emperors in a small space of time, takes us back to the matter raised at the outset of this chapter: the matter of respect for the source of law. We have to the left, below, what may be called the legitimate, to the right, pretenders; and of course the lists are not complete.

Maximinus 235–238	Quartinus 235	
Pupienus Balbinus 238		
Gordian III 238–244		
Philip 244–249	Iotapianus 248–249	Pacatianus 248–249
Decius 249–251	Licinianus 250–251	
Gallus 251–253		
Aemilianus 253	Uranius (248?) 253–254	
Valerian 253–260(?)	Ingenuus 258 (259?)	
Gallienus 260–268	Regalianus 260	Postumus 260(?)–268
Claudius II 268–270	Aureolus 268	Odenathus 262–267
Aurelian 270–275	(?)Domitianus 271(?)	Zenobia 267–273
Tacitus 275–276	Florianus 276	Laelianus 268
Probus 276–282		Marius 268
Carus 282–283		Victorinus 268–270
Carinus 283–285		Tetricus 270–273 (274?)

One rival pair was to hold out for a time in the northwest (Carausius and Allectus, 287–296), another briefly in Egypt (Domitianus and Achilleus, 297); and transition from the First Tetrarchy to the unchallenged rule of Constantine was not accomplished without more civil strife. Still, with the accession of Diocletian, the worst was over. Its full count is usually averaged out to an emperor per year for half a century.

Its necessary and its probable consequences have often been discussed. One can almost be documented. News of the death of an emperor would take two to five months to percolate into the consciousness of a city of central Egypt.[70] That delay must have compounded chaos, especially among people at all cut off from main roads and ports. "The emperor and his associates and their devil's dance, which we hear of in our gatherings, are mere names. That there will always be an emperor, they [the common folk] know well enough. We are reminded of that yearly by the tax collectors. But who he may be, they have no clear idea." [71] Too many claimants would have confused them or, for that matter, would confuse the loyalties of governors, procurators, and troop commanders; too little continuity would have made attachment impossible; and, as imperial portrait distribution lagged months behind the beginning of a reign, politics would often be a faceless story. The machinery of administration could simply stop.

A second set of figures suggests effects to be felt at the very center of government. A question concerning law, if it arrived or arose there, had the less chance of being answered during the crisis, because of the natural rhythm of activity: rising from nothing on the first day of a new reign to a peak, let us say, about eighteen months later; thereafter, or at any war, distraction, or disturbance, dropping back to a lower level. Such patterns can be traced in the Codes from the later second to the later fourth century. For example, the Justinian contains 369 rescripts in a decade of Alexander Severus as compared with 9 in the 270s.[72] Thus a ruler whose occupancy of the throne never lasted into the peak months, or was continually disturbed by the need to take the field, could never attend to problems crying out for his commands. On the other hand, with Diocletian we have evidence for enormous activity— many hundreds of rescripts by chance preserved from 293– 294—to take care of the backlog of business, and with Constantine, a significant shift of energy to *constitutiones*.

These, as opposed to rescripts, made for broader, swifter change.[73]

Against the background of what has been said about the implementing of laws, it may be wondered whether the flood that issued in the time of recovery did not overburden the machinery of government. Complaint about the sheer number and resulting chaos of laws begins in the early fourth century and carries forward to a sort of climax in the 370s, with the statement to the emperor that "from Your Serenity there remains one remedy for the alleviation of your subjects' concerns, that you should shed light on the jumbled and contradictory decisions in the statutes."[74] No one who has spent an hour dipping into the Theodosian Code can fail to find some simply unadministrable ambiguity or vagueness in it, a perfect invitation to the abuses ever ready at the edges of the tribunal, ever darkening the office doors of the emperor's agents. Equally in an era of too much as of too little law, between the intent and the execution fell a shadow.

5

MONEY

The heart and brain of the empire lodged in its cities; and the heart, swelling with pride in the amenities, and the brain, determining where the greatest nourishment should go, together insured that not even the most distressed decades of Roman history should bring urban civilization to an end. That meant fortifications, up to perhaps 290 or so. We will return to the subject later. But the Tetrarchy could spare energy for the embellishment of Rome, Milan, Trier, Antioch, Nicomedia, Thessalonica, Carthage, Perinthus, all in the traditions of more peaceable centuries. To these sites was added Byzantium, greatest of all declarations that the ancient tasks of the emperor were to be taken up again in an era of calm, repair, and new achievement. There, in 330, tremendous displays and celebrations took place to mark its inauguration as a second capital; to a wider audience coins showed its significance as a Rome renewed and mistress of the seas; and its founder

numbered himself in an edict among "those whose zeal
it is to establish new cities or decorate the old or renovate
the half defunct." [1]

The extraordinary effort needed in the 320s and 330s
showed in the jerry-built nature of some of its structures
and in the patching together of pillage from other centers.
*Constantinopolis dedicatur paene omnium urbium nudi-
tate:* [2] meaning not merely the tripod stripped from Del-
phi, originally set up to commemorate the Greek victory
at Plataea; not this porphyry column or that statue; rather,
meaning the inflow of fresh inhabitants, many of whom,
with their wealth and distinction, could be ill spared by
their proper homes. They were drawn to Constantinople
by offer of special privileges, in themselves a cost on the
empire: by a corn dole on the model of Rome's, diverting
thence the harvests and shipping of Egypt and other eastern areas; by state-built mansions for Roman senators who
made the move; by exemption from taxes and municipal
obligations; by outright cash grants; and by requirements
that lessors of crown lands should erect a second residence
in the capital.[3] Some of these measures needed no direct cash outlay, being in that respect characteristic of
straiter times. The creating or enlarging of an urban center by enforced migration begins in the third century; the
reuse of statues, marble, and columns filched from neglected sites likewise typifies the later empire. And none
other than Constantine, guilty himself, forbade it.[4] In the
mobilization of artisans of all kinds he has frankly to con-
fess how rare and precious their skills have become, of
architects especially but of plasterers, masons, mosaicists,

sculptors, and many others as well.[5] He has no cash to offer them, only the indirect reward of certain immunities and study-scholarships in the course of training. But for Gaul, in the wake of much earlier destruction, his father had had to borrow teams of just such craftsmen from Britain.[6] Constantine over his own vaster area of rule managed to find the means to restore not only the cities re-named in thanks—Constantine (Cirta and Arles), Con-stantinople, Helenopolis (Drepanum)—but others less favored in Italy, Asia, Africa.[7] The tradition behind his energy was the same that had inspired three centuries of rule before him; unthinkable, no matter how strained his resources, that he should not perpetuate it. Even as the crisis set in, the advice still thought fit for the throne was that "such expenditures somehow contribute to a sense of awe among our allies and panic among our enemies."[8]

That thought may explain the immense gift of "bread and circuses," most of all, bread, to the "new Rome."[9] Constantine it was, however, who initiated similar systems in several other large centers and continued in the old Rome the provision of foods beyond the bare staples. Aurelian, beset by financial problems, had earlier in-creased them by putting pork on the menu for the Roman plebs.[10] In the decade just before him, Alexandria and other Egyptian cities received a dole on the Roman model.[11] No one would expect to see obligations so numer-ous and heavy assumed by emperors struggling with money shortages and inflation. Such extravagance can only be interpreted as an attempt to secure the political support of urban populations when prices were rising

and grain supplies were often interrupted. Whether or not
the political considerations were really as pressing as the
emperors believed, the expenses involved were certainly
very large.

It is easier to explain Constantine's preparation of a
proper harbor in Thessalonica. That was for use in his
war against Licinius.[12] Since transport by water was so
much cheaper than by land, especially for the bulk requirements of a civil population or of military campaigns,
this too was a major item in the budget right through the
Empire.[13] The third century, however, sharpened these
needs by bringing the emperor, along with his civil retinue or army, to many points where he had earlier been a
stranger. The sheer multiplication of "wearers of the
purple" (using that courtly phrase to include the more or
the less legitimate) meant more capitals; civil wars meant
more staging areas and winters quarters suddenly in need
of more billets, more food, stables, fuel, and so forth.
Tangible proofs of these emergencies can be seen in the
great stone storage barns at centers like Trier; better, in
the dozens of palaces known to have been erected by the
Tetrarchy at Aquileia, Nicomedia, near Sirmium, and
elsewhere.[14] Spalato is the most familiar, perhaps the
largest, too. But it does not misrepresent the general type
of structure on which enormous sums were lavished, suit-
ably to house the divine presence. Not only were its proportions overwhelming. The smallest details of decoration
were of rare and showy workmanship; so too the costumes
and jewelry of the courtiers who thronged its halls. All
combined to explain items at first sight incongruous in Con-

stantine's list of essential workers: artisans in gold, silver, glass, and ivory; mirror makers; furriers; and purple-dyers. Freedom from compulsory services granted to them by his decree was ordinarily reserved for persons considered of prime use to the state. What could possibly be the need for rich vestments, inlaid floors, or gilt ceilings? The answer was *kataplexis,* the "astounding" of all who would question the authority of the emperor and his agents. In the chaos of the third century, challenge was only too often offered to him, and response returned with increasing emphasis—and expense. Thus, from "bread and circuses" down through the building of harbor facilities for the launching of a fleet, and so to the subsidizing of apprenticeships in luxury manufactures, the costs of facing the crisis not only rose with it but could be justified in familiar terms—familiar, at least, to its contemporaries.

The number of palaces, or of capitals, or of emperors that they represented, suggests another special expense of the 200s; for each center of power strove to command the full list of agencies and operations and servants that had once belonged only to Augustus. Lactantius' often quoted saying that those who live off the treasury are more numerous than those who pay into it,[15] points up the consequences. He cannot be taken literally, of course, nor, till a century later, do the sources allow even the most tentative count of the civil service. But it cannot be doubted that the multiplication of pretenders produced a major increase, made permanent by the Tetrarchy in different forms and under different titles, with more than one capital, with more than one praetorian prefect and set of central bureaus, and with the radical subdivision of provinces. Given especially that latter change, which in turn made necessary an intermediate diocesan level, government personnel surely doubled over the half century before Diocletian's abdication. No absolute figure can be calculated, but a relative one suits our purpose just as well.

It is not surprising, as the next consequence, that people unable to meet the demands for tribute abandoned their homes and fields, or were thrown into jail, or sold their children into slavery. Those who had a chance to address their oppressors on the throne congratulated him for supposedly doing what they dared not accuse him of failing to accomplish, the appointment of governors "not mere collectors of wealth. And you will speak, too, regarding the tribute he imposes, and that he plans out how his troops can be provisioned and at the same time how his subjects may easily and lightly afford it." [16] In truth, Romans seem to have been at no time able to support taxes "lightly." Remissions of back dues suggest as much, as likewise the public auctions of palace valuables in moments of emergency.[17] We need not rehearse all the facts and texts. What is essential to establish is the ever-present background of financial strain against which must be understood the special demands of the crisis period.

In the passage just quoted, the train of thought from tribute to troops is unconscious, natural, and clear. It is encountered in other ancient authors who considered the imperial budget as a whole.[18] It should be listened to, at least to the point of accepting the troops as the direct cause of a majority of the emperor's expenses in the first two centuries, after which pay rises tipped the scales still more heavily in the same direction. If we continue to concentrate only on the *proportion* of imperial expenses accounted for by the army, further related difficulties appear less serious. The number of denarii in the rises granted by Commodus, Septimius Severus, Caracalla, and Maximinus is not in every case clear,[19] but it could take on significance only if other figures were known also. In the first place, we must know the total available normally, or annually, or in a specific year, for all imperial expenditures combined. But after Augustus' reign, for which plausible conjectures can be sketched at least in outline, the data on which to base an estimate of the yield of taxes direct and indirect, of inheritances, and of rents from crown lands, recede beyond our reach. Trajan's ambitious building or Septimius Severus' gains from confiscations indicate the great range of variation from one period to another. That must discourage generalization.

In the second place, if we knew the army pay total in, say, 235, we would have to determine its buying power before considering whether it represented an increase over that of some earlier reign. Calculations would have to allow for inflation of prices clear across the empire's history, from Augustus on. While the fact of that inflation is accepted, its degree is another matter. Most likely, the cash the soldier received bought less after all the pay rises than a smaller sum had bought under Vespasian or Antoninus Pius.[20] The percentage of the imperial budget, then, represented by the cash part of the military payroll need not have inceased in value. Perhaps it actually diminished.

In the third place, however, payments in kind constituted a growing item in the soldier's salary. Since their
equivalence in weight of silver or in the debased coins of
the third century is equally difficult to reckon, their meaning within the state's budget over all can hardly be fixed.
The problem appears in terminology itself. Third-century
writers like Herodian speak of the soldier's "keep" (*annona, trophe, siteresion*), not his wages, "because by the
time of Herodian . . . *annona* had become such an important part of military pay."[21] To it were added other
items that we will return to: uniform, armor. Donatives became annual, just when in the third century is not known,
and partly in precious metal, partly in debased coinage,
according to proportions and practices likewise unknown.
We confront then a variety of factors quite outside of base
pay in denarii; we lack the means of translating them into
any numerical terms; and in our predicament we can
find help only in a nonstatistical fact. Recruits continued
to come forward. There is no hint in the sources of resort
to the press-gang or of draft-dodging before the fourth
century. Thereafter, only young men of the decurion class
avoided the army—and not all of them, by any means. It
follows that the remuneration of the soldier, however
variform it must have been, made up an attractive pack-
age. Though officers got less in the later Empire than in
the earlier, the man in the ranks cannot have been much
worse off than those predecessors of his who mutinied for
a raise at Augustus' death.

  That broad fact—not a number, not a value, not economics—nevertheless can be put to further use. For if it is

accepted, and if the size of the army increased (as it certainly did in the third century), then military expenses as a whole join the parade that we have been inspecting so far, a parade of mounting expenditures in every chief aspect of government during the period of crisis. There remains a last factor to be considered, no doubt the most subject to change of all, namely, campaigning costs.

Given a standing army whose forces were not specially augmented for war, and then reduced again, it is at first sight puzzling why a legion should cost more on the march than in its barracks. Surely loss of materiel and premature retirement bonuses for the incapacitated cannot have amounted to much. The fit men were paid no more, they ate no more, they were not issued special equipment for fighting. Nevertheless, we must again listen to contemporaries of the Roman scene. It is axiomatic among them that wars raised taxes. Taking up the evidence only from Severan times forward, we have Dio's verdict on Septimius' eastern advance; Caracalla's and Maximinus' wars alleged by their authors as the excuse for heavier tribute; and the accumulated experience of the next century, leading to the conclusion that "wars are the fathers of taxes." [22] Modern historians for their part are agreed that Hadrian turned his back on Trajan's expansionism as having strained the empire's economy too obviously; perhaps Commodus' courtiers put forward the same line of reasoning to ease him into the retreat he desired anyway; Domitian's earlier wars took a heavy toll which Nerva had to deal with in his reign.[23] And if we look beneath these broad statements and events to a succession of local scenes in distress, especially as recorded in inscriptions, papyri, and laws responding to individual complaints, it is the legions that are most often to blame, and their passage that is most bitterly remembered, when peasants had to surrender their draft animals to the quartermaster's wagons, or when the decurions had suddenly to collect from the community food representing months of the normal supply.[24] Herodian, describing Alexander Severus' preparations for the invasion of Persia, reports "there was a tremendous disruption throughout the whole empire." [25]

And well there might be. Consider only the peacetime effect of having the emperor in one's midst. In northern Italy in the 290s Milan had to be equipped with a perfectly huge granary as the natural adjunct of another great building, the palace;[26] and in the whole region round about, "in order that the army and the emperor—who were always or generally present—could be provisioned, a new law was introduced into the tax system." [27] On the move, emperor, court, and armed following cost still more —so much that ad hoc levies had to be made along their path or collected in advance to pay for their transitory presence.[28] Special structures served and memorialized the requirements of thousands of men: grain depots (perhaps fortified), hostelries, and stables.[29] From such better-recorded testimonies to the expense of shifting the center of government itself, we may understand what was involved on a smaller scale when, for example, merely a single regiment was summoned to a remote campaign. We may apply what we learn to the question, Why did wars increase costs over peacetime? The answer, or at least the chief part of it, must lie in transport: of military baggage (troop units being without heavy wagons and mules, the higher officers being encumbered with many belongings and luxuries); of provisions taken along the road; of provisions brought to halting places, sometimes from great distances. It was a cliché of praise that the good ruler demands supplies for his armies only from their close neighborhood. There were indeed limits to the loss and dislocation he could inflict on his subjects even in the cause of defense, limits to what he could demand without payment. Somehow, in proportions unknown to us, he and his people shared the burden. In the period of crisis, frenetic with hurryings of defense and attack now to this front, now to some other, it must have been almost heavier than the empire could stand.

The increase in the army budget is neatly illustrated by money itself. Toward the middle of the third century, the depiction of imperial largess on coins replaces a civilian recipient—the Roman people—with a military. Personified Abundance clasps the hand of a soldier.[30] The same relationship can be read on an archaeological map. Where there are big permanent camps, there are a dozen signs of wealth in the vicinity: lots of rich pottery, rich villas, rich tombstones, at least in the provinces that have been well excavated in modern times. At individual sites, the presence or absence of a nearby garrison registers in the size and constituent coins of hoards, at, for example, Vindonissa over the second and third centuries.[31] In the fourth, imperial mints are set up where Constantine is assembling his power (Sirmium, in 320) to attack Licinius, or they are never attested at all because the provinces where they might be expected lack a large military establishment.[32] Most clearly of all, eastern mints, both imperial and municipal, are slack or busy according to the chronological patterns of Rome's great collisions with Persia, at points strung out along the chief routes of approach in Syria and Asia Minor. Cities normally issuing no coins spring into activity, or add issues of silver to their usual bronze, often with types that commemorate the legions in their passing: Nineveh under Trajan, Antioch under Caracalla, the whole phenomenon rising to its peak toward the mid-third century.[33] The underlying cause for coining is the need of the army payroll; the momentary occasion may be a donative or imperial anniversary.[34] The connection between political events and necessities on the one hand and the numismatic record on the other grows increasingly close as a result of the emperor's presence at the scene. During the emergencies that the third century witnessed in every decade, almost in every year, the emperor (or pretender, or barbarian king), and armies, and great concentrations of precious metals, and mints, and history, were all tied together in single knot.

Such a close connection serves nearly as well as statistics to prove a fact of economics: crisis had become a ruthless creditor. It pressed for payment with a harshness peculiar to the period of our focus. And that same fact brings to an appropriate end our survey of imperial expenses in general. Looking successively at its principal categories— the care or expansion of cities; the supply of free food to their inhabitants; the construction of roads, ports, palaces, and storage buildings; the number of civil servants; the size and payroll of the army, and campaigning costs, mostly of transport—we see them all enlarged, to what dimension it is every observer's right to conjecture on the basis of the evidence thus far outlined. That the government nearly doubled its obligations over the course of the crisis seems to me quite credible. And even in earlier centuries, its difficulties in making ends meet—that is, the difficulties experienced and expressed by the taxpaying population—are amply attested. It follows that only very radical budgetary measures would suffice for the 260s or 290s or 320s.

As the objects of expenditure differed in these various decades, so did the means of extending the state's ability to pay; but the easiest, the most tempting, and the first in sequence was adulteration of the basic silver coin. This was the denarius, up to the second quarter of the third century, when it gave way to the antoninianus (first minted in 215–219, revived in 238). The latter was put out as a two-denarius piece, though weighing considerably less than that. Its dictated and artificial values raise problems to which we will return. Here it is only necessary to say that it went on losing its precious metal content just like its predecessor, and contained barely detectable amounts by the late 260s.[35] The consequent saving was enormous, up to that date. The state had stretched the quantity of precious metal in its control many, many times without giving rise to inflation on anywhere near a corresponding scale. To the people who advised this process, it must have seemed that the experiments of their predecessors (all but the bold Septimius Severus) had only shown but never opened the door to virtually limitless wealth.[36] The procedures involved were relatively simple. Through taxation, coins of the old weight and purity flowed naturally to the mints, were there melted down with an admixture of cheaper copper, and were then brought forth again in new form for payment to the army. Certain rules were of course to be observed. People trusted the familiar, especially the handsome, coin.[37] They were more easily deceived by an increase in base metal than by a loss in overall weight that they could measure by the feel of it. But Trajan's calling in of better denarii in 107, to emerge from his decoctions with both less silver and less weight, or Septimius Severus' robbing of as much from the denarius in 194/195 as had been gradually withdrawn over the preceding century and a quarter went off without a hitch.[38]

Late in Gallienus' reign, all measures were carried to the point of frenzy—quite understandably, if one recalls the political context. Very large increases in the production of Egypt's tetradrachms, despite the first clear signs of real inflation, were now ordered, and again resumed at a higher level in the 270s.[39] Outside Egypt, the silver coin, the antoninianus, poured out in quantities from Rome, Cologne, and other centers.[40] For a generation, quite radical tampering with currency had been going forward, the results of each previous decade being sucked up and in a more worthless product spewed out by the mints with rising speed and in rising amounts. Along with their content, style and uniformity had been lost.[41] At an ever faster rate of recirculation and deterioration, in a fever that threatened to kill off the very idea of money, gold and silver coins by Aurelian's reign presented him with a disastrous proof that debasement could be carried no further. Not that his expenses were any less than those of his predecessors —that was by no means the case. But he could not cover them by further stretching of his supplies of precious metal.

He resorted instead to a different inflationary attack on the chief element of the currency, the silver—but with innovations intended to stabilize it. Though what he did is not perfectly clear, very likely in 274 he began the re-minting of all the now utterly debased coins that reached his mints so as to issue two new denominations, one marked "regular" (*usualis*), showing the emperor crowned with a laurel wreath, and set at the same value as the antoninianus (two denarii), the other somewhat less than twice that weight, equally negligible in silver content, but handsome and uniform. It showed the emperor wearing a radiate crown. To distinguish it from the antoninianus which it otherwise resembled, it bore the mark XXI, that is, "Twenty-equals-one," upon it. The "twenty" were ses-terces, the "aurelianianus" equaling five denarii.[42] Though it therefore represented a further inflation of 150 percent, it was accepted quickly and fully and remained in abun-dant use till Diocletian's reforms twenty years later.

What is chiefly interesting about the aurelianianus is the declaring of an announced value on it, just as if it were a paper bill. Government had come to grips, how-ever unsuccessfully, with the idea of a universal fiduciary system. The background to this lies in provincial responses to imperial monetary policy.

Over some generations prior to 274, the traditional permission to coin for local needs, in bronze, was exploited
by eastern cities in a curve that rises to a peak—some 360
mints simultaneously in operation—under Septimius Severus, with further but less prominent high points later.
They are best connected with the abundance of imperial
silver put in circulation in the region by wars civil and
foreign; and as this would both increase prices and call for
interpretation into the small change of the marketplace,
the natural response was to set the city mints to work.[43]
Generally speaking, their products were not meant for
wide export, and they therefore did not require fixed
rates of exchange with each other. Where necessary, translation could be taken care of by local money changers. For
each city, the principal anchorage had to lie in the imperial currency, with which some conscious relationship
was established. It proved fatal. By 270 virtually all city
mints had been driven out of business through the operation of Greshams' law: their own better bronze had been
suppressed by worthless antoniniani. But in their last
struggles to keep up with devaluation of antoniniani, besides diminishing the weight of their own coins, they
made quite frantic use of types issued, or subsequently
overstruck, with numbers to revalue them upward.[44] The
numbers announced "One-equals-three" or "-five" or up
to "-ten", making quite obvious to us their intent if not
the precise worth of the coins on which they appeared.
They announced, even while trying to master, the dizzy
progress of inflation, sometimes even by countermarks
struck on top of countermarks. Despite every effort, such
coins could at last only be minted at a loss. Their place

was taken for minor transactions by an inrushing tide of now quite debased imperial "silver." It too was counter-marked, as we have seen: "Twenty-equals-one."

In the West, coining of all sorts was a state monopoly. In law, there should have been no local issues. From the mid-third century, however, hoarding, inflation, and the irregular working of the mints and channels of distribution had brought a dearth of currency upon many regions. Tolerated or perhaps encouraged by government, counterfeiting supplied the resulting need in abundance.[45] Patterns of this activity are eccentric; much depends on distance from points of supply, on the absence of troops with their payrolls or of pretenders with their treasuries; and there are first- and second-century anticipations on a small scale. North Gaul is a special source of production; the decade of the 270s brings the phenomenon to a height, though not to an end, thereafter.[46] Generally the decisive factor in the West, as in a few small pockets in the East, is the absolute necessity of having a medium for minor, everyday transactions. If the necessity could not be recognized by the government, then private initiative assumed a supplementary or even completely dominant role. Upward revaluation by countermarks or other frauds is attempted in the West on a small scale only for a short period after Gallienus, by Gallic pretenders, but in time to have served as a model for Aurelian's experiments.

The decade that followed gave the empire an intense course of instruction in the idea of value as something arbitrarily fixed upon currency, and as something nevertheless ever changing; for prices rose with a new velocity.

Their incomprehensible behavior matched that of the coins that people were now used to; for as they had seen the distinction disappear between silver and bronze, so also had the distinction disappeared between different denominations. A coin was a coin. More than that, who could say?—looking at some botched, anomalous, trashy bit of metal in the hand, the work of an emperor, it might be, or of a pretender, or of a counterfeiter. How much it was worth, apparently anyone could declare, or try to declare, by putting a mark on it. That was one lesson learned by everyone. But would the tariff be observed in daily buying and selling? Apparently not. That was a second lesson even more thoroughly driven home. Before the economy could ultimately regain its health, economic man would require a long-drawn-out reeducation.

When Diocletian made his attacks on inflation in 286 and 294, in the new fashion he stamped a number on his aurei (seventy, soon thereafter sixty) and on his now really pure argentei (ninety-six, to the pound). On his almost silverless 10gm "follis" he stamped "Twenty-equals-one" (namely, twenty sesterces or five denarii); but as it was laureate, not like Aurelian's radiate XXI coins, it implied some retariffing of the latter, probably downward from five to two denarii. In effect, the empire recovered its three-metal curency, though the bronze contained an insignificant admixture of silver.[47] The nightmare of nominally silver coins becoming bronze, and chasing the latter off the market amid dizzying price rises, should have ended.

Several questions arise, however, and the government's

failure to master them prolonged its difficulties. The first to consider is the interrelation of the metals. How many silver coins would buy a gold one? How many bronze? The answers in our sources are too many, which is to say, equivalences might be legislated but smiply would not stay put. It was the market itself that fixed the rates. Significantly, then, in the Edict on Prices, gold and silver do not appear directly after the introduction but are tacked on near the end; like every other item on the list, too, they are expressed in terms of bronze (that is, denarii, with only an accidental trace of silver in them); and no usable relation between them is indicated. One aureus would buy 18.12 argentei! From all of this, we can only infer that the two precious metals were treated as commodities and even differed in price from one region to another as from one time to another.[48]

These particular commodities, like others as well, government of course had the power to demand at any price it wished, through requisition or taxation—though in fact political considerations set some limits even here. When government acted as paymaster, on the other hand, it enjoyed no such invulnerability to the economic forces rampant around it. Soldiers and officials had to be given money that meant something in the market, which thereupon asserted its supremacy over the emperor's currency at its weakest point: small change. Aurei and argentei were not the media of everyday business. They did not issue or circulate in great abundance toward the turn of the century. Despite or rather due to being as generous in weight, as handsome and pure as Parsifal, they were bid

up to greater and greater prices in terms of the metal in
which lay most of people's wealth, bronze or near-bronze.
And it was this latter, the denarius or its multiples of 2,
2½, 5, 12½, 20, 21, 25, or whatever at different times may
have been the intended value of different billon coins,
that did abound in hundreds of tons. The economy was
committed to its existence, committed by the ever-more-
debased and copious floods of currency that had poured
out of the mints in the effort to pay for a half century of
crisis.

Faith in base metal should have been bolstered by the
introduction of pieces new and striking in appearance,
and by deflation of at least one of their multiples.[49] That
was all to the good. But the sheer quantities of emission
and the doubling of another multiple by fiat in 301 followed the now established and disastrous tradition. Price
spirals in the early 290s and the opening years of the
fourth century resumed their rise.[50] After Diocletian,
civil wars brought a succession of abrupt cuts in the
weight of base-metal coins, right through into the 320s.[51]
Prices were reckoned separately in the precious metals,
which appear to have floated free from each other on the
market. Their ratio showed abrupt changes, for example
(though the picture is confused), from 1:10 in 301 up to
1:18 in 323.[52]

In these troubled times, how much someone would pay
for a pig or a shirt depended on how many coins he had
in his pocket, and on his readiness to spend all of them
that day. It depended, in other words, on quantity of currency and velocity of circulation. Both factors might be

violently affected by the government. The first in actual fact had evolved gently over a long history through the diminishing of weight and purity of coinage, until the third century, when inflation was made inevitable by progressively larger numbers of coins on the market. The second, velocity, would in any case have responded to the first, with an increase of some degree; but uncertainties about the value of coins, as they changed in appearance or in tariff, provided an extra stimulation. Government for its part reacted like a frightened child at the controls of a runaway express train, pushing all sorts of levers and knobs. One such had never been, perhaps is still not, correctly understood: the adjustment of the gold and silver coins to each other so as to maintain a stable relationship between the two metals. More often than not, if issues of one were lightened, so was the other. This can be seen happening, however, when circumstances allowed it for reasons other than of set policy, for instance, when an empty treasury needed the stretching of supplies of both metals. It seems safest to say, then, that emperors had never paid much attention to parity as expressed in weight of precious metal; and as expressed in the number of coins (twenty-five silver to one gold), the matter had taken care of itself till the onset of crisis. Thereafter, as we have seen, gold broke free from debased denarii and antoniniani.[53]

As to other knobs or levers, Roman government had from time to time forbidden the setting up of brand-new municipal taxes, the issuing of debased municipal silver, the rejection of imperial coinage or excessive charges for converting it into local currency.[54] These constraints had all operated directly on the local level, according to imperial rights certainly claimed but seldom exercised. At any rate, they produced no visible check on the actual course of inflation in the third century, when they were most needed, nor is it easy to imagine how powers of enforcement as we know them could possibly have insured the acceptance of coins at a legislated rate, once they had entered on their steeper path of debasement.

The citizen, for his part, was equally helpless to control, though he could not ignore, the effects of adulterated coins. He naturally took account of changing prices everywhere, "in individual cities and regions, especially of wine, oil, and grain," as even a jurisconsult had to acknowledge.[55] Cash handouts on festivals and fines for violating tombs had to be jacked up; municipal contracts for labor had to be renegotiated.[56] In the third century, references multiply to "new" and "old" currency, as antoniniani and aurelianiani and overstrikes and adulteration all forced themselves on the popular consciousness,[57] and the often gigantic sums they involved made people think in totally new terms, of millions of denarii or, in a necessary shorthand, of "bags" and "myriads."[58] By the close of the third century, without arbitrary retariffing, it would theoretically have cost sixteen tons of bronze to purchase fifty pounds of wheat; and, theory aside, the unhappy banker handling his wares, those great, wretched piles of shoddy change, "will be so weary he will not know what to do."[59] Such were the mechanical difficulties that flowed from debasement.

Rapid changes in value required other adjustments, however. In Egypt, loans of money are made for shorter terms in the third century and still more markedly so in the fourth, when house leases grow shorter, too, and land leases begin to stipulate payment in advance.[60] Over the space of a year, an agreed sum might lose half its meaning. For that reason the 6.5 percent surcharge on what the state deposited for expected deliveries of goods, representing the interest the money might otherwise have earned, was simply abandoned; for annual inflation rose at more than that rate.[61] These items give us a glimpse into the consequences of inflation for people who had and handled money.

It is often assumed that these classes suffered particularly —as doubtless anyone would whose wealth consisted in debased silver hidden under his bed. On the other hand, large surplus sums were normally not hoarded but turned into bullion or real estate, both of which would appreciate. In the meantime—to judge from the quantity of cash transactions undiminished over the period of our study, and from the call for cash to which the irregular issues in the West testify in such bulk—everday business for the ordinary man continued to depend on currency, especially in small denominations.[62] It was these that made trouble for anyone who had to deal in them daily. Over all, then, it seems likely that the small creditor class and urban professional (a teacher, for instance), but neither the peasant nor the magnate, suffered as the result of inflation.[63] Despite the great historical significance of the question, Who lost most? it is so entangled in the distribution of tax

burdens and other factors that it does not permit more detailed discussion.

Nor was the state in a better position than ourselves to
judge just what was happening. Perhaps reports from
Egypt showed a province little shaken by economic misfortune in the third century.[64] To the west, the capital of
newly defined Libya Pentapolis in the generation after
290 or so enjoyed prosperity.[65] Beyond, Numidia and
Proconsularis in the same period could boast at least
certain regions that flourished, as well as a growing export in fine pottery and mosaic arts.[66] Britain did not fall
back in the third and moved ahead in the early fourth
century in villa- and city-building,[67] Italy in its north and
south had more than Milan and Piazza Armerina to show
for its economic health from Diocletian on,[68] and in Gaul
and Germany, again there were isolated points of prosperity unbroken or reviving under the Tetrarchy: Arles,
Autun, Toulouse, Trier.[69] Here and there in Asia Minor,
too, rich new buildings were rising at least a generation
earlier than the well-attested good times of the mid-fourth
century.[70] A glance around the empire in this cursory
fashion discovers not enough, by any means, to discount
the whole fact of crisis. It does, however, suggest how confused the testimonies may have been, from which government must form its picture of the state of the economy.

Add in particular the distortion due to the treasure that
flowed in on each emperor, on the army in whose midst
he was generally careful to place himself, and so on the
city and territory that might hold them both. Besides the
palaces, storage barns, and other facilities that their pres-

ence gave rise to (somehow paid for, and therefore a means of putting much money into circulation locally), the imperial retinue and guard had a payroll to spend. The results are visible in the boom and bust, the destruction and renovation, the wars and affluence, that agitated and eventually ended by enriching the whole northern belt of provinces stretching from Noricum to Bithynia.[71] Their ties grew closer with the less afflicted East, more tenuous with the West, as power and wealth and history focused on the Hellespont. The Via Egnatia across the Balkan peninsula yielded to more northerly lateral links for the same reason, now favoring cities like Serdica and Philippopolis. In Pannonia and Thrace, manufacture and export took on a new vitality, so also landed investment. Most of all, Constantinople, and the earlier-favored capitals like Sirmium or Nicomedia, made the line of prosperity rise on the economic graph beginning with Diocletian and accelerating under Constantine. An emperor resident anywhere along the Danube might therefore be excused if he found the evidence hard to read: from cities and farms nearest around him, only signals of wealth undisturbed, or growing, or rapidly recovering; from large cities or whole provinces elsewhere, the same; but quite contrary signals of desperation and poverty reaching him from still other areas. Where we have no direct proof of physical destruction caused by invasions, we are to this day hard put to decide how serious were the effects of the economic crisis on the Roman world taken as a whole, despite obvious dislocations of advantage from one class to another, or from one region to another.

How well government could gather and sort out information has been described in a previous chapter. We have gone on to indicate the perplexing nature of what actually might have been learned about the economy in, say, the year 300. It remains only to sketch the economic theory then existing, into which information (as much as came to hand) could be fitted.

While the Romans were used to quite complicated ways of registering and transferring sums of money, their understanding of its behavior was limited. They knew that prices rose and fell according to demand, and they could express that as the gain or loss of money's buying power;[72] they knew that abundance lowers prices, including abundance of money that lowers interest rates;[73] and they knew about artificial shortages of goods or money created by hoarding.[74] They could see the interdependence of different areas of the economy—more crudely, that cities needed the countryside to survive.[75] It was almost a cliché of praise, too, that good rulers had account books for the entire empire, showing where their profits and losses lay.[76] These were drawn up under headings like "Navy," "Army," "Tax Income," "Cash in Hand," "Gifts," "Outgo," "Province Such-and-Such," quite reliably attested through the first century and, less so, later. Hadrian is said to have known them as well as any careful family head (*paterfamilias diligens*) knew his own household (*domus privata*)—which puts the whole matter suddenly in perspective: the bureaucracy merely as bailiff, the emperor as a sound man of property. Always uppermost among his concerns would be the balance sheet, to see if his realm was a paying business—not to make it so by adjustment of internal tariffs, infusion of fresh capital, or tinkering with the gold-silver ratio. Had one of his budgets survived for inspection today, not only would it be a most summary document, surely, but those in charge of it could have considered its meaning only in the simplest terms. Moreover, after Alexander Severus, it is not even mentioned any more. We would hardly expect it to be.[77] Government's grasp on the economy was loosened by shocks of its own making, and a vast range of problems developed in the third century beyond its comprehension.

Diocletian's Edict on Prices and its attendant measures provide the most familiar illustration.[78] Together, they show a certain limited intelligence, not much above cunning, on the government's part. Revaluation of the currency it rigged in favor of creditors, among whom, itself was of course the greatest; and the price of *frumenta fiscalia* and transport charges generally were disproportionately depressed. In these, too, the state had a vital interest.[79] Listings of items were as minutely detailed as any army of clerks could devise. But if in Egypt the market and those who supplied it actually did declare their stocks in hand as they were supposed to, in a fixed, sworn formula right up to Constantius' reign, yet the last sign of obedience to the decreed price levels flickers out a generation earlier.[80] What we miss (leaving aside the question, How soon and how fast did the dam of the edict burst and inflation crest in new waves?) is the broader application of more appropriate measures actually in the government's

grasp. It was no secret that the more money people had,
the higher they would bid for whatever they wanted; no
secret that inflation was connected with the great pressure
of demand created by imperial spending, above all, in
regions where the court or troop units were resident.[81]
All this was common knowledge. It was not put to work.
Instead of reducing the money supply by reducing expenditures, an opposite policy was pursued. And against its
inevitable consequences only a blast of execration and re-
proof was let loose in 301.

The reason for such disastrous miscalculations lay partly
in the range of rising costs earlier surveyed, some quite
unavoidable, some accepted out of reverence for tradition.
City building, for example, was thought to be inseparable
from the role of emperor. But traditions of another sort
imposed their limitations on the emperor's vision. As
paterfamilias of his people he was indeed accustomed to
intervene at will in the economy, but without any in-
tention of controlling it. As he had the knowledge to do
more, so he had the power, without exerting it. Ordinarily, his laws declared in favor of laissez-faire, reserving
only the right to punish speculators or provide emergency
relief in times of famine.[82] From Republican days on, cer-
tian expenditures for luxury, certain rates of interest, were
looked on as outrageous. They too continued to be regulated far down into the Empire, for moral and humani-
tarian reasons, not economic. A whole list of state actions
bears the same character of casual paternalism whereby,
in really pressing need, urban finances were investigated,
and the power of cities to exact the fulfillment of in-

dividuals' campaign promises, or their capacity as corporate bodies to take bequests, or their obligation to restrict their spending, were all secured.[83] The right to institute periodic internal markets (*nundinae*) was controlled, simply to protect the health of existing ones against needless competition,[84] and as to external markets, the state kept them in check as a police measure against infiltration of barbarians across the frontiers.[85] Exchange only of strategic goods was regulated, with very little regard to protective tariffs.[86] Practical sense, an unsophisticated shrewdness, a care for the well-being of the jewels of the empire, the cities, and a thrifty use of the resources of aid and oversight mark the emperors' approach to their responsibilities. It proved quite good enough for ordinary times. Extraordinary times, with expenses and inflation to match, were something else again.

One clue to a new approach is the inclusion of gold in the list of contraband in the fourth century.[87] Its outflow to foreign nations had been a cause of occasional concern earlier, but it constituted a far more precious asset when Roman coinage in other metals deteriorated. It began to be collected (sometimes along with bulk silver) by special requisitions and taxes in Egypt in the early 300s.[88] A striking unanimity in written sources underlines the still more active raking in of gold by Constantine, so much emphasized even by his admirers, and through methods so various and thorough, that it must have been highly successful. Temple treasure and two regular levies (on merchants and on senatorial lands) were the chief but not the only sources of his supply.[89] Emperors thus joined their own subjects in the rush to secure wealth incorruptible, which, as it lacked effective anchorage within the currency over all, of course behaved like any other commodity. As against denarii, it rapidly doubled and trebled in price beyond the level prescribed in the edict.[90] The course of this development constituted one of the closing chapters of inflation: for the prominence of solidi in transactions of every sort drew them away from other coins. The same development also wrote one of the earlier chapters in the drift toward a natural economy. It could be read in the numbers stamped on the new issues of Diocletian and Constantine, or in the latter's new submultiples, all declaring their relation to the pound, not to each other. And when fines were reckoned not by counting but by weighing, when coins were pierced and worn for jewelry, when soldiers got their salary, or part of it, in ounces, or in rings and gilded armor, then the old ideas of currency were dissolving and the detemination of value was passing from the mint to the marketplace.[91]

Such signs of change can be seen from the very beginning of the crisis. They seem not to gain official recognition, however, until Diocletian's reign. They carry us then into the final phase of the story of money in the third century: the first, greater expenses, next, inflated prices floating upward on floods of debased coins, and last, flight from them to other alternatives. This did not involve, for the private citizen, a radically altered way of life. As we have seen, he continued to use cash, with however great inconvenience, or adjusted his business dealings in relatively simple ways that we will return to later (chapter 9). The government was in a different case. To exist, it had to buy force, before that latter could be used to seize the means of its own repayment. Army and civil service, in return for their allegiance, therefore got real value. It was supplied to them increasingly in goods, of which the most precious was gold, pointedly specified as the form of reward to essential groups.[92] Army donatives gave rise to Constantine's new taxes. But both lower-ranking soldiers and bureaucrats were by the end of his reign (through previous stages hidden from us) getting the bulk of their remuneration in a second form, provisions.[93] Higher-ranking officers and officials likewise received the best part of their salaries in kind: luxurious uniforms and armor, as we have just seen, plus multiples of a single man's food allowance (annonae).

What their total salaries amounted to in buying power, say, in the year 300, we have no good means of telling. As an example of the problems involved in any estimate, we may bring forward a statement made at about that date that the emperor's private secretary got 300,000 sesterces. That would make him, in second-century terminology, a *trecenarius*. But the word had surely lost its numerical meaning to become a mere title. If not, the salary attached would come to something like one pound of gold, not the sixty-six and two thirds pounds it had meant in better times; in terms of wheat, not 100,000 measures but now a mere 750.[94] Incomprehensible as this evidence seems to be, it may still serve some purpose. It proves once more how ideas of currency had melted into fresh shapes. Further, it indicates that in the wake of crisis the upper levels of government service were far worse paid than their predecessors, at least in terms of money; and this fact, scattered evidence throughout the rest of the empire's history does confirm, though in no very precise form. In his efforts to keep up their pay, the emperor had therefore to supply them with servants, with richly dyed or embroidered garments, with silver brooches, horses, tableware, and so forth, not so distant in value of gold from the lump sum of money received by equivalent officers in the Principate. If the Dominate could not produce a coin that had meaning, or if it lacked the solidi to meet its debts fully, it could find quite adequate substitutes.

With these, officials trafficked like merchants. A favored device lay through the translation into cash (*adaeratio*) of taxes or salaries due in kind; or vice versa, as advantage might suggest. But whose advantage? The instances of adaeratio, which rise in number after 255 in Egypt, and the repeated worrying of the problem in laws of the Theodosian Code, later, have prompted many explanatory interpretations.[95] The small taxpayer would be glad to be rid of bad coins in bronze or near-bronze, the big taxpayer would want to hang on to good silver or gold, the tax receiver would be governed by the same calculations in reverse, and all three parties would have in mind the nearness of harvest that would lower the rate of exchange with grain; and we cannot tell if that rate was a fair one or not. Among so many variables, there is no hope of understanding the history of adaeratio in any detail. Only its general significance is clear. It shows a flight from the uncertainties and perils of cash dealings and, for goods, a matching competition that the state could forbid but not control.

One early law, of 325 (*CT* 7.4.1), lifts the curtain on some curious goings-on. Troop quartermasters are selling to tax receivers grain never given out to the rightful consumers, while the receivers raise cash for the purchase by adaeratio of the tax they exact. The losers are common soldiers at one end and peasants at the other. In the middle, the military and civil higher-ups make their profits. As the portion of pay in gifts and commodities leads on to adaeratio, so adaeratio leads on to corruption—all, nonmonetary means of reward. Unable to check corruption, government could legitimize it, making it a source of gain as regular as an employee's monthly wages.[96] Bribe taking, long customary, attained quite new and gross proportions; and so did the scramble for opportunities opened up by a rank or title. Titles could be given out like salaries. Constantine in particular was very free with them, in full knowledge, we may suspect, of just what he was doing.[97] But at this point, economic history mingles with and is lost in a richer history of later Roman society as a whole.

6

TAXES

From what has been said so far of Roman administrative procedures, they cannot be imagined responding to a long-drawn-out emergency with much success. They suffered from loose connections—between theory and practice, between what was known and what was applied, between appearance and action, above all, between the grandeur of their responsibilities and the pennywise inadequacy of their staff. They sufficed only for the essentials defined in terms of the *pax Romana* and secured by the efforts of conquest and settlement to which Augustus' reign served as climax and conclusion. He or Hadrian or Antoninus Pius might in all serenity thumb through the pages of the imperial budget and find it a good working document—for peace.[1] Their ease of mind might extend to a matter always of the first importance, the annual balancing of that budget. It was adequate so long as no loose connection developed between tax and pax.

Just this point of vulnerability must be emphasized once again. "Wars are the fathers of taxes."[2] It is appropriate, then, to begin this chapter with the military side of the emperor's concerns.

Some of the army's extraordinary requirements included equipment, discussed elsewhere. The main item, however, was food. When a centurion for the *annona* office picks up oil or wine from storage or the same account in Egypt acknowledges payments in kind at some time in the last quarter of the second century, we catch a glimpse of a new method of military supply aborning. Its further rapid growth in Egypt under Septimius Severus can be followed in receipts for grain, wine, oil, meat, fodder, and cash, exacted in addition to the land tax. It is the *annona militaris*.[3]

The annona militaris was exacted in the provinces partly through existing machinery: government transport systems and storage depots,[4] the gearing in of city senates (Severus established them now in Egypt), and the use of liturgists to help in collection. Procedures are hard to trace at first, because terminology is ambiguous. *Annona* by itself may in the second or third century mean *militaris* or, again, grain for the urban population.[5] Irregular measures of army supply continue right through the third century as if the new process were hardly understood, even as if it had never been developed.[6] But some progressive rationalizing of it by Severus must be conceded in the form of a supertax imposed on landed property,[7] sufficiently flexible to yield not only staples but cash or leather and recurring so often as to become, in the course of the third century, virtually annual.⁸ In its more developed form it did something to legitimize army provisioning, to diminish the element of quasi-pillage, and to reveal the possibilities latent under a tax title that specified neither wheat nor cash but simply "needs." It did nothing to distribute broadly or fairly the burden of meeting those needs.

Besides the old machinery of collection that the annona militaris used, new machinery developed. The soldiers themselves menacingly confronted civilians. *Actuarii* and higher ranks appear in this role with growing authority. The army becomes a branch of the state's fiscal power from Severus on.⁹ It was Severus also who regularized the leasing of camp lands to tenant farmers. This device of direct supply was controlled by *primipili* at first, passing some generations later into the care of civil officials and eventually to liturgists. At some point in the history of these duties, the primipilus extended his responsibilities more widely over the procedures of collection and transport. A tax named after him appears in our sources, without the surrounding detail that we would wish for. This much is clear, however: even the convenient shapelessness of the annona militaris had proved inadequate to cover all needs. A further item had been added to the list of payments that the state might levy on its subjects at will.¹⁰

The list that we call as a whole "Roman taxation" was indeed very confused, even casual. The cause lay in a philosophy of government prevailing among the conquerors: "get the most for the least." So, in the course of expansion, as little as possible was added to the bother and business

of rule. Could the Romans have exacted more profits
without correspondingly heavy costs in administration?
They did not think so. Their subjects certainly dinned
into their ears the impossibility, the extortionate irrational-
ity, the savage cruelty of tributes demanded; [11] they lied
in their tax returns, forswore themselves solemnly, submitted to beating, adulterated their grain deliveries, or
failed to make any delivery at all, due, of course, to somebody else's (always somebody else's) lamentable delin-
quency.[12] It is not hard to explain the government's per-
petual problems of arrears, with special collectors assigned
to them, or the periodic remission of taxes accompanied by
the ceremonious burning of great files of bureacratic documents.[13] Nor is it hard to explain why traditional systems
of taxation were as little disturbed as possible. To have
redesigned them in the interests of uniformity would have
aroused even sharper exasperation among newly incorporated members of the empire. The structure that grew up,
then, combined long-established diversity, alternating
strictness and relaxation, demand pressing upon resistance,
and makeshifts responsive to temporary needs. Those last
underlay the annona militaris, by far the most important
example of expedient become institution. What the entire
structure of taxation lacked, of course, was logic. But em-
pires founder on just that rock.

We find in Egypt an extraordinary welter of taxes, taken
over by Augustus with no great reforms. There was not
even uniformity within the province from district to district. In Judaea, people paid a poll tax, that is, a fixed
sum on each person differentiated according to age, a

land tax differentiated according to the use of the land,
plus other taxes left over from Seleucid times.[14] In Africa,
people paid a poll tax and a land tax in kind, in various
articles, especially grain;[15] in the province of Asia, a
land tax, perhaps recognizing differences in land use and
probably paid in money, though evidence is slight;[16] in
Cilicia and Syria, 1 percent of assessed wealth plus a poll
tax;[17] in Bithynia, perhaps a tithe;[18] in Pannonia, a tax
on land differentiated according to use;[19] elsewhere, unspecified, "a fifth, a seventh, or cash portion" of the harvest;[20] from many further areas, especially the Greek East,
a poll tax at differing rate.[21] It is tempting to claim at
least this as something universal within the empire; but
then, the ages between which its was owed were not everywhere the same. Moreover, Tacitus' mention (*Ann.* 4.72)
of the tribute exacted from the Frisii, in the form of so
much leather for the army's use, reminds us of the tribes
and places with an economy too primitive to be fitted
under the complicated machinery of exploitation that the
Romans had inherited from the Carthaginians, from King
Hiero in Sicily, or the Seleucids. It might be thought that
backward peoples as they developed, and advanced econ-
omies at any time, could have been reshaped to uniformity. No doubt something was accomplished along these
lines—but on no wide scale. Considering the publicity
given to any step that lightened or made heavier the in-
cidence of taxation, surely significant changes would have
been recorded. In fact, we find none. So it seems an acceptable argument from silence to project the better documented second-century system forward to the eve of Dio-

cletian's reforms. The chief characteristic of that system was variety.

In addition to provincial tribute, regardless of where they were, Jews for a long time paid their annual two drachmas, slaves yielded a tax through their masters [22] and again on the price of manumission,[23] heirs upon inheritance,[24] and merchants upon crossing toll districts or external boundaries of the empire.[25] Transport tolls varied from place to place, manumission and inheritance taxes from time to time. At unpredictable intervals the crown tax fell due, upon the ruler's accession day, at least in the earlier Principate; but it became more and more frequent, and by Severan times annual.[26] And there were unexplained "extraordinary indictions."[27] On the other hand —not to paint the picture in colors less grim, rather to bring out its complexity—many people enjoyed exemptions from one or more taxes by reason of their civic status, or individual grant, or membership in a favored community.

Floating loosely above all the particularities of region or status are general statements in the sources that bear on taxes. As far as concerns terminology in them, *stipendium* and *tributum* had become interchangeable by the early third century. The latter word grew to be more commonly used, to indicate one's total taxability (meaning neither one's financial capacity to pay nor the sum of one's ordinary obligations, but rather one's broad duty to meet the demands made upon one in the name of the state). Papinian, for instance, declares, *ut omnes pro modo praediorum pecuniam tributi conferant.*[28] Two implications here, that taxes were thought of chiefly as falling on landed wealth and were paid in cash, are both confirmed by other writers, though the evidence cannot be pressed very hard.[29] Perhaps, too, the use of the plural, *tributa,* in, for example, *CIL* 11.707 and 13.5092, shows a sense of the word covering a number of liabilities under different headings in different regions. But within one given region, except for some freedom under the annona militaris, administration was imprisoned in long-established tax usages. So far as we know, the bargains struck at the time of conquest under the Republic remained everywhere undisturbed throughout the entire Principate.

A minute's thought suggests a dozen questions of the most fundamental importance that simply cannot be answered, regarding the translation of this or that tax into credit toward another, the fair apportionment of dues within and among provinces, or the relative yield of different types of due.[30] What can be said about the whole system as it existed on the eve of the empire's crisis is this: that a substantial part of its yield came in as cash and supported a variable expense, the military. We have seen how the latter bulked large in people's minds, not only as a stable item in the imperial budget but as one subject to sudden increase in times of active campaigning.

The dependence of the budget on cash flow, however, opened it wide to attack by inflation. The first gentle stages of this may have contributed to steps taken by Septimius Severus. He placed greater administrative burdens on the urban upper classes and initiated far-reaching changes in army supply. Thus he obtained services and goods in kind. His son Caracalla increased the rate of certain money taxes, whether because of an absolute or an inflationary rise in government expenses, we cannot be sure. Thereafter, signposts are a little more often encountered. In Egypt in the course of the third century a variety of changes were attempted with no consistency or long success: trades taxes and poll taxes were increased, the age of exemption from liturgies was raised to seventy, and Philip briefly established a new, more efficient system of land assessment and taxation—while on the other hand, forced assignment of vacant land (*epibole*) did not become a major feature of life for the peasant, nor were his taxes in kind increased.[31] From Judaea came ever-sharper reports of suffering under taxes;[82] of more general import, the statement that "from Gallienus' day on, the state was in a wretched condition, with the treasury exhausted and the rich attacked as by a flash flood."[33] Decius' declaration that "indictions ordinarily fall on property not individuals"[34] has sometimes been understood as the death knell of levies in cash, a turning away from a debased and inflated currency; but, however logical the interpretation (the date is too early for the worst fevers of the economy), in fact Egypt at least went on with its old mixed ways. Decius may only be saying what had always been true, that landed wealth was the preponderant base of assessment. In sum, our evidence for response to crisis in the tax field could hardly be less satisfactory; yet surely it points to just the difficulties we would expect to find in a complicated, regionally varying, many-layered system developed in and for a period of sound coinage and tolerably fixed expenses. That such a system should have proved quite inadequate for the third quarter of the third century is what anyone would predict.

Diocletian's tax reforms usher us into a time of abruptly better documentation. So intricate are the puzzles concealed in the evidence that these documents—rather, a few of the more illuminating ones—must be looked at individually. Since they have been minutely examined by scholars over a century without consensus on many major and still more minor points of interpretation, there is small reason to hope for anything better now. As a reflection of the shape of crisis, however, they are not only of importance in themselves but suggest what form must have been taken by the economic difficulties of the decades preceding Diocletian.

To begin with Gaul: an orator addressing Constantine in about 312 [35] thanks him for great benefactions. Autun, the orator's home, has been subjected to "a new tax survey." [36] The fields had been described according to the general formula for Gaul, and the registering of the number of inhabitants and the measure (*modum*) of the lands is not challenged; [37] but for various reasons, great difficulties had arisen in paying taxes. Now the emperor has canceled five years' worth of back dues and reduced the census by 7,000 *capita,* more than a fifth part, so that children hold dear their parents, husbands their wives, parents their grown offspring—all rejoicing in the burdens lifted from them.[38]

In this story, the use of round numbers by the administration may suggest a rough-and-ready estimate of Autun, adding together its work force and territory. Both elements would be known from old or specially revised records, perhaps compared with inventories of other cities, subjected to challenge (Autun had none to offer), and assigned an overall taxability in fixed but arbitrary units of calculation, capita—necessarily large units, if so substantial a city as Autun and its surrounding territory had only 32,000.[39] On these would fall the obligation to pay whatever was fixed for the year by the indiction: so many gold pieces much reduced by Julian, as we see the system in operation in the 350s.[40] Julian's concern about high taxes is described in several passages of Ammianus, who uses *tributum* and *capitatio* apparently as equivalents and who depicts the latter, at least, as supplying army needs.[41] *Capitatio* seems thus to derive naturally from *capita* and naturally to indicate liability in a broad sense, if it underlies the chief charge on the imperial economy, the military.

Census in the oration as elsewhere should be taken to mean registered taxability.[42] It evidently counted persons of both sexes and all ages, along with their land. If for any reason land ceased to be cultivated or the work force diminished, the city's total of capita should reflect the fact. Protestations to that effect surely were needed to reduce Autun's total to 25,000. But in the meantime, the community shared out the obligation in such a way that a big family paid more than a small—hence the orator's description of resentment within families at their own number. The *Gallicani census communis formula* must therefore have counted each adult citizen as a fixed fraction of a *caput,* grouped under the head of the family, owner of the property they lived on. That latter, constituting a fraction or a multiple of a caput, would have been added in to make the total of the owner's capitatio. If we try to understand how it might work, we may imagine for the sake only of illustration one Marcus Gallicus, registering himself, his two sons, and his fields, probably with specification of their type and use.[43] Let us imagine that the three adult males, just as in the towns around, each counted as one fifth, their property, two fifths; total, one caput, one thirty-two–thousandth of the municipal whole. If the whole is reduced to 25,000 capita, the number of people may remain the same on the registry rolls, but adjustment will be made to increase the area equaling one caput. Thereby each family will be liable to a smaller annual payment on the landed portion of its taxability.

No doubt this model appears and actually was clumsy to handle. By analogy, that is still acceptable. For in the diocese of Asiana a number of fourth-century inscriptions[44] contain declarations of taxability according to several patterns expressed in very minute fractions, at the extreme, one two-thousandth. The land unit is, in some, the ἰούγερον, in others, the ζυγόν (*iugerum* and *iugum*), further defined in terms of land use for pasture, grain, olive, or wine production. Some of the inscriptions also record κεφαλαί (*capita*) of living creatures in great variety: declarants and family, πάροικοι or γεωργοί (*coloni*), δοῦλοι (*servi*), and livestock. At Tralles they are combined to one total, according to formulae that cannot be reconstructed. Area may be totaled in portions of a κ(εφαλο)ζ(υγὸν) at Thera; ζυγοκεφαλαί at Astypalaea combine in one sum both main elements, "heads" and land. One estate lists ἀνθρ(ώπων) κ(εφαλαί) one half, one fourth—that is, three fourths—indicating that a human counted less than one full "head." [45] The word *zygokephale* appears later in laws to mean "heads" only.[46]

Thanks to careful study over the past generation,[47] the meaning of these lists and of the technical terms in them has been cleared of much obscurity. Several forms of registration for tax paying are represented, implying not different systems of assessment, perhaps, but different stages preliminary to one system. On details, certainty does not seem within reach. The simplest model to imagine, however, is one whereby a declarant submitted to the authorities for public view and challenge the whole of his taxability. This included the various elements we have seen grouped into fractions of a head or of a "yoke" of land (or giving each item as a unit, to be translated later into fractions according to a formula we cannot reconstruct). In the last stage, at which the amount of tax would be reckoned, heads and yokes would be added to one total in "yoke-heads" or "head-yokes," indifferently. Some certain quantity of land would necessarily (but not in a round number) owe the same amount of tax as one head; some certain fraction of a head would necessarily owe the tax of one yoke. To that degree and no more, we can speak of equivalence between the two. We cannot go further, to say that a head equaled a yoke in its theoretical productive capacity or in the amount of taxes it paid.

Measurement by yokes had a long history. An inscription of 370/371 from Ephesus in Asia describes territory there in iuga, not as bare units of area but (through *qualitas*) as units of productivity. Each iugum paid a certain number of solidi.[48] Here, *iugatio,* as it is termed in the text, recalls the Gallic tax units producing so many aurei. And the several Asianic types of agricultural use—pasturage, vineyard, arable, and so forth—recall the system applied in Syria; but the Syrian iugum works out to about two fifths the size of the Asianic.[49] What begin to emerge through comparison are certain consistent principles, tolerant of regional diversity.

Rather less is known of Africa, but that diocese like others had its own character. The chief tax, considered the only "regular" one, was raised on land in kind, and most of it went to the feeding of Rome.[50] It applied to areas defined in *centuriae* or subunits, *iugera.*[51] While of course people registered their households (women, children, slaves) in the city rolls and rendered services such as corvées and money under such headings as the trades tax, there is no trace of the totaling of their capita and centuriae.[52] The much older system appears to have survived, of personal and property taxes separately; the latter rested on units of area which perhaps reached back to the Republican centuriae of 200 iugera and were in any case different from units in other provinces.

In Egypt, finally, we encounter under and after Diocletian yet another set of fiscal practices, very richly documented though still not understood in every detail. As in Africa, both persons (until about 313)[53] and *arourai* of land (at least under Constantius)[54] were registered, the latter under newly elaborated headings of differing use[55] but in simplified categories of ownership [56] and under a simplified list of tax headings.[57] Thus, according to whatever the governor of Egypt announced as the formula (διατύπωσις, *delegatio*) for the year, individuals paid not only a personal tax (until about 313) but a range of other taxes as well, falling upon their land and arranged (perhaps in Diocletian's time, certainly in Constantine's) into three broad groups. A landowner might find himself billed, let us imagine, for one-tenth recruit, one-tenth load of hay, one-tenth jar of wine, one-tenth transport cost for a load of wheat, and one-tenth army uniform per aroura, all of which he might pay in money.[58] The most important group supplied food to Rome and Constantinople; the second most important, army needs of all sorts; and the third, a catchall of minor taxes.

Papyri show abandoned experiments, fumbling, and change especially in the earlier decades of this system. The whole required resurveying the resources of Egypt more than once (above, p. 66); and there are scattered hints of assessment edicts now lost to us.[59] Scholars nevertheless deny any basic departure from past practices in Diocletian's measures [60] or, for many decades, any introduction of iuga or capita. We may of course see in the aroura Egypt's equivalent of the African centuria or the Syrian iugum. Such the aroura was in function if not in extent; but it was not added to a poll tax to yield some fraction or multiple of a new, combined unit of calculation.

Our short survey of four areas brings out the continuity and therefore the diversity of the empire's tax structure across the bridge of Diocletian's reign. The obvious question arises, how he and his successors coped with this diversity in edicts issued from their central headquarters. Whatever the answer, it does not seem to be within our reach. We have no description of the administrative structure in the round. It must instead be assembled in our minds out of tangential references and hints and glimpses, and they are simply too confused to yield any sense.

Two laws of Constantine concern exemptions to veterans so as to relieve them "from the registry and payments" of annona to the extent of several capita, their own plus that of relatives, one caput for each or the equivalent total of capita if the relatives did not exist.[61] They were forbidden to transfer any of their credit to someone else's property (*res aliena*). Since human beings could not be moved around, this mention of property proves that the caput could mean or be translated into landed assessment.[62] Moreover, several capita were envisioned as conferring in some cases a credit greater than an individual could make use of (the recipient might have extra left over, to assign fraudulently to another person's account), or in other cases less than an individual could make use of (the recipient might wish to take over the immunity bestowed on a nonexistent wife's caput). That could only be assigned to a man if it were a fixed, published quantity of credit.

We have here a set of implications and inferences which must, every one, fit into a single description of how taxes worked, and that description in turn must fit with what is known of practices looked at region by region. The most satisfactory model seems to require that caput in

Constantine's two laws should mean a part of taxability sustained by a person as such (that is, for Marcus Gallicus in our earlier illustration, one fifth of a caput in the broader sense that included also property). Let this be called a "personal caput," as opposed to the taxability unit (caput) that determined what Autun owed to the government.

It might be expected that the personal caput underlay poll taxes surviving (perhaps with some changes) from the very widespread *tributum capitis* of the Principate. That levies were indeed raised from persons as such is amply attested. We have the fourth-century mentions of the registering of slaves and tenants by the landowner; [63] or of a *capitatio humanum, animalium,* or *plebeia;* or again, in the description of Galerius' harsh census in Bithynia. It fell principally on small farmers, *enormitate indictionum consumptis viribus colonorum.* Their vines, fruit trees, and fields were entered in the rolls—but also their livestock and their selves, *hominum capita.*[64] And a part of Autun's rejoicing, *cum plures adiuvant obsequia paucorum,* is echoed in a later law, *privilegia paucis personis in perniciem plurimorum.*[65] The two texts agree in showing that some portions of a city's burdens over the empire generally became easier to bear, the more people it was shared among. Obviously their names appeared in a separate list of some sort, subject to a levy.

Still further: a distinction is made, within overall taxability, between the land-based and other kinds. So we have the phrasing, "the *capitatio,* not only under the *annona*-heading but other forms and payments as well." [66]

From that former, more central aspect, immunity was very sparingly granted, at first not even to veterans and priests, though they were exactly the classes of citizens whom Constantine considered the most eligible.[67] It is true that during his reign, traders' tolls are not heard of, and hardly at all throughout the fourth century;[68] he extended to new areas Diocletian's exemptions from *capitatio plebeia;*[69] but on the other hand, it was he who instituted the glebal and lustral taxes, of which one fell on land without regard to its use or yield and the other on humble artisans and similar, quite unpropertied persons.[70]

All this evidence demonstrates, first, that urban and rural residents alike were fully and separately entered in a city's census books and, second, that they owed money to the state on their heads, their capita.

We can absorb that conclusion into others that concern Gaul, Asia, Africa, and Egypt. We can absorb it into the texts that concern veterans' immunities. To offer once more an illustration of what they might mean: a soldier with a wife and father living on a farm might gain credit for each of them, for himself, and for his deceased mother, totaling four personal capita (but four fifths of a caput as the taxability unit that lay on his city and its territory). By a formula—for instance, one personal caput equals twenty acres of arable—a percentage of the farm would benefit from the mother's caput. A device of this sort, that could translate a human into an inanimate resource, serves to explain the conflating of persons and lands under the term *capitatio* (or under *capita* as taxability units) in Gaul, as well as that monstrosity, the "yoke-head" in Asia.

But what cannot be absorbed is the iugum. It raises insoluble problems, seemingly from the earliest stages of Diocletian's tax reforms. For when we find in Asianic inscriptions the *zygon,* surely that translates into Greek a land measure taken over from Latin. By 340, the term turns up in a law declaring that *immunitas iugorum* wipes away one's capitatio and tax registration.[71] Iuga here cover one's entire taxability and limit it to land. That fits with the fact that iuga in 341 are being sold at auction.[72] It fits with the fact that *capitatio* likewise occurs very early as meaning landed taxability.[73] *Capitatio* and *iugatio* as synonyms in all these contexts could be understood easily enough if Diocletian's tax system bore only on the real estate one owned. There is evidence for Africa by the mid-fourth century that seems to show just that,[74] and a later law reads, "Let a tax be levied upon the taxpayer's iuga, or his capita, or however else they may be called." [75] The interchangeability of the terms is seen in the phrase, *capitatio vel iugatio,* or *capita vel iuga,* quite often encountered in the Codes. The sum of this evidence would show that, though local custom gave different names to taxation taken as a whole, it grew out of the old *tributum soli.* When is impossible. For we know that taxation bore on land *and* persons.

A wealth of thought has been spent on the vocabulary of the puzzle. Iugum is a square measure, true; it is a measure of agricultural resource, much of arable or less of vineyard; it is a measure that adds together so much area plus so many men or oxen, subject to a given levy. It is, then, a tangle of contradictions. And similarly, caput: a

registered head or unit of calculation that includes more
than one head or that includes heads plus real property.
How each meaning can be reconciled with every other
and within a believable system of taxation, no scholarly
consensus as yet declares.

But two points must be made. First, regional diversity
ruled in the empire after Diocletian as before. That must
certainly go far to explain the contradictions above. The
iugum as a land measure had different sizes in different
provinces.[76] Senators paid less glebal dues in Macedonia
and Thrace than in other provinces; trades tax exemptions were greater for clerics in Gaul than in Italy and
Illyricum; residents of Lycian and Pamphylian cities for
some period were paying taxes from which other cities of
the Oriens diocese were exempt; Oriens, excluding two of
its provinces, might pay the army equipment tax in
money, but at a higher rate than Thrace; certain eastern
provinces, but not others at the time, received a lowering
of their tax liability; and military remounts were levied at
different prices in different African provinces.[77] In Africa,
Gaul, Asia, and Egypt, as we have seen, different traditions carried forward from the Principate into the Dominate different ways of assessing types of land use. Somehow,
unbearable inequalities of tax burden were made to seem
bearable.

Second, official language was tolerant of almost unlimited inexactitude (above, p. 84). To the astonishment
of any sane observer nowadays, terms of great importance
in public enactments were employed with loose interchangeability or in several meanings. Taxability as defined

above, the citizen's overall obligation to regular government tax demands, appears now as *tributum*,[78] now as *indictio*,[79] now as *census*,[80] now as *canon*,[81] now as *annona*,[82] now as *capitatio;*[83] or (it follows naturally) one term may stand for the other.[84] On the other hand, these sometime synonyms may occur as opposed to each other, or as mere parts or aspects but not the whole of each other (that is ,of taxability).[85] And wrapped up inside them are quite various roots: for example, *annona* indicates not only the supply of the capital(s) and army but a rations unit, just as *caput* may be one's liability under *capitatio* but likewise a rations unit.[86] The so-called glebal and lustral and crown taxes all peek through clouds of periphrases. Government's stylistic habits in even the most technical documents of the labor Empire are notoriously ill suited to the job of making clear their intent.

The modern student wants to draw out the intent, upon the supposition that, in its rational essence, hidden within official communications, it really exists. Confusion, however, may be rather his than the Romans'. Consider a law which direct quadruple penalties at "wealthy men" who fall behind in their taxes, while "the lowly" are to pay no more than the actual sums due.[87] Nowhere do the Codes define a "wealthy man." Though the matter is not important in itself, it suggests a way of thinking quite strange, one that leaves to local interpretation an adjective full of legal, not to say painful, consequences. And that interpretation is better called political than administrative: the official in charge is expected to ask himself, not what exactly are his instructions, but what, within vague

TAXES   149

limits, he can get away with. A second illustration may be
drawn from instances of tax abatement. Many, many laws
and other kinds of sources report the abrupt giving or
taking away of exemptions; far better for our purposes,
certain passages indicate the scope of such actions: a sudden 50 percent tax, a halving of Thracian taxes, a 56 percent tax cut in Gaul in a few years, a sudden 25 percent
tax cut by Constantine.[88] These figures sound unbeliev-
able. For that matter, it is not very easy to comprehend
the varying assessments we discovered in different regions.
Perhaps what counted for the Romans was not so much
logic at the center as feasibility at the local level, where,
with scourgings, tortures, and imprisonments, with super-
exactions and "rake-offs," with arbitrary "extraordinary"
taxes, and with contrary remissions of uncollectable arrears, taxation like politics was practiced as "the art of the
possible." [89]

Diversity in practice and inadequacy of expression do
not, however, take away all meaning from imperial tax
legislation. When every allowance is made for what does
not make sense (either in truth or because of our mis-
understanding of the subject), enough remains for some
judgment on Diocletian's new measures.

They called for reports on the state's needs to be assembled in the great bureaus; authorizations to levy taxes
issued thence, ending in the governors' hands; the governors added together the totals of taxability units in the
cities under their authority; and that total, divided into
each heading of need, each *titulus,* determined the citizen's obligations for the year. Nothing prevented the

system from producing anything whatever that the government required: pork, textiles, ships, uniforms, or horses —all specified as regular, "canonic." [90] If the objects to be levied came only in expensive packages, they could be divided into make-believe fractions, of a horse or of a recruit. By the device of *protostasia,* a "little head" (*capitulum*) grouped together several smaller landowners jointly responsible.[91] Large levies of labor were possible, assigned *per singula capita.*[92] Most common of all were levies of grain. True, from all the pieces of evidence lying at hand, we cannot reconstruct in our minds the machinery of assessment; but we can see in use in the central bureaus and in some of the provinces a key concept, *iugum* or *caput,* that allowed government to take account of, add together, or intertranslate every element of productivity: a farmer, a draft animal, an irrigation ditch, an olive tree. The notional unit (as it is sometimes called) is an invention really new and really important.

It addressed itself to one of the great problems of Diocletian's earlier lifetime, rotten currency. To bypass that, and to put the budget of needs in direct contact with goods and services, was clearly the idea behind the caput. In theory, government henceforth could function perfectly well within a natural economy. In fact, most money taxes had died a natural death in the later 200s. In debased coinage, they were valueless. More were done away with by Diocletian. But not only did the system itself, in its joints, so to speak, continue to require some old-fashioned lubrication by cash equivalents or exchanges; the state's chief creditors, its soldiers and officials, demanded gold.

So while the Egyptian poll tax was disappearing in the East, in the West Constantine was instituting a new levy in that commodity, and in his later reign did much to reduce the domain of a natural economy.[93] For all his successes in this, however, the main elements of the Diocletianic reform were maintained and extended to the whole of the empire, perpetuating into the fourth century and beyond devices shaped by the third.

Besides rotten currency, a second major problem confronted Diocletian, war costs. For these, a second invention, capitatio, was produced. It asserted in its vagueness an unlimited right to demand in a regulated manner what had earlier been wrung from the emperor's subjects more by force and fraud and bureaucratic makeshift. The edict of 297 published in Egypt by the prefect was for that reason not hypocritical in announcing a new census as a measure of justice: "Our most provident emperors, having learned that the levies of the public taxes were being made capriciously, decided to root out this most evil practice and to issue a salutary rule." [94]

No one can imagine the drama of crisis without assigning to its darker scenes every sort of sudden pillage inflicted in the name of survival by the defenders upon the defended. But such pillage is not merely imaginary. It is easily documented for the first half of the third century, and thereafter we hear less of it for a space only because the voices of its victims are exhausted. By some better means, the legitimate requirements of security and recovery had to be shifted from the areas physically wasted to the areas less sharply attacked. Somehow the snug and the rich had to pay their share. Hence even Italy, under Diocletian or Constantine,[95] had to submit to taxation, and the senatorial class to endure under Constantine a special levy on its estates. Nor did capitatio stop there. It embraced in its thoroughness the value of labor, without which a field was no more than so much dirt. It embraced, exploited, but at the same time protected the landowner's tenants and draft animals. In administrative theory, at least, there was to be no more *angareia,* no outright seizing of transport or recruits or any other thing by armies on the march. All necessary items were raised under a lawful title in kind or cash, and in equal shares from every source within a province.

Certainly the development of this system of revenues, begun around 290,[96] took many decades. Certainly it required for perfect success more administrative efficiency, less corruption, more support, less evasion, than it received. But its logic was powerful. Diocletian might acknowledge his extensive concessions to rooted customs that detracted from his logic, and the debt he owed to the model of the annona militaris, which anticipated much of his work. But caput and capitatio were marvelous inventions, one to respond to the crisis of rotten currency, the other to respond to war costs. Together they constituted a workable plan for survival.

7

GOODS AND SERVICES

With needs increasing and the money to pay for them sapped of buying power, government was bound to turn to exactions of a new sort, or more accurately, to make much greater use of the old that suited the times better.

Raw materials of many sorts flowed in from crown preserves and monopolies. There were big herds to provide meat, leather, wool;[1] quarries to supply fine building stone and, by the second century, enormous productive capacity concentrated in a cluster of imperial brickyards around Rome, with others in scattered provinces as well.[2] There were, from at least Alexander Severus' reign, imperial purple fisheries.[3] We should mention, too, properties that produced such less important things as salt, papyrus, perfumes, timber, minium, and spices, though they are not generally attested beyond the second century.

For labor, the state could use convicts (especially after 250, but perhaps the persecutions distort the record).[4] In the Principate they are found in mines and quarries, rarely in other work.[5] Corvées are attested for city wall building in the second half of the third century [6] and for transport duty, beyond the *angareiai* that become especially notorious in the third century.[7] In Egypt, liturgists supplied teams of free workers for all kinds of short-term assignment besides the immemorial cleaning of irrigation ditches; but for quarries, only from the beginning of the Dominate.[8] A great deal of work the army took over: large-scale projects like canals and roads, harbors and drainage and surveying.[9]

Two lines of development cross: that of the state's material resources falls away in the course of the empire, as they are sold off or leased to private enterprise for exploitation or as they simply disappear from the surviving record. The line of the state's use of forced labor, on the other hand, appears to rise from the mid-third century on. Were this the whole story, however, the state would certainly have been ill equipped to meet its needs in such conditions as beset it after 250.

A more significant means of supply was taxes, with which requisition must be considered jointly; for ad hoc levies dissolve into abrupt demands for whatever an emergency might require, and we are often unable to say whether suppliers were remunerated fairly, or at all. The bulk of the evidence comes from Egypt, not only because of the survival of papyri but because of special institutions there which the Romans inherited and maintained. These permitted them in the second century to raise army uniforms under one title, "Public Clothing," sometimes for

shipment to very distant points;[10] thereafter under another title, "Army Clothing," from the later third century.[11] Still a third title, the "Anabolic Tax," begins about
the same period, perhaps under Aurelian, and raised not
only clothing for the troops but raw linen.[12] On occasion
it could be paid in cash, most necessarily when assessed
on one's extent of land;[13] for fairness demanded that a
small taxpayer should owe only a fraction of a cloak, or
the like, which had to be translated into money. Fractional payments in money become more common in the
fourth century.[14] It seems a likely explanation for the
military-uniform prices in Diocletian's Edict, that they
were meant to fix the terms of the necessary translation.[15]
As with crown monopolies or convict labor, we have no
way of estimating here the total production figures. We
can only focus on administrative devices and precedents
available to the emperors when needs increased and normal currency and market habits were disturbed.

Egyptian clothing taxes could involve an alternative
route to delivery, through guilds of weavers put under
contract to weave the articles demanded of taxpayer
groups.[16] When the levy was laid on towns and villages,
they might be given no choice but to produce the actual
completed garments; and, themselves taking in the money
from their citizens or, in the earlier history of taxes in
kind, perhaps taking it in from the state as a requisition
price, they negotiated with local craftsmen for the quantity they needed. The state strictly controlled the quality
of its receipts.[17]

The two methods seen here, of goods obtained direct

from the taxpayer or indirectly through artisans' associations, are very widely diffused across the empire in the wake of inflation. Diocletian's Edict sets prices for "indictional" garments, pointing both to a government levy in kind and to the free buying and selling of such garments by private citizens, most likely in order to acquit themselves of their tax obligations.[18] By 323 a tax called *vestis* is being referred to casually as "canonic," regular, and turns up in later laws under a system that exacted so many cloaks, and so on, per unit of land, just as had been done in Egypt since the third century.[19] Its main purpose was the initial outfitting of new recruits.[20] We have seen in the preceding chapter how the yield was exacted through capitatio.

But certainly by the earlier 300s free weavers in groups were placed under specific obligation to deliver to the state an annual quota of their goods,[21] and some part thereof was worked up further in state factories. To *gynaecia,* as they were called, and to dye works, convicts were being sent in Diocletian's time.[22] Two dozen of these workshops are mentioned across the fourth century, most of them located in major cities. They produced uniforms elaborately embroidered and colored for high officials and for the emperor himself. Perhaps that constituted their main output, not coarse clothing for army privates. At any rate, the materials for manufacture included gold thread and purple dye, over which the emperors after Constantine are seen exerting a monopoly.

State *fabricae* to make weapons and armor are likewise first encountered under Diocletian.[23] Before Constantine's reign is done, a good number of them have made their appearance in our sources. Possibly the bulk of nearly fifty were then in existence that later can be counted in the Notitia Dignitatum and elsewhere. They were run by small staffs of army officers set over workers free, valued, even prosperous, but under compulsion to offer their skill and a fixed annual quota to the emperor. Very likely their factories looked like those that legions had built and run during the Principate. The practice of setting an officer to round up artisans of a city for emergency manufacture of arms was not unknown, too, in those days; and the imperial palace had always held silversmiths such as later made gilded or chased helmets for the Dominate.[24] It was once more Diocletian, however, who put together all those precedents into one single organization to supply the items of payment for army and civil service that were described in an earlier chapter. And most likely mint workers too were conscripted by him. In any case, by 317 they were permanently tied to their jobs at various centers.[25]

There is something instructive in the recommendation of a bureaucrat of some sort, author of the treatise *De rebus bellicis* of the 370s, that mint workers who were not making coins *comme il faut* ought to be shipped off to work on a desert island. The shipping in of British labor to Gaul in the 290s, to patch up the ruined cities there, fits well with this casually dictatorial attitude toward essential skills.[26] Their scarcity in the later Empire and their importance to such imperial concerns as currency production, embellishment of palaces, and manufacture of luxurious

equipment of all sorts brought them into a chancy prominence, in which they might equally well receive abrupt
orders or special favors. Both testified to the effect of
crisis. Loss of private wealth to the demands of war, the
scattering of the rich from many cities into rural estates,
and the gathering of a larger proportion of the empire's
total economic power into the emperor's hands had diminished the patron class necessary to nourish architects,
jewelers, and mosaicists. And the emperors themselves
were used to demand services unrequited. In fact, sometimes they did pay. As will be seen later, they paid in the
form of privileges of many kinds. That cost them nothing.
In the whole process by which silver was got by the Count
of the Sacred Largesses (as a tax) and given to be worked
into a helmet, then returned to the Count as a tax or quota
from the smiths, and again given by the Count to a high
officer as salary in exchange for the latter's loyal exertions
and support, no money changed hands. Therein lay the
clue to the understanding of the devices so far sketched.

Under Aurelian, when the story of outright conscription
may conveniently begin, we see Rome's wall built by
corvée exacted from the city's many guilds; in Egypt, we
see reorganization or new invention of taxes to yield both
the raw materials of cloth manufacture and the finished
product; and a famous revolt of mint workers took place
in the capital, of which we can make nothing, except to
say that a very large workers' association, and one connected with currency, and one whose misconduct was
brutally crushed by the army, all fit the times. Ten years
later began a reign in which the tax system was radically

rethought so as to facilitate the exaction of any goods or services whatever, in addition to cash and corn. State factories of many kinds were built and workers' associations were meshed into their service, along with the harsher use of forced and of penal labor to keep them going. Granted, Diocletian's methods had their limitations. Constantine is later heard complaining that scarce artisans are being enticed away from the cities they have served; he must establish training programs for architects, who simply are not to be found for the cities' needs in Africa; and he must guarantee that artisans in a very long list shall be free from all civic obligations so as better to practice and pass on their skills to their children. His continued legislation on these problems betrays its own weakness.[27]

Besides his servants, military and civil, the emperor's subjects in Rome and Constantinople also had a claim on him that had to be recognized. The administrative devices that we have looked at thus far, mostly concerned with manufactures, can be seen in operation also for the supply of food to the capitals. To collect it at the threshing floor, take it thence to granaries, measure it, approve it, store it till shipment, embark and sail it to Rome, unload it and measure and approve and store it, and finally deliver it to bakeries for eventual distribution among more than a hundred thousand ticketholders, required a large and intricate organization of many kinds of workers. It has often been described.[28] Two of the groups involved can be picked out to illustrate the way it operated.

Navicularii owned ships that could carry grain, were therefore at least modest capitalists, and provided something vital directly to the Roman plebs, indirectly to the stability of the throne. The wealth needed for this role was exempted from taxes by Nero; possible losses at sea were underwritten by the state through a measure of Claudius —who also extended to shipowners immunity from the Lex Papia Poppaea if they were citizens, citizenship to Latins, and the *ius quattuor liberorum* to women.[29] Hadrian added immunity from municipal obligations. The grant was defined and approved by many later laws, freeing the beneficiaries even from the decurionate.[30] They had of course to be in genuine and active service to the supply of Rome, with the majority of their property devoted to it; and they had to build ships of an adequate size. Benefits fell to the individual who thus qualified, not to navicularii corporately. But the spontaneous tendency of shippers—like entrepreneurs and craftsmen of every sort at all—to join in associations gave birth to a fateful confusion by the end of the second century. Law speaks of "the associations which extend exemption, such as of navicularii . . . in order that they may afford the needful labor to the general good, *publicis utilitatibus.*"[31] We have seen in chapter 2 how *utilitas publica* received more emphatic advertisement from emperors of the crisis years, and can imagine how it might be easily stretched into the form of bonds to tie men to their duty. Probably through legislation of Diocletian, navicularii guilds became subject to constraint.[32] There continued to be shippers unconnected with the state; those otherwise, continued to be paid for their voyages just as they always had been in the past, even if a large part of their reward consisted in their

various exemptions; and they did not give all their time
by any means to the provisioning of the capital.[33] But they
were bound to their occupation, bound by *origo,* their
very birth, and their landed possessions with them, so that
there was henceforth assured to the state a registered number and replacements to that number of men, ships, and
supporting acres of land in pledge for their feeding of
Rome.

How violent was the introduction of this entire system?
Its elements were in fact not all new. The right of the
state to make its subjects build ships by corvée was long
familiar.[34] Moreover, the *annona civica* had of necessity
involved supporting workers in a close, subordinate relationship to it from Augustus on, a closeness demonstrated
in a hundred ways—on an especially grand and moneyed
scale, in the grain convoys that plied from Alexandria and
Carthage under ultimate command of the *praefectus
annonae.* If captains were to claim the privileges that had
been legislated for them, surely there must be some public
record not only of their names but of the location and
extent of their estates in pledge for their *bona fides.* On
the other hand, for the *compulsory* attaching of land and
persons to the system there is no proof before Constantine,
no hint (a little short of proof) before Diocletian. Innovation by the early fourth century is thus very real, though it
followed natural paths.

The new policy may be examined in one other group,
the *pistores* who prepared bread for distribution to the
Roman people. Like ship owners, they were granted important exemptions in the second century for active opera-

tion of their business. If their associations threatened strikes in the provinces, governors stepped in.[35] In the third century their menial ranks drew on corvée labor and, under Constantine, on convicts also;[36] their upper ranks owned property subject to fixed obligations. But a law in 319 (CT 14.3.1), by then evidently according to established practice, forbade pistores to escape their guild by dropping below the required capitalization, through fake transfer of their estates to some friend. This recalls a similar reference of a century earlier, regarding cloth dealers (centonarii): members of their association shall enjoy immunities only if their wealth does not exceed a certain amount, and they must not conceal any so as to qualify for immunities.[37] The wealth and work of citizens who contributed to the public interest are thus seen to have been a normal sphere of interference by government in the middle Empire, leading easily to some measure of dictation by the later Empire.

One last point: to dwindling associations of centonarii and builders throughout the empire, Constantine ordered woodmerchants to be simply conscripted, in 315; minters to be forever tied to their occupation, in 317; and pork butchers to be similarly tied along with their property, in 334.[38] Government appears to have suddenly enslaved the economy. But in the first place, it must be remembered that a good degree of spontaneous continuity or stagnation was normal in trades throughout antiquity, so that the fourth-century sons who followed their fathers did not differ greatly from their predecessors in the second;[39] and a section of a city called the Bakers' Quarter or a whole town called Kilns only provides another clue to the same traditionalism prevailing in the economy.[40] Diocletian and Constantine thus need not be imagined as having abruptly to freeze every citizen in some job he would otherwise be likely to leave. In the second place, much freedom remained perfectly open and legal even in occupations such as those connected with Rome's provisioning, where we would least expect it; or it was asserted more or less blatantly in the face of prohibitions.[41] Both the difficulty and the completeness of conscription of labor in the wake of crisis should therefore not be exaggerated. Indeed, given the limited powers of enforcement that have been so often underlined in earlier chapters, we would expect developments to proceed slowly, stumblingly, and within restricted areas of special need.

In the very government itself, some of the precedents and principles of a bound condition had emerged without constraint from above. The lowlier attendants of magistrates in the provinces as in Rome organized themselves in benevolent societies [42] and openly bequeathed their jobs "with perquisites." [43] Inheritance was to become compulsory under Constantine: "Those born of members of any office whatsoever . . . shall proceed to the place of their fathers." [44] Like cloth dealers, too, certain minor bureaucrats formed into guilds in Egypt were required by Hadrian to demonstrate some minimum of property.[45] The purpose of this rule, however, was different from that laid on *centonarii* (above, p. 162). It recalled a Republican tradition that only people of some wealth should be put into positions of responsibility, partly because they

might be less swayed by bribes than a poor man, partly so
that they might provide some attachable guarantee for
their good behavior. Precautions along these lines led to
the stipulation in Egypt that citizens rendering compulsory public services, liturgists, should have a sure income
matching the size of their jobs [46] and that town accountants in other provinces, formerly most often slaves, should
under Diocletian be chosen rather from the ranks of the
freeborn.[47] With these persons, we pass from imperial
service—generally the object of eager ambitions—to municipal service that people tried to avoid. The two nevertheless have in common, for our present purposes, certain
features that bound them into groups easily dealt with by
government and that brought them under some gentle
supervision in the Principate. With the Dominate appeared emperors of more predatory needs and dictatorial
tendencies, to whom any already organized association
proved very vulnerable.

No group counted for more, none was more prominent,
than the urban elite in their senates. Without them the
empire was ungovernable. "A person born in a village is
understood to have as his *patria* the city to which his
village answers," says a jurist, making the key role of cities
explicit; and "cities are set up by the state in order to ex-
tort and oppress," says a rabbi, making the same point
with slightly different emphasis.[48] Taxation it was, of
course, that constituted the salient aspect of municipal
government as an extension of imperial. And just as there
was a tendency for the latter to dragoon private collectors
of taxes, *publicani,* to stay with their jobs and contracts

against their will,[49] so it naturally put pressure on city officials to do the same. That pressure was bound to become intense in the third century, in which our jurist and rabbi speak; for the alternative, a corresponding increase in the emperor's own means of enforcement, was too costly to consider. Though the civil service did grow bigger and though soldiers were more often employed for administrative purposes, the state's response to its personnel problems lay in the drafting of town leaders into its own designs. It made them extensions of itself or, as the rabbi would have said, the instruments of oppression.

And they, like the bakers, smiths, shippers, or weavers whose fate we have already outlined, traced a similar descent into servitude by similar stages. They came into close, natural, and ordinarily beneficial contact with the emperor's agents in, say, Trajan's day; they sought his intervention spontaneously, when they were in difficulties; they elaborated their internal organization to meet the responsibilities of peacetime with more efficiency, thereby offering to intervention a more convenient handle on their communities; and they accepted imperial appointees in their midst without objection. At the same time, traditions of civic duty that had habituated individuals to emergency deliveries of clothing or to emergency building of ships made private citizens take up a hundred public functions unremunerated. Such functions, qualified people were specially pressed to assume—qualified like shippers and bakers by wealth that incidentally afforded a grip upon them, if they proved derelict in any way. All these matters have been carefully studied by many scholars, just like

Roman trade associations. We need touch only on a few points specially illustrative of developments in the period of crisis.

By then, the actors were settled in their roles: decurions with a subcommittee of the Top Ten (*decemprimi, decaproti*); magistrates in varying posts and numbers elected by and from decurions, thereafter forming a pool of candidates for the decemprimate—though by no means every municipality had so orderly a constitution. Jurists had to acknowledge local variations.[50] In most localities by the earlier 200s, decurions cannot have been very easy to find. The dearth of them here and there had been reported for a century and more, and emperors had begun to apply pressure to recruitment.[51] Still, in particular contexts, the decurionate is treated as an honor and expulsion as a penalty right up to Diocletian's accession.[52] Thereafter, the picture turns unrelievedly black. An illegitimate and illiterate son of a slave was not only thought worthy of the post but absolutely forced to accept it if he held as little as ten or fifteen acres of land.[53] Nominated, he could not refuse, and (though unenforced precedents appear as far back as Severan times) his sons no matter how young could not avoid the same burden. Their birthplace claimed them forever—perhaps from Diocletian on, certainly under Constantine—as their estates had begun to claim them for their city yet earlier. As *originales* and *possessores,* they might thus be liable to service in two cities at once.[54] To immobilize them in their function took no great edict. Like craftsmen around them, they lived in a world by our standards stagnant. Wealth once gathered tended to pass down the generations undisturbed, along with rank; and, unlike craftsmen, decurions had land they could not hide from census takers (who were themselves, incidentally, of the same afflicted class).[55] Their conscription proceeded therefore in gentle degrees, hardly across the social grain, though very much against the economic: for the final tightening of laws took place in just the period of greatest improverishment and dislocation among the urban elite.

The Top Ten as a finance committee elected by the city senate existed from the first century (though in Egypt, only between about 200 and 307). They were especially concerned with the raising of taxes. As a body they pledged their estates to make good any shortfall in the cities' deliveries. Their duties counted at different times as a *munus personale* (by which one agreed to do something for one's native place, for example, go on an embassy) or as a *munus patrimonii* (by which one agreed to give it something, for example, a year's supply of wood for the public baths).[56] Such a group, as opposed to individuals answerable to the state, offered it obvious advantages. Parallels emerged from the mid-third century within villages. We will return to them shortly. But further than that, the Top Ten were slowly transformed into cogs in the machinery of imperial tax collection, chosen on the basis of the lands they owned inside the city's territory and in effect subject to election because of their wealth. Their *munus,* from being an obligation in a municipal sense and sphere, developed into an obligation toward the state, assigned to them just the way tax dues in grain or money might be levied.[57] The chief legists around the emperor can be heard discussing and eventually agreeing on this change over roughly the second quarter of the third century. It illustrates a general policy surprisingly harsh. Though *munera personalia* continued to be waived for this or that favored class or occupation—the veteran, for instance, as we saw in the preceding chapter, or the professor of rhetoric—the total number of them diminished, and *munera patrimonii* increased, from which exemptions were almost never granted.[58] Anyone with a patrimony, woman or child, was by definition liable to them. Moreover, the governor was expected to use force if need be to restore rich people to their place of birth, there to shoulder the burdens of citizenship. Such had been the law as early as Severan times.[59]

Munera made up a long, long list: the offering of one's house as a billet to soldiers, the assuring of a cheap and steady supply of oil to the town's gymnasium, or going along on a grain barge to a point of delivery. At best, such tasks took one away from one's normal concerns. At worst, they could be ruinously expensive. At the ceremony of nomination, the victim may therefore be found in the third century offering to prove himself less able to bear the burden than someone else, volunteering to exchange estates for the year involved; but even if he accepts the job without making this desperate challenge, his nominator is still liable as reserve surety behind him. There was no escape from rendering full payment of time or money.[60] How tangled and acrimonious the resulting struggles might become, to avoid duties or at least insure their fair assignment, can be sensed in the minutes of a meeting held under Diocletian in one of Egypt's four chartered cities:

> The assembly cried: "Noble syndic! You have adminis-
> tered well; witness has been made to one who is true and
> upright and a patriot. . . ." Menelaus, syndic: ". . . You
> remember when I distributed the album of magistrates
> between the two tribes and the matter was referred to my
> lord the most eminent Prefect, while the voting on their
> apportionment was going on. . . ." As he continued, the
> assembly cried: "Noble syndic! You have administered
> well! Hurrah for the patriot! Hurrah for the man of
> initiative! One who is worthy of the Prefect by a unique
> discharge of the syndicate! Just such men as this are
> needed. . . ." The members of the first tribe cried: "Yes,
> noble syndic! You have administered well!" The members
> of the second tribe cried: ". . .You have acted unfairly."
> . . . Menelaus, syndic: "In general, those from the album,
> having been submitted to my lord the Prefect, all took
> part in meetings, and those who did not were posted up."
> Pactumenius Nemesianus, former hypomnematographus:
> "This should not have taken place today." Menelaus,
> syndic: "Do not disturb the assembly." Nemesianus: "Do
> not set pitfalls for the assembly. . . . It is with the inten-
> tion of shielding these people that you have done this to-
> day, after your syndicate is over. . . ." Menelaus, syndic:
> "The beginning of conspiracy and confusion is already
> here. . . ." [61]

The workings of the system are revealed by another document, or rather, set of documents. It returns us to our starting point a few pages earlier, the raising of taxes. With this business, an obscure rank of liturgists were concerned, collecting dues called *primipili*. Successive mentions in the Justinian Code refer to a widow's inheritance seized by the treasury to make up what her husband had not been able to collect, under Caracalla; to children whose estates had liens on them, for the same cause, under Aurelian; to dowries held as pledge for full delivery of the tax yield, under Carus; and to orphans dunned for such payments and grown men bankrupted, under Diocletian [62]—from all of which we learn how fine the snares had become that caught the defenseless, entangled their property, and secured always one further group or person in reserve to meet the government's demands.

In one of the later of these texts occurs a phrase, *obnoxius necessitati,* used with chilling frequency in fourth-century laws—used of a craftsman "answerable to his lot," or of a decurion, or of the son of a veteran, or of a shipmaster. Or of their wealth. That was a point of vulnerability that no citizen could defend. He could not hide his house or his farm, upon which fell the envious eye of his neighbors, quick to spy out his qualification; upon which fell the imperious eye of the state as well, quick to exact full service according to one's degree of riches.

Much has been made of the tyrannous cruelty of Roman government in the period from, let us say, 250. But if an emperor were before us to offer his own defense, he might say he was himself *obnoxius necessitati.* It would be no more than the truth. He too was victim of crisis. Beyond that, he might have us look not at the cruelty but at the sheer intelligence of a system so well known to modern scholars, so easy to misjudge, that made all ranks of his subjects feel not only the exigencies of the time but the directing force latent in the very term "Dominate." Most of its devices had developed without compulsion. They were the easier to accept, then. Particularly important was local government's right to expect heavy contributions unrecompensed from richer people in the community. These, second-century emperors were already enforcing for the cities' sake. More recent was the right of the emperors to demand for their own purposes the same sort of contributions, assessing them directly on an individual's land but delegating all the labor of collection to the city senate. What body could do the job more equitably—or more conveniently? Administrative services could be in this way exacted like manufacture or transport. They were levied like a tax, so much per acre; and the decurions were treated just like an association of weavers, corporately guarantor with their wealth, *obnoxius necessitati.* By Diocletian's reign the system was in working order. Where, a century earlier, a well-to-do citizen might owe it to his town as a munus to supply a cart driver from his farm for delivery of wood to the public baths, under Diocletian he owed it to the state as a munus to come forward with a recruit for the army. The system had unlimited possibilities.

It meshed with special smoothness into Diocletian's tax machinery, which has been seen yielding articles of every sort.[63] We are now in a position to see how it might yield a quantity of government itself—a year's term in administration, let us say, just as if that work were so many silver coins. Considering the nature of those coins, however, the desirability of avoiding their use is understandable. They bought too little. Needing reinforcement in handling its many tasks, government simply bypassed payments in money and got help direct, by drafting into its ranks the necessary number of private citizens unpaid.

It had long been a right of the emperor to exempt essential workers from their local municipal obligations. When munera in the second half of the third century emerged as obligations—and more costly and laborious obligations—due rather to the state, then exemption from them took on a much greater value. It could be offered as salary to a high bureaucrat or army officer instead of silver coins.[64] Thus, by one more device, the economic problems of the time were confronted and a way round them discovered. It proved almost too successful. In flight from munera, people would go to any lengths, exert any amount of influence, pay any size of bribe to get themselves a palace post.

In surveying in a single chapter the goods and services exacted by the emperor from his subjects, jewelry and cloaks and marble columns provide a convenient point of entry to the subject; but they must give way to a more important matter, the food supply of the capital. That in turn must yield to the mechanism of levy that had to produce the food, the men, and their labors in the first place. Underlying the whole structure of the Roman world was the peasant. We turn at last to his conscription into the "force" economy of the Dominate—not to the whole history of the colonate, so much and so often discussed, but to the new regulation of agriculture growing out of the period of crisis.

That the peasant fully understood his own role is clear in the threat he often made when his back was to the wall. "I will have to flee the land," he mutters, when taxes grow too heavy. And flee it he did, in desperate protest. The evidence comes from many different provinces and decades of the empire, most of all from Egypt, where custom had given rise to a special term, *anachoresis*. Emperors for their part acknowledged the threat in legislation to insure that the fields should not be deserted.[65] Exploiters and exploited (if one wants to put it that way), or agricultural management and labor, or owner and worker engaged in a more or less constant tug-of-war. Inevitably, government took sides against the peasant. It wanted its taxes; it was directly involved as a landholder itself, of crown properties by the hundreds of thousands of acres; and moreover, it was run by a class of men virtually all of whom had personal experience with the problems of getting their rents in.

It might be expected, in all periods of the Empire, that scientific land management might be legislated. Indeed it was, but rarely. Best known is Domitian's effort to limit wine production, perhaps only to protect then existing big vineyards of Italy.[66] Irrigation sometimes received imperial aid, especially in Egypt, where emperors like Augustus and Probus conducted widespread campaigns of canal clearing; but similar attention is occasionally attested elsewhere, on a specially large scale in Pannonia under Galerius.[67]

Ordinarily, however, government intervened with a much cruder touch, directly to increase its income by putting more land under cultivation. Where the destructive passage of war had left it vacant, the emperors drew in new energies, Hadrian by favoring regulations in Egypt,[68] the Severi by attracting settlers to recently pacified areas of Africa,[69] and many other emperors, particularly from Marcus Aurelius on, by opening border provinces to barbarians along the Rhine and Danube.[70]

Where not war but economic causes were to blame, from the beginning of the Empire, a tax on marginal land that farmers left untilled in Egypt forced them to get what they could out of it after all; and even more effectively, unworked state lands were assigned for compulsory labor by individual abutters or by whole villages as the responsible units.[71] Outside of Egypt, from the first century on in Africa, anyone who took up vacant land and worked it would receive short-term tax exemptions and long-term occupancy that was his to bequeath to his heirs; something very similar turns up in a Severan inscription from Greece, and Pertinax advertised that vacant (probably crown) lands in Italy and the provinces would be generally available for ownership after ten years of tax-free farming.[72] Aurelian, with offer of only a three-year exemption, obligated cities to farm vacant land in their territories, and his law was confirmed and adjusted by Diocletian and Constantine.[73]

There was of course something circular in all this. Taxes had been at least partly to blame for the *agri deserti* that a new tax title throughout the empire, on the Egyptian model, now forced back under the plow. And it was the state that was saddled with properties of its own seizing: it had always asserted its claims over a farm left without heirs, or indebted to the fiscus. Deserted lands were simply one category of state lands, and the owners, the emperors, had to make them pay. They began to do so, however, from the 270s on, in a fashion characteristic of the times, by laying responsibility on a public, visible body of people, the decurions. The procedure, using either associations of "state farmers" or entire villages, had been long familiar in Egypt.[74] There, it advanced a step further in the early fourth century, as the state parceled out its various kinds of holdings to private ownership.[75] "State farmers" then disappeared, villages came to the fore, collecting taxes from their community of private owners. At least in theory, there remained no acre untilled anywhere in the empire, no acre failing to yield income through the efforts of some answerable citizen.

On crown estates as distinct fror *ager publicus,* it would be natural to look for similar measures of conscription, since there the emperor was master in every sense. He made use of tenants contracting for an agreed span of time. Most went by the name of *coloni.* Far up into the fourth century, some of them as *conductores* (lessees, perhaps hiring subtenants) simultaneously worked his land as well as land they owned themselves.[76] No doubt the majority of imperial coloni, however, were landless. They undertook to deliver a tithe of produce, a sum of money, ten days' labor on their master's home estate, or any mixture or variation of these elements. They had always been under pressure to renew their lease.[77] If they left before it was up, then by long-established law they lost any pledge they had deposited and could be taken to court.[78] Presumably there might be some sort of distraint on them not to leave, too, before their dues were all paid—their *reliqua,* as the term appears in various laws; and the government always had first claim on these as creditor.[79] That might explain the command of an imperial official in Egypt in 247 that tenants of an imperial estate should be tied to their lease till they had paid off their taxes.[80] Right up to the fourth century, however, this is the only instance of such force being applied, and in Egypt, periodic orders to return to one's place of registry had been long familiar, intended to control the problem of tax arrears and flight. What we are really looking for, some general rule that bound the peasant to the land, cannot be found as yet, neither in this special province nor on crown properties.

Tax obligations point to another context in which someone who hired land might lose his freedom. Had he been a slave, of course he could always have been sold with an estate as part of its working equipment. Along such traditional lines, Constantine's recommended format for transferring title of abandoned, confiscated estates to his subjects specified inclusion of "the slaves appertaining." In a later law he forbids "slaves assigned to the tax rolls" to be sold outside their province.[81] Here again, he has in mind the same purpose, the assuring of an estate's productivity. What if that purpose were expanded from servile to free labor? In many small, natural ways, free farm workers tended to be thought of almost as slaves even by much earlier jurists.[82] Just like rural slaves on whose economic value the master paid taxes, coloni also produced taxable value that landowners were responsible for in at least some areas, before 300 as after. Law recognized the analogy.[83] And a sort of intermediate status of person, the *inquilinus,* could be found, too, in Ulpian's statement that everyone shall be personally held to tax liability if he has not registered such an occupant of his property.[84] The inquilinus under Marcus Aurelius could be bequeathed "along with the properties to which he is attached," though not without them. He was to the latter extent a free man.[85] No very clear picture of his rights emerges from our evidence, but at least he makes clear to us, as he doubtless did to those who employed him, how easily the landless could be subjected to something like serfdom.

Scholars have often argued that the unresisting dependence of poor tenants clinging to someone else's acre with all their strength because they had no other home or possession and had perhaps improved it with extra effort, with a hut, or with a well, brought them into a kind of voluntary servitude; and this their master was the more inclined to take advantage of, as his own obligations to the state grew heavier. Habits of mind would therefore develop in fact, long before they developed in law, and would prepare the moment when government could support a landowner in forbidding a colonus to leave. Law, after all, had undeniably acknowledged a man's right to hold on to a slave or inquilinus. By such intermediate developments, social and economic forces were bound to prevail over the legal and administrative.

Our search for the bound tenant can be pursued a little further through certain third- and fourth-century texts of the Greek-speaking East. Here, a variety of words are used of tenant farmers, stressing their nonresident, landless status.[86] Added to the Latin vocabulary of the West, they prepare us for the loose, confused terminology of Constantine's order in 325 that, on "patrimonial and emphyteutic" property on the islands off Italy, "slaves, registered (*adscripticii*) coloni, or inquilini" are to be assigned to private owners along with the estates they work on, having no regard to their wishes or liberties, though without breaking up their families.[87] The emperor's view of their rights appears even earlier, in 319, when coloni of the *res privata*-estates are whistled back to their proper work, "to be assigned to Our farming exclusively." [88] The two laws together employ three different terms for state land, as well as three for workers. The former set of terms, it should be noticed, is subject to the same careless use as the latter. In fourth-century texts, as law becomes a less disciplined study, a number of terms and concepts of real property grow blurred in outline: *fundi fiscales* and *patrimoniales, dominium* and *possessio, emphyteuticarii* and *coloni,* tenancy *iure perpetuo* and *locatio-conductio.*[89] The efforts of generations of scholars to attach precise boundaries to all of these, through which the peasant's conscription must be traced, have thus produced no consensus at all. The fault lies not in any lack of modern learning, but rather in the ancients of this particular period. Just the same difficulties of interpretation arise in the study of tax terminology (above, chapter 6). In the empire's crisis and in the government's desperate exertions to rise above it, one thing that proved (or was thought) quite expendable was "the endless haggling of the law experts."

The opinion is Constantine's,[90] the very man whom one should least look to for a body of well-drafted, internally consistent legislation—above all, least when he is dealing with his own tenants. Whatever they called themselves, it made no difference to him. What mattered was the yield of their hands. Let them just stay put.

To sum up: in *agri deserti* claimed by the fiscus as their owners fled from war or from the burdens of tribute, precedents for conscription had first emerged. That we have seen under Aurelian. Tribute itself played a second and more active part, by tightening the landowner's grip on the labor he needed if he were not to be driven to flight himself. Law permitted this in every century of the Empire. That too we have seen. To begin with, slaves, then (at least from the second century) inquilini, and finally coloni were placed under the landowner in the local census lists. But whatever the obligations to till deserted fields in addition to one's own, whatever the free tenant's interest in submitting to the renewal of his lease, government itself did not attempt to immobilize the agricultural population by decree until Constantine, beginning with his own coloni. Their status, dissolved among inquilini and slaves, and their rights, eroded by emergency, were forfeit from at least 319.

It has long been conjectured that this change was made somewhat earlier, by Diocletian, to insure that the effect of the recensusing of the empire, and the tax program built on it, should not be lost straightway—as surely they would have been lost if every hard-pressed peasant could move about at will.[91] Such a conjecture is attractive. It may be right. But the first explicit reference we have to the colonate—Rome's version of serfdom—comes only in Constantine's announcement of 332 (*CT* 5.17.1): land-owners who shelter any colonus belonging to someone else (*iuris alieni*) must send him back and pay whatever capitatio he had fled. The law is pretty clearly aimed just at tenant farmers who have no property themselves, for a number of texts already mentioned demonstrate after 332 the continued existence of coloni who possessed their own estates and were very far removed from serfs.[92] Quite un-disturbed in whatever degree of liberty they had earlier enjoyed, they joined other categories of humbler land-holders variously attested through the fourth century, coloni in the sense only of lessees, but not without prop-erty. They cannot all be imagined in a condition resem-bling servitude.[93] Indeed, whole areas of the empire into the later 300s remained still to be subjected to the col-onate.[94] The Roman countryside was not by any means enchained overnight. Rather, Constantine (if not Dio-cletian before him) looked solely at taxpayers who had no security to offer and for whom someone else with land must be made responsible. It was the guaranteeing of taxes combined with labor, on his subjects' farms as on his own, that the emperor now intended. Strictly speaking, he asked no more than the renewal of leases presently in effect—but renewal indefinitely into the future. And the analogy of heritable constraints on soldiers' and decurions' status, and the harsh wording and penalties invoked in Constantine's law, point to a quite tyrannous object in mind.[95]

What set some bounds to Constantine's policy was more

than the limitations on his power of enforcement. It was custom. The rural scene, and relations there between master and man, great and small, had always been governed not by Rome, in the sense of a central authority, but by regional tradition. Central authority had to concede as much, in many legal opinions of both Principate and Dominate.[96] It could not decide the number of days' work that belonged to a year's rental, or a thousand other questions that concerned the inner workings of a farm. More detailed interference than Constantine attempted was not feasible. No doubt in many areas, too, the labor supply was adequately insured through still-functioning rules for the cultivation of deserted fields, through the immemorial due of villages to the great estate that adjoined or enfolded them, or through other arrangements about which we know nothing. Here the colonate would not be needed. But as a means of guaranteeing that no registered acre should lie idle for lack of a hand to guide the plow across it, the colonate proved its worth in its slow, steady spread from province to province and, later still, in institutions that derived from its presence and parentage in both East and West. It brought forth, from causes the most natural—liberties dissolved and commands more abruptly given in emergencies, state needs more pressing, and therefore more pressing needs for a tax yield secured by real property—the bound tenant, that creature of crisis. His bent figure joined the bound decurion, soldier, and shipowner. Together, their shadows projected onto the landscape of the fourth and later centuries the events of the third.

8

DEFENSE

In the eyes of Rome's governing classes, the peasant was—at a proper distance—a most admirable creature: so tough, sturdy, simple, strong, and sheltered from the debilitating concerns and temptations of a more refined life. The ideal army would have consisted solely of sons of the soil, the aristocracy supplying the officers.[1]

An ample pool of recruits was felt to be necessary. Augustus introduced famous legislation to discourage divorce and infidelity and to encourage large families with rewards of privileges and exemptions—families with full Roman citizenship, which of course changed meaning after 212. As late as Constantine, the father of five was excused from *munera personalia,* and in 363, the lucky father of thirteen could get out of the town senate entirely.[2] It was "in the public interest" that young women should have dowries so as to find husbands, and against the law to procure an abortion.[3] Orphan relief set up by the state in the 90s in Italy, in Antinoopolis in Egypt by Hadrian, and by numberless private benefactors throughout the empire to the end of the third century had the same purpose in mind, to increase the size of the citizen body; and when they all ceased their functions, Constantine stepped in with orders directing poor parents to apply for emergency food to the local authorities, rather than let their children starve.[4] It was acknowledged as a good citizen's duty to produce lots of babies,[5] partly in the vague sense that a great nation needed them, more plainly in the recognition that they grew up to be soldiers. Pliny saw Trajan's endowments as supplying "a resource in wars," and Macrinus' measures explain the normal age at which state aid ceased: "up to draft age." [6] Reception of barbarians within the borders was cause for courtly congratulation: the emperors had secured a reserve of future recruits.[7] All this evidence traces in an unbroken line the government's intent to nourish its armies, under Augustus as under Constantine.

What connection there may have been between this policy and real facts, we cannot say. On the face of it, there can hardly have been a shortage of citizens in each and every generation. A real case, however, can be made for an absolute decline in the empire's population in the period of crisis. Malnutrition and higher mortality rates would follow in the wake of economic decline; violent deaths would rise in times of barbarian raids, of more frequently attested brigandage, and more or less constant civil wars; and in about 257 a plague set in, to spread widely and devastatingly from the eastern provinces across to the western.[8] It is equally impossible to estimate or to deny the impact of these simultaneous phenomena in demographic terms.

In administrative terms they added up to a very large problem. How that was addressed, as far as it concerned the agricultural labor supply, we have seen in the preceding chapter. As far as it concerned the army, it called for better methods of recruitment. Along the northern tier of provinces in growing numbers and significance, from the later second century until the final collapse of the frontier, bit by bit, in the fourth and fifth century, whole tribes of barbarians were admitted as settlers, generally with the understanding that they would supply some quota of their young men to the empire's defense.[9] Their contribution, earning an occasional high command before the end of the third century and the throne itself for their descendants before the end of the fourth, has often been described. But voluntary and, very rarely, something closer to forced enrollment in the legions worked well enough to need no further aid before Diocletian.[10] First in 292/293, mention appears of a munus, a municipal job of producing recruits or an enlistment bonus with which they could be rounded up.[11] Since these methods were modified or supplemented in Constantine's later years and again in the 370s, the scattered fourth-century laws cannot be combined as if they all belonged to one unchanging system. All that is clear is the apportionment of the administrative work among liturgists, and of the expenses among landowners, these two avenues of exploitation especially favored by the Dominate.

And the third, heritability of function, was not neglected, either. Soldiers' sons had carried on from their fathers, spontaneously and more and more regularly as time went on. A law in effect by 140 tended to steer auxiliaries' sons toward enlistment.[12] At some date before 313, veterans' sons were made to assume as a munus either military service or the decurionate,[13] though likewise by Constantine's reign, decurions are seen fleeing their duties into the army. Government seems troubled not so much by shortage of volunteers as by lack of funds for the initial outfitting and enlistment bonus of new draftees, and by uncertain priorities: now the decurionate, now the army, is short of men, and laws tip toward one or the other according to the times. With barbarians available in those provinces where the greatest forces and greatest call for new men existed, and with the recruit tax, and finally, with compulsory enrollment in one's father's profession, the empire's needs were well taken care of.

A closely connected question, How big was the army? really cannot be answered. If we start with a figure generally accepted by scholars, a Severan total of legions and auxiliaries just over 300,000, we might in the half century thereafter expect it to grow larger, as civil and defensive wars raised their demands. Some such increase should be accepted, though on the basis of rather shaky evidence.[14] Further expansion was accomplished by Diocletian and possibly yet again under Constantine. For all that, the better-attested numbers engaged in fourth-century battles never approach those of Pompey or Augustus.[15]

The apparent contradiction between more men under

arms, but few actually fighting at a given juncture, is resolved through the separate development of a mobile army. The outlines of its history are well known. One of the early though not the very first chapters was written by Septimius Severus when he assembled in camps in Italy but regularly used on his campaigns a crack force amounting to over 30,000, in which cavalry, especially from Africa and Osrhoene, predominated.[16] By his reign, legionary detachments (*vexillationes*) to any seat of war had also come into more significant and regular use, necessarily involving "barbarians," that is, the less Romanized peoples within the frontier provinces. Traditional legionary cavalry was quite inadequate. Under Alexander Severus, the non-Roman term for these mounted units, *cuneus,* first appears in inscriptions; and he led them, in his last three years, on marches totaling well over 3,000 miles. That figure suggests the demands that might be made during the period of crisis. His successors in the next few years began to draw still more such units from true barbarians living beyond the borders.[17] At least in embryo, all the elements are in the field at the beginning of the crisis period that were to be developed by the 250s into a regular cavalry army: mobility (and actual need of it in long, hurried movements back and forth across the empire); cunei, with their implications of foreign origins and styles of combat; vexillations, with the eroding of legionary strength that they entailed. For defense against a pretender, the praetorian guard had proved far too small, far too pampered, fractious, and expensive; and for defense against external attacks, particularly simultaneous ones on more than a single front, the thinly strung-out stationary lines that had been posted along the edges of the empire in the first and second century could not be relied on, either.

An inner elite corps of *protectores,* serving also as a pool of officer candidates, and a largely mounted army with its own commander appear under Gallienus, justly advertised by coins showing Pegasus and bearing the legend "Speed." [18] The coins issued from Milan, to which —historic event—the emperor's mint and headquarters were moved in 258. The center of events had shifted now decisively away from Rome. And Milan was to put forth coins of more emphatic import, stamped "Bravery of the Cavalry," "Loyalty of the Cavalry," "Peace within the Cavalry," [19] trumpeting the power not only of Gallienus but of the mobile army's marshals Aureolus and Aurelian later. Their source of principal strength was further explained on their currency, too, in the legends *Genius Illyrici, Pannonia, Dacia.* These were their great recruiting grounds.[20] The answer to the empire's weakness in arms was to be sought in a body of troops ready for instant motion, drawn from and based in a strategic zone on which events were increasingly centered, or from which events could be most swiftly touched, in the north-central provinces.

Aurelian was to carry forward all these processes: the use of foreign contingents, the advancement and diffusion of Illyrian units, and reliance on an army of action; but of this last, some portion melted away into garrison duty in the reconquered East. How much Diocletian did to restore the loss, ten years later, is not clear. That he maintained and indeed added units to the army as a whole is certain. On the other hand, he also dissipated portions in postings along the frontiers and in towns. For his own or his fellow Tetrarchs' campaigns, the usual field armies of cunei, *promoti* from legions, and various other types of unit were assembled, and the select guard corps would, as had long been the practice, call themselves "the Emperor's Own" (*comitatus*). After campaigning ended, so did their special assignment. By Constantine, probably in preparation for the march of 312 into Italy and with an overwhelming prominence of Germans in its makeup, such an army was again organized. But this one was destined for a very long and honored role, enjoying a formally higher rank within the military. After 312, it was made larger, not returned to its origins. It received in due course under Constantine its own commanders; and enrollment in its infantry legions or *equites* meant promotion and better pay. By the end of his reign it constituted a good quarter of the armed forces and was itself perhaps one-third mounted—a very full elaboration of the idea that Gallienus had introduced in the 250s.[21]

The usefulness of such an instrument of war hardly needs emphasis. Lodged in a limited number of centers in the most strategically important sectors of the empire, and on main highways, it could move rapidly against any danger. Rewarded with special exemptions, relatively good salaries, prospects of further promotion, and proximity to the centers of government, it felt favored, and in consequence could be trusted to exert its strength for the throne. It provided an equally good answer to revolt and to in-

vasion. Moreover, it included the most up-to-date special-
ists: fully armored cavalry, horse and rider equally in-
vulnerable,[22] and experts in siege-craft, both first attested
under Constantine.[23] For these and other corps, the new
equipment was made in Diocletian's new government factories, in turn supplied with materials and labor by his
new and improved forms of requisition. It seems likely
that Diocletian and Constantine belong in the list of emperors, virtually all of the third and fourth centuries, who
personally took an intelligent, probing interest in the military arts.[24]

But there was also the second-class army of *alae* and
cohortes—second-class indeed, in the wake of disruption,
dislocation, and demoralization that marked the half
century after Alexander Severus. When invasions swept
across a frontier zone or pretenders split the loyalties of a
legion right down the center, or when Zenobia or Postumus
or Carausius organized their separate realms against the
Sacred Augusti, many a private in the ranks must have
simply decided to give up the trade of war and drift off
home. From the Low Countries in the late third century,
from a great expanse lying between Rhine and Danube in
the 230s and 260s, from Dacia in the 260s and 270s and
most of Moesia in the 270s, from most of Mauretania
Tingitana in the 280s, Rome herself, as a state, withdrew
for good and all.[25] A less clear retreat of troops also took
place from border installations to walled cities. Whatever
the promise of the mobile striking force, evidently in its
earlier form it could not save, nor in its developed form
could it later recover, much of the empire permanently

lost. For that task, only an army of occupation would do
—which, tested over the third century, proved quite inadequate.

Part of the cause no doubt lay in its too-close ties with
surrounding civilians. During the crisis, the unarmed population around a fort might seek in it a momentary protection, even permanent residence. They settled in on top
of the soldiers, who had themselves grown partly civilian-
ized since at least Severan times. Children's shoes, weaving
combs, and spinning whorls and jewelry and agricultural
tools turn up in a garrison post on the lower Danube, as
they may equally well at any point along the border north-
westward clear to Scotland.[26] In Phoenicia and Arabia,
strong points were built by soldiers with an extra compass
to accommodate fugitives; in hilly terrain, convenient
heights were crudely fortified by farmer folk to receive
them in emergency.[27] The mixing of functions bore a
character of haste and unprofessional makeshift.

A more obvious refuge from the flux of fighting that
went on throughout the crisis could be discovered in
walled cities. No doubt a hundred such sites could be instanced, though due note should also be taken of those
whose defenses long predated that period.[28] In Italy,
Gallienus got credit for Verona's walls, Aurelian's procurator for Pisaurum's.[29] Methods of all sorts were applied
to the fortifying of the empire. The central government
provided direction or force or money (or part of what was
needed) or supplied army architects or army labor. The
results can still be seen in many monuments today. An
architectural fragment from a temple is incorporated into

a tower; a section of the whole defensive circuit turns out to be nothing but the outer side of a municipal theater. Anomalies like this make visible the frantic joining of civilian and military in a single response to danger.

The rapprochement is still more complete, and from the government's point of view planned and intentional, when walled cities are assigned as homes to units pulled back from the outer edges of the empire. In eastern provinces, urban billeting was long familiar. No doubt it spread more widely in the course of the third century, until Diocletian and particularly Constantine decisively encouraged it. From Diocletian up to the 350s (to look no further), evidence of the new army emplacements comes from histories of the period, from papyri, archaeological traces, inscriptions, and, by retrojection, from the Notitia Dignitatum.[30] It clearly represented a major policy of redeployment, touching all areas though best seen in the northern provinces. It is hard to estimate how many troops it involved, since both Diocletian and Constantine were immensely active in true frontier fortification as well. But we know they had raised more troops and fragmented older units so as to give themselves flexibility in the disposition of soldiers both on the outer boundaries of the empire and in the interior centers.

There was an obvious saving and practicality in putting contingents right in among the city population. They could be helpful to each other in defense and supply; and the walls were there around them, ready to be manned by professionals. Ammianus, however, has some sour remarks to report about the effectiveness of the garrisons,[31] and

Vegetius later echoes similar views, though he may only have picked them up from second-century writers like Tacitus and Fronto: city life corrupts. There is a hint that he is right, in the third-century history of Dura-Europus. Papyrus fragments from that post contain complaints about soldiers straying off the base, and the need for *disciplina*.[32] The grand experiment, then, in resettling the nonmobile army proved less than a complete success.

Some similar mixing of soldier and civilian in the countryside was likewise familiar before the crisis and was likewise pressed forward to a greater extent in the period of recovery. Its ultimate result, seen only after the mid-fourth century, was *limitanei* stationed in frontier areas and closely tied in with the farming population. It represented the rural equivalent of that urban defense in depth just described. And it grew so naturally out of common sense and precedents they may almost be said to have forced it upon the government. Quite unprompted, except by the danger of the times, third-century landowners in the northern and western provinces were to be seen putting walls around all or part of their estates, in addition to the strong corner towers on their main residences.[33] In a number of these have been found inscribed material of nearby legions and *auxilia,* though it is hard to tell if veterans are owners or if serving soldiers have remade a villa into a military road station. The ambiguity of the archaeological record, rarely earlier than the 230s, only underlines how conditions of unrest forced the same response upon the state and the private citizen. In isolated regions, both equipped their centers with great, strong

granaries, high lookout turrets, and some sort of mini-
mally defensive compound to take in outlying peasant
families.

The key question remains, however: were those peasants
themselves soldiers? To this—except as concerns the owners of farm tools found in fortlets, where it is difficult to
escape the notion of a farming militia—the answer seems
to be no. On the other hand, the vacuum between gar-
risoned cities and camps right on the Rhine and Danube
had somehow to be filled. Here, men whose hands were
accustomed equally to the sickle and the sword were
planted of set policy: first, barbarian tribes with defense
contracts, so to speak, and second, veterans. As to some
member of the former group, "if you call him to arms,"
declares an orator to Constantius, "he comes running . . .
and congratulates himself on serving us in uniform"; to
the latter, veterans, Constantine offered a discharge bonus
of either free, vacant land, a hundred measures of seed,
and 25,000 *folles*—or, if they chose some career other than
farming, a flat 100 *folles*.[34] There can be no doubt of his
wishes for their future role!

Finally, in the North African frontier zone, blocky farm
buildings still stand today, fit for a siege; and inscriptions
and bas-reliefs in and around them make it certain that
their native occupants once served as guardians of their
own land and thereby of the more Romanized country behind them.[35] They were in some districts first settled, in
others first organized, in Severan times. In Tripolitania,
they appear to have been reinforced in the fourth century,
or to have rebuilt their huts into little stone dwellings.

Among them were scattered officers to provide military direction and oversight. In the series of fortified residences, from the smallest and simplest to the largest and strongest, no line can be drawn to mark the transition from that of a farmer to that of a company of soldiers; and no agricultural implements conveniently survive to show the activities that went on among any group of occupants; so we are left to guess whether the soldiers ever worked the land with their own hands. It is unlikely that they did, at least till long after the close of our period of study.[36]

While the mobile, elite force can be called an invention, the stationary army is rather a development, and not so much a single one as a variety of arrangements and experiments applied and improved at different times and places. Its essence is defense in depth. The brittle logic of the second-century frontier broke in the third century. What survived behind it was self-help: on deserted lands, immigrant barbarians; on imperial estates, circuit walls, ditches, and palisades, watchtowers and small forts put up with the labor of coloni; these same structures erected by private enterprise, or hilltop refuges; around cities (often protecting only a portion of them, for reasons of economy), walls that might incorporate any handy, big civic building. But the stiffening provided to these many expedients by emperors from 200 on, through the posting of small troops units in a thousand villages and towns, brought self-help under central control and joined soldier and civilian in a closer union for supply and protection. Makeshift had been successfully rationalized.

9

SUMMARY

There are many stretches of history in which the surface events and dominant personalities are known in too little detail to be strung into a satisfactory narrative. They do not satisfy curiosity, they hardly arouse interest, because the inadequacy of the evidence is too obvious. Such a stretch the historian meets with from the 230s up to the 280s. As to its difficulties: if he assumes, for illustration, that the *protectores* were invented by Gallienus, he may argue that they represent a revival of Alexander the Great's Companions, in the entourage of a Hellenizing emperor, or that they represent Germanic sympathies on the part of a Roman willing (so the sources tell us) to marry the daughter of a Marcomannic chieftain. Either line of interpretation may, in our ignorance, be spliced in to equally gossamer threads of intellectual or economic or art history, with equal fatuity, or at least futility.

And yet no more than a glance at the happenings in

Gallienus' reign, or in the generation earlier or later, is needed to convince the most unimaginative observer that exciting, tragic, striving, strange, variform, sudden, and profoundly significant things were going on in the Roman world; and the observer, the historian, "simply knows"—which is to say, he feels sure but he cannot prove—that these things have a pattern lying within the normal boundaries of causation by which he can and must make sense of them. If he is unable to find the necessary flow of evidence in the surface events and dominant personalities, then he must seek it in the level just below, in government. That had no name, no face; but it never died, was never assassinated or deposed, and in a thousand little bits and pieces has left to us the materials for its biography. Its every generation had a heritage in which it was raised; schooling in rule books or juristic treatises or bureaucratic form letters; a corporate mind to be trained, tests to be passed; responsible work to be entered on thereafter, and duties and loyalties to be lived up to. It was in touch with the great, like Gallienus; and together with him in his capacity not of general or statesman but of governor, it exercised initiative or influence or choice in various directions of obedience. All this, through government's recorded acts and words, can be traced in enough detail to make a story.

That story offers one of the more obvious lines of continuity in a half century noted for the opposite quality—noted or notorious for a tumbling succession of emperors thrust up or struck down in never-ending conflicts; noted too for continual invasions. It was a time of wars. With these, however, planning at the center had to reckon in its own way, not by leading the troops to victory but in seeing that there were enough of them and that they were on the spot, paid, fed, and equipped. Such concerns, focused on military needs, became again what they had been at intervals in the past, the chief business of Roman government. They entailed others subsidiary: the raising of taxes, recruitment, supply and transport of arms and provisions, the striking of coins, account keeping, oversight and promotion of civil and military personnel. More remotely connected with national defense was the matter of loyalty. For that, there must be ceremonies, announcements, didactic use of all public occasions. And the Roman plebs must be pampered lest its shouts shake the throne itself. The amenities of life in the capital, rather than being cut back, as might have been justified at any point in the period, were actually increased. Aurelian refined the dole; Diocletian built the gigantic baths named after him.

Even in peacetime it is illuminating to look at government through the eyes of those subject to it. What did it do? It took one's money away. That was the apparent object of its existence, that was certainly the bulk of its business. "What are kingdoms but great robberies?"[1] Rulers rose and fell, taxes went on forever. In wartime, they were bound to become more oppressive and various, more loosely defined to include demands for more kinds of contributions. Government as taxation may be said to have followed out its destiny to a logical conclusion over the period of our study, at the end of which anything at all required for the saving of the state was flatly declared "canonic," "regulation tribute."

But that was a development very natural, given the

character of the period that set in after the death of Alexander Severus. A dynasty ended and, for adventitious reasons, not from any deep fault in the empire that had not existed earlier at the death of Nero or Commodus, no successor line was able to establish itself with any tolerable speed. Maximinus pressed his needs too hard on the population, revolt and drawn-out instability invited invasion. A spiral of disasters set in, none of them new in kind but many new in degree. To government fell the task of coping with them in new ways. It is not too forced, from this point forward, to treat government as hero in a drama. The last act, a triumphant one, sees stability restored in a state transformed by Diocletian and Constantine. The period 235–337 has its own unity.

At the beginning, the problems to be solved seemed and were familiar. No one could be blamed for not predicting their consequences or for not understanding as one whole the layers of difficulty that were subsequently to unfold. Hard times there had been before. If some particular affliction roused the fear that "the inhibited world" approached the hour of its death, there was little the emperors' jurisconsults or chief accountants could do about it. They had troubles enough of their own. Rumors and visions they left to the masses, something a little more conventional remained for them. They had their national faith and their national history.

Neither served pragmatic analysis of the contemporary scene. By belief in the power of the gods, the intelligibility of history in terms that one could act on in this world, this dying world, was diminished. Priceless energies were

squandered on the persecution of the Christians, because
their atheism, and divine wrath, and the defeat of the imperial armies were seen as a chain of cause and effect; and
if the resources and population of a city were known to
have declined in recent years, "the divine fortune of Our
Majesties" could be trusted to set everything right without
need of merely human exertion.[2] As to knowledge of the
past, it was indeed treasured; but for most people it consisted of tales told only for their edifying conclusions or
for exemplification of virtues by Regulus, Scipio, Trajan.
Saws and saviors offered very little for citizens of the
third century to think about and apply to their own condition. Thus, in a mixture essentially moralizing made up
of religion and exempla, of faith and history, solutions to
problems like the flight of peasants off the land, or rising
prices on the marketplace, were sought through preaching. Granted, that was the tone expected by its audience.
Emperor worship, worship of Jove or Jupiter, a loving
veneration for stories of national heroes, a backward
glance to golden days in a mythic past, all could be ap-
pealed to with success, to stimulate actions and feelings
that might serve the state. Within the limits of existing
media, government did exert itself and did no doubt
know what language to use in its messages. They were
well suited to the times: brief ones in coin legends and inscriptions, "Restitutor," "Pannonia," not merely traditional
slogans; long ones, like the preface to the Edict on Prices,
transmitted in new ways, notably in more hortatory law
texts.

But the contrast surprises, between the well-chosen tone

and symbols of propaganda on the one hand and, on the other hand, its written style. Like Latin in Europe only a generation or two ago, a few tags of which proved one a gentleman, so the swollen language of the Roman upper classes in the later Empire served more than the purposes of communication. It proclaimed rank; and rank was an obsession among those of any place in society at all, of any ambitions or any claims. They made it visible to the passer-by in the street through items of costume too expensive for the common man or items preserved by custom or even by law to one higher station or another. Their way of talking and writing resembled the gorgeous colors of their dress; as they sewed ornamental patches on their gowns depicting Dionysos, for instance, so they embroidered their letters and speeches with exempla and *topoi.*[3]

The prestige, expense, and years of training involved in the acquisition of literary skills crowded out other skills that would have stood the governing aristocracy in better stead. They might better have learned how to evaluate the information spread before them by their subordinates: how many acres there were in the territory of a city, how many miles separating it from its nearest neighbor, how many its rural inhabitants, urban residents, slaves, Roman citizens, equestrians, and senators, and how much land each owned. They had this information before them, at least in the early third century; but it is clear in various ways that they could not make full use of it in military and economic planning, simply because the language of numbers had been so badly drilled into them. Their subordinates—imperial slaves, town accountants—knew more than they

did. After 250, statistical services probably deteriorated
all over the empire, manifestly so in Egypt. The average
citizen's literacy and numeracy continued their own steady
decline, too. The consequences were perhaps not ap-
preciated until Diocletian. In his reign were compiled
several route maps as hand accompaniment to much road
repair, and a recensusing of the provinces very like
Augustus' was undertaken, to bring up to date the picture of imperial resources. The job was done with enormous care. Characteristically, however, in an edifying
edict, it was explained to its subjects (like pigs being
weighed before slaughter) as a project of pure beneficence.

It is interesting to discover, in what ought to be a sketch
of the administration, that extraneous strands of aristo-
cratic culture weave their way through its workings:
pride in rank, a taste for letters but not for numbers,
nostalgic identification with remote models of leadership,
certain views about religion and historical causation, and
so forth. Government was Roman, like (and touched by)
everything else in Romans' lives. It is therefore idle to ask
of it some abstract or absolute good sense in response to
particular emergencies. Both its strengths and its weaknesses, and there were many of each, could not be
changed without some very powerful force.

No strength was more characteristic of Roman civilization than law. But here too, emergency exposed weakness.
Law gave its best to civil matters, to the concern over contracts, bequests, leases, legitimate issue, and the like that
most occupied the propertied classes. They spoke the same
language as their judges, they were not unwashed rascals,

they came to court of their own will. Over their litigation government presided with thought, care, and discipline. Over its own relations with its subjects, not theirs with each other, however, government left to its agents great freedom of action. No body of rules, at least no science, was developed.

In a period of protracted emergency, naturally it went hard with civil law. The series of distinguished jurisconsults, in which the later members Ulpian and Modestinus had begun to apply their minds to hitherto neglected problems and in particular to those that a provincial governor had daily to confront, now ended. The quantity of litigation for which emperors had leisure fell off abruptly. No so the pressure of their demands. We must suppose that just as many, or rather, many more, executive decisions were made without anyone bothering to think through, justify, or so much as record them. There was no time. Not till after the worst was over could any attempt be made to survey the consequences methodically. Under Diocletian, retrospective compendia of civil law received little attention, but the promulgations of the emperors received a great deal, in the form of at least two Codes. In the compiling of them there was no rich inheritance of technique to draw on, only a tradition of peremptory command. Thus law had to stand on its weakest leg, in the third century. The consequences became clear through many complaints of arbitrary and unjust decisions, and of confusing, contradictory ones as well.

Before judgment is passed on these faults, it should be recalled how stubborn local custom and jurisdiction were, and how long they had had to entrench themselves. No amount of force from above ever succeeded in ironing out all their differences; therefore, on many vital questions, no decree could ever apply universally. The lack of clarity that appears in so much third-century and still more fourth-century legislation must be blamed not only on inappropriate tricks of style, not only on the tradition of tyrannous powers accorded to magistrates and the consequent stunting of developments in criminal and administrative law. A kind of carelessness, too, was to blame, arising from the knowledge that, whatever was said, it would necessarily require interpretation in different ways by the governors of different provinces. So diverse were the parts of the empire, so hard to reach, and in Trajan's or even in Constantine's day so hit-or-miss the processes of enforcement, that the emperors must sometimes have felt that they were talking to themselves rather than commanding their subjects.

For ourselves, such a condition of things is very hard to imagine. We may fairly ask for some supporting parallel from within the area of Rome's departed rule but within the reach of our own more recent knowledge. No further back than the beginning of our century, an observer of Turkey writes:

> The system of administration is so disorganized and out of gear that no real amelioration is possible: the Grand Vizier may give as many orders as he pleases, but as any subordinate can neglect them or appeal direct to the Sultan, there is an end of the matter. The Sultan in the meantime can always say he instructed the Grand Vizier

and he is therefore not to blame. No minister has any intercourse with the Sultan, except those who for personal reasons blindly follow his policy of inaction and retrogression, the rest, among them being the Grand Vizier, being mere cyphers without a vestige of authority. [And around the Sultan, in a mixture of all kinds of ability, are persons] ignorant and servile, but grasping and corruptible in the extreme.[4]

How could such a realm be run? But without the thrust of European powers into Turkey, there was no obvious reason why it should not have continued its shambling, somnambulant course through history into an indefinite future. Analogy so clear and close to us makes it much easier to understand what the Roman empire was really like, when in its turn it was confronted with European powers: Alamanni, Franks, Vandals, Goths, Carpi, and so forth, to say nothing of African tribes to the south and a revived and vital Persia to the east.

The shock of their attack induced a number of overdue changes. At long last, perhaps not much to anyone's regret, senators were displaced from high commands by candidates chosen from a far larger, more deserving pool of candidates. Government in general grew steadily bigger. It narrowed units of responsibility. It separated the civil and military, from Gallienus on; within the military, it split the tactical from the stationary, during the same reign; with the civil area, it subdivided financial business, under Constantine; and the provinces were subdivided too, by Diocletian, to a much greater extent than by earlier measures of Septimius Severus or Domitian. The list of improvements could be drawn out further, but even in a shortened form it shows how Rome, once fairly into the midst of its troubles, could rise to meet them energetically. The two generations from Gallienus forward produced transformations not matched by any similar period since Augustus had established the Principate.

The area of broadest and most radical reform, however, may be called taxation, in a peculiar, new, and all-embracing sense. Other than food for the capital and army, whatever the state needed it had always bought with money (whether or not at a fair price). The means of purchase was the yield of tribute. In the period of our study, food continued to be a large item, indeed a growing one, as the dole was extended by Constantine to cities other than Rome. But the disastrous results of coin debasement turned government from its old ways of supplying such needs as equipment for new recruits or manpower to work the quarries. Forced and unremunerated labor was the cruder alternative. Evidence of its use is easier to find from 250 on to the early 300s than at any period either earlier or later and fits nicely in the interval between the first perplexities of inflation and later, more sophisticated solutions. The building of Rome's circuit walls by requisition of work from crafts associations in the 270s is perhaps the most spectacular illustration, though at least one very close parallel can be found a little earlier.[5]

Fortification involved no ongoing demand; nor was convict labor regular and predictable—not a fiscal item, we may say. In contrast, we may instance the order that deserted lands were to be obligatorily farmed through the direction of city senates—farmed and of course thereafter taxed. The order was Aurelian's, the effect was to draft individual peasants and whole villages into an enlarged agricultural labor force. Or we may instance the anabolic and the army clothing taxes in Egypt. The date of their introduction is uncertain, though Aurelian's reign seems likely. Reaching beyond tribute in cash or grain, they raised as a regular, fixed exaction the materials for clothing and the finished product. The latter, as the levy subsequently called *vestis,* is indicated by 301. The former, raw materials, certainly imply some further system either of factories or of an annual work quota demanded from weavers' associations. The first mention of factories being built occurs under Diocletian.

Pressing this and other evidence as far as it will allow brings us repeatedly to his reign as the one in which the devices were adopted officially that were to be more widely spread about and further developed, without fundamental change, into the sixth century and beyond. In the process of constructive reaction to the chaos of the third, and in the series of emperors who took significant steps that we know of, to resist or repair its damages—Gallienus, Aurelian, Probus, Diocletian, Constantine—it is Diocletian who stands out as chief. No matter that his colleague Tetrarchs or officials or existing practices may have suggested various administrative expedients to him. He could look and listen. His mind was open to the bold elaboration of a score of schemes: to remodel the empire's stone defenses according to the most up-to-date developments in fortification; to declare on coins and actually achieve

their regulated weight; to draw up in unprecedented detail the inventory of landed resources; to codify administrative law; and to subdivide rule so that the throne
now stood on four legs. The list of innovations could be
lengthened. He was a man of ideas, for historical stature
fully the equal of Augustus.

But how different, since the times demanded it! Where
Augustus proceeded gingerly in his rebuilding of a riven
nation and had fifty years to do it, Diocletian must act
abruptly, placing or displacing all the resources of his
realm like little chessmen: here a castle, there a knight;
here a pawn, there (in a mine, a quarry, a *fabrica*) a
bishop. All must serve his purposes. When Constantine
had added his own measures, then indeed all his subjects
not actually administering the system, and even some of
its ranks, were meant to move about and have their being
only as he directed them.

Here is what we find: a fully unfolded theory of
requisition—call it tax, if the word is not stretched out of
all meaning—based on a minute assessment of what every
citizen could contribute, whether in baking, weaving,
keeping municipal accounts, transporting grain, making
a helmet, finding a recruit to wear it, plowing a field, or
whatever. The very work of the assessment was itself subject to requisition of the most important and burdensome
variety, exacted from decurions. A person liable under one
title of this "tax" code was granted exemption from some
other. There was a rough-and-ready justice in the sharing
out of obligations, justice refined according to the stridency
of complaint. Enforcement was insured, or at least in-

tended, through two devices. Property which could neither hide nor flee was registered. It served as pledge for the performance of a service as well as determining the nature and extent of the service. The census therefore underlay munera and tribute alike. Second, it was groups of people mutually watchful, mutually liable, that the state commanded, so that it could better control even the propertyless. Villages or guilds or city senates or government bureaus were forced into corporate shape and responsibility; they and their descendants were immobilized in corps of tributaries; and if one group proved too small for its job, new members were moved into it along with their estates, if they had any, from another group that was thought at the moment to be unnecessarily large—all, pawns.

To appreciate the magnitude of invention achieved in this whole system, it must be compared with the empire's capacities for survival in, say, the year 200. Thereafter, anticipatory bits and pieces, experiments and expedients in this province but not in that one, began to appear. The period ca. 290–315 sufficed to assemble them, or at least constituted the crucial quarter century. Thereafter there were to be further adjustments and diffusion to previously resistant or neglected regions; but the outline had been fixed.

To appreciate its actual effects is another matter. On the one hand lie the weaknesses of earlier administration, as we have seen. Most of them persisted in the fourth century. There were technological limitations, cultural factors, the high cost of a big bureaucracy. We feel the con-

tradiction latent between all these, and the extraordinarily
ambitious plans elaborated by the Restorers and Renova-
tors of our story. The more credit to what was in fact
done! There were inconsistencies in application, too. Custom proved ineradicable, uniformity beyond reach. But
much more was attained than ever before. Finally, there
were aspects of the new system quite repulsive to the observer today. Who would want to live in the empire of
Constantine? But of course, who would want to die?
That seemed the alternative to measures introduced, after
all, to save Rome from ruin. Hence, both motivation and
(had emperors and their officials cared about our opinion)
justification for the sacrifice of so much that their world
in peace had once enjoyed.

At any rate, there were plenty of exits from the great
structure of force and demand that in theory gripped so
much of the lives of so many people.

One consequence of both the crisis and government's
response to it was the eroding of the middle ranks of
wealth. This, in an economy chiefly agrarian, meant the
small landholder. He by no means disappeared from the
scene, but in different regions with differing fortunes, he
was less and less often to be met with. In Egypt, taxation
was to blame. He surrendered his property to somebody
better able to make it pay, enrolling himself as tenant. So,
unexpectedly, *anachoresis* is not heard of so much under
the Dominate as before.[6] The failed farmer would not so
soon flee into hiding as take refuge with a more powerful
neighbor. A convenient illustration of what was going on
is the complaint of the village community of Philadelphia

in 332 that it was losing its people to a certain Eulogius, from the gates of whose estate village officials were driven by violence.[7] It sound as if Eulogius had walls around him and armed servants inside, a kind of private guard better attested in later times. In other provinces, the small-holder was more sharply touched by inflation, taxes, and the passage of war to and fro: in Palestine, for example, in the later third century, in Pannonia and Gaul from the same period on, and in Italy a few generations later.[8] The large landholder was the gainer.

The ability of the large landholder to rise above the times he owed in part to his self-sufficiency. Producing most of what he needed on his own property, and dealing with tenants and neighbors in terms of exchange in kind, he was to that extent not hurt by what was happening to currency and prices or dependent on links with the city. His private response to crisis has often been emphasized.[9] Moreover, he served as government to himself, judging, preaching to, imprisoning, or exploiting his dependents as if he constituted the Dominate in miniature.[10] It was difficult for the emperor's agents to treat a figure like this as if he were a pawn—though difficult too, it must be admitted, to form any clear picture of how pervasive his type had become, say, in the year 350.

His powers as adversary of the Dominate are revealed early, and grew steadily. Taxes he simply forgot to pay. Arrears piled up on the local account books till a general amnesty started another round of his triumphant intransigence.[11] Summoned to court, he ignored the summons [12] or bought acquittal for himself or his dependents

"who call in the patronage of the mighty," *potentiorum
patrocinium*.[13] Inside municipal administration, he saw to
it that those weaker, that is, poorer than himself had to
shoulder the heavier burdens,[14] despite a stream of laws
and protests from the emperors; and if he succeeded in
reaching the Roman senate [15] or, more easily, won appointment to the staff of some imperial official, then he
could truly count himself among

> potentes maxime terribiles, duces potentes et adminis-
> tratores fortes, magnorum virorum amici et pleni gratia,
> noti potentibus viri, magni potentes, maximarum civitatum
> vel imperatorum vel potentium virorum negotia tractantes,
> qui regum actus sua intercessione disponant, exactores
> regiarum annonarum vel pecuniarum fiscalium, provinciis
> civitatibus praepositi.[16]

The source here is the same that was quoted at the very
beginning of our study, a treatise on horoscopes in the
earlier part of the fourth century. It provides a sulfurous
list of terms to conjure with in its day: "dukes," "collectors of taxes," "governors of provinces and cities," and
again and again in its phrases as in the law codes and
papyri, mention of "the powerful."

This composite person it was through whom and on
whom the whole array of new government measures had
to work. And he was everywhere. He could be found in
the senate of Rome, in a vast rural mansion, among
decurions of Carthage, or in the emperor's own palaces.
In the upper reaches of his arrogance, he baffled the imperial will directly, though not until Ammianus takes up
the tale after 350 do we gain any great depth of detail.

In the lower but not less important reaches of administration, we catch an occasional glimpse of what was happening. Word would go out that everyone was to declare himself for taxation—in 309, for instance, in Egypt. "And there has been no one else living with me for a long time," obediently reports the taxpayer at the end of a list of his household.[17] But in the same year for the same census, one official writes to another, "You also surely are aware, brother, of the command issued by the divine and heavenly Fortune of our Lords and Monarchs, to surrender to the most sacred fiscus, for five *folles* each, all strangers who are found in the villages, . . . with sturdy good sense *instead of extortion*." [18] So government had calculated what bribe was usual to buy silence, perhaps four folles, and just topped it. There would be doubts still, and strangers able to pay six to be forgotten. Some of that sum might be the price of freedom to a colonus who wished to shake off the shackles of his condition. Coloni are in fact found changing jobs and residence quite freely.[19] Or part of that sum might work its way up to the *duces* whose bribery rates were fixed in a law of Constantine.[20] That would help to explain why the treatise on horoscopes specified their rank among the better fortunes that the stars might grant. And, outright venality aside, the correspondence of army officers, senators, high decurions, bishops, and rural magnates holding no office at all is at hand—most of it post-350 by accident of survival only—to show how a word in the right place by the right person could be confidently expected to produce results.

Let Constantine survey the structure of compulsion

that he and his predecessors over the past few decades had built in response to the crisis: a structure of grand dimensions and many parts, assembled out of trial and error, in circumstances of great urgency, constraining all citizens in the most painful obligations. It had served its purpose. An army sufficient to meet Rome's enemies external and internal; resources to pay for it and keep it loyal; the means of producing these resources, and then of exacting them from the producers; finally, reverence for the ruler, to make his commands over the whole effective—such were the chief elements in Rome's recovery. They took the form of institutions with a life of their own, developing further for centuries, quite beyond the logic that had given rise to them in the first place.

An earlier government ineffectual enough to bring to mind comparison with Turkey, as it was no more than a few generations ago, had been braced up, made stronger, extended in the range of its demands, and justified in crisis. But experiment had barely hardened into institutions before crisis passed and people began to look for a way out of the structure that had saved them. Evasion proved easy. Of what effect was the colonate, then, how workable were laws directing the supply of provisions to border militia through their commanders, if the *potentes* could find an escape for themselves and a back door, too, for the humble folk under their protection? Roman government and people had risen to the challenge of the third century. When it was overcome, however, they relapsed together into a Roman Sultanate.

NOTES

Works ancient and modern appear in standard abbreviations, possibly excepting three that may be less familiar:

FIRA[2] *Fontes iuris Romani anteiustiniani*[2]. . . , ed. S. Riccobono et al., 3 vols., 1941–1943

ESAR   *An Economic Survey of Ancient Rome,* ed. T. Frank, 6 vols., 1933–1940

RIC   *The Roman Imperial Coinage,* ed. H. Mattingly et al., vols. 1 (1923)–

CHAPTER 1

1 Complaints that evidence runs out: P. Lambrechts, *La composition du sénat romain de Septime Sévère à Dioclétien* (1937) 86, the cessation abrupt after 235; S. J. De Laet, *Portorium* (1949) 447 f.; G. Alföldy, *Noricum* (1974) 176, sharp decline in Samian production from 240s on; on data regarding city elites, A. Mocsy, *RE* Suppl. 9 s.v. Pannonia (1962) 697, or B. H. Warmington, *The North African Provinces* . . . (1954) 29.

2 Cypr., *Ep.* 62.1 (ca. 253, barbarians in southern Numidia); cf. other captives taken in Pontus, Greg. Thaumat., *Canon.*

215

Ep. 1 (ca. 258); and other examples of captives taken, G. W. Clarke, *Antichthon* 4 (1970) 79.

3   *CIL* 8.5290, Numidia in 294–305.

4   P. Oxy. 3065 (third cent.). P. J. Parsons ad loc. compares P. Ross.-Georg., III, 1 (third cent.), involving some fighting; and cf. no. 2, a related text. Both deal with events at Alexandria. The dating ca. 270, and other interpretations proposed by C. H. Roberts, *Aus Antike u. Orient. Festschrift W. Schubart* (1950) 112–114, seem to be weakly supported.

5   I draw on bk. 3 only of Firm. Matern., *Math.* For dating, see MacMullen, *Anc. Soc.* 2 (1971) 111.

6   Dio 72.15.6 (192); *ILS* 4424, *felicissimum saeculum* of Severus and his sons; cf. Herod. 3.13.4, on treasuries and temples "overflowing with riches" in the Severan age.

7   Tert., *De anima* 30.3 f., ca. 211.

8   G. Alföldy, *Historia* 22 (1973) 480, citing *Apol.* 32.1 and 39.2, and the anon. *De laude martyrii* 8, *clades saeculi, mala mundi, ruinae orbis.*

9   "At the outset of the third century, the problem of the world's end was a perfect obsession within the Christian community," G. Bardy, *Hippolyte, Commentaire sur Daniel* (1947) 10. Bardy (p. 11) dates the work to 202–204, as do others also, whereas S. Mazzarino, *Trattato di storia romana* 2 (1956) 313 f., prefers a date under Alexander Severus. On millenarianism of Severan times, see further Alföldy, *Greek, Rom., and Byz. Studies* 15 (1974) 93, and MacMullen, *Enemies of the Roman Order* (1966) 154.

10 Min. Fel., *Octav.* 9.1.

11 F. Cumont, *Rev. hist. relig.* 103 (1931) 60, citing *Cat. codd. astr.* 4.118; cf. Tert., *De anima* 30.3 f., *querellae apud omnes* that precede collapse.

12 Orig., *In Matt. Comment., Series* 36; Cypr., *Ad Demetr.* 10 f.; Lact., *Div. Inst.* 7.15.7 f.; Alföldy, *GRBS* 15 (1974), 492, on Cyprian; and S. Mazzarino, *The End of the Ancient World* (1966) 54.

13 Mazzarino, *End of the Ancient World* 21–40, collects and comments on many authors, and the subject has been often investigated. See e.g. Sen., *Contr.* 1.2.20. 2.5.7, and 10.4.18;

Ep. 51.10, 86.6, 89.19–23, 95.13–36 passim, and 114.9–13; Dio 71.36.4; and Aurel. Vict., *De Caes.* 28.3 f.

14 Tac., *Ann.* 6.12; SHA *Aurelian* 18.5, 19.1–6, 20.5–7, 21.4.

15 The basic text is Mt. 24.7 f., with derived pictures in Cypr., *De mort.* 2; *Ad Demetr.* 2 f., 5, 8 f., and 10; Orig., *In Matt. Comment., Series* 36; Victorinus, *Comment. in Apoc.*, ed. Haussleiter (*CSEL* 49), pp. 68–70; and Lact., *Div. Inst.* 7.15.10.

16 Orig., *In Matt. Comment., Series* 36 (*PG* 13.1649 = *GCS* 38.68). On the text, see J. Quasten, *Patrology* 2 (1953) 48, dating it to shortly after 244; A. Souter, *Journ. Theol. Stud.* 35 (1934) 63. E. R. Dodds, *Pagan and Christian in an Age of Anxiety* (1965) 12 n.1, Alföldy, *GRBS* 15 (1974) 95, and H. Chadwick, kindly giving me his views in a letter, all accept the Latin as at least a close paraphrase of the lost original.

17 In Euseb., *H.E.* 7.21.10, trans. Oulton, dated to 262 by H. T. Lawlor and J. E. L. Oulton, *Eusebius, Ecclesiastical History* (1928) 2.251, and S. I. Oost, *CP* 56 (1961) 10.

18 Cypr., *De mort.* 2; *Ad Demetr.* 3, 5, and 7; Victorinus, ed. Haussleiter 72; Arnob., *Adv. nat.* 1.3 and 9; Lact., *Div. Inst.* 7.16.5 f., derived from the East, Cumont 76; Ambrose, *Expositio evang. sec. Luc.* 1506 (*PL* 15.1807).

19 From Lk. 21.10 f.; see e.g. in Cappadocia, persecutors and earthquakes associated, in 235, reported by Firmilian to Cyprian, *Ep.* 75.10, cf. *frequentius terraemotus* in Orig., *In Matt. Comment., Series* 36; Cypr., *Ad Demetr.* 3; *De mort.* 2; Victorinus, ed. Haussleiter 72 and 77; Arnob., *Adv. nat.* 1.3. As an inevitable accompaniment of bad times and wars, quakes are attributed to the empire post-180, Herod. 1.1.4, and to the year 260, SHA *Gallienus* 5.2.

20 Min. Fel., *Octav.* 34.2; Cypr., *Ad Demetr.* 3 f.; Alföldy, *Historia* 22 (1973) 497.

21 On Rome as child, adult, and aged, see e.g. Tac., *Ann.* 2.88; Hippol., *In Dan.* 4.9.2; Lact., *Div. Inst.* 7.15.14–16; W. Hartke, *Römische Kinderkaiser* (1951) 396 f.; R. Häussler, *Hermes* 92 (1936) 314 f., 319 f.; and A. Demandt, *Zeitkritik u. Geschichtsbild im Werk Ammians* (1965) 119–138. On organic determinism, seeing the very *kosmos* as mortal, add Aelian,

Variae hist. 8.11, to passages discussed by Mazzarino, *End of the Ancient World* 21.

22 Oral circulation of Sibyllines: W. Bousset, *Der Antichrist* (1895) 39; J. Gagé, *Basileia* . . . (1968) 296. Cyprian's contacts with Firmilian and Demetrian recall the audience that Arnobius addresses, or Augustine's much later, in showing how panicky rumors could be elaborated in various communities and ultimately require reasoned opposition. See *Adv. nat.* 1.1, for Arnobius, and, for Augustine, J. Hubaux, *Rome et Véïes* . . . (1958) 18, with reff.

23 For illustration of a familiar phenomenon, see Arnob., *Adv. nat.* 1.1, on "popular sayings," and Orig., *C. Cels.* 8.73, on demons.

24 Cypr., *De habit. virg.* 23, dated to later 240s by K. Götz, *Gesch. der Cyprianischen Literatur* . . . (1891) 5 and 8, and V. Saxer, *Vie liturgique et quotidienne à Carthage* . . . (1969) viii; *De opere et eleemos.* 18, dated to 252/253 by Saxer and to around 250 by P. Hinchliff, *Cyprian and Carthage* (1947) 60—both passages contradicting *Ad. Demetr.* 3, *deficit in arvis agricola, in mari nauta, miles in castris.* Compare Origen in the later 240s detecting "the onset of ills," above, n. 16, but in the same period congratulating an audience that "life holds so many good things" for them: *Dial. with Heracleides* 27, dated in the edition of J. Scherer (1960) 21 to A.D. 244–249, and by J. E. L. Oulton and H. Chadwick, *Alexandrian Christianity* (1954) 454, to the same period.

25 Under Decius, note *Ep.* 58.7, 59.18; calling Decius *ipsum anguem, metatorem antichristi,* 22.1; and *occasum saeculi atque antichristi tempus adpropinquasse,* 58.1.

26 Alföldy, *Historia* 22 (1973) 485 and 489; idem, *GRBS* 15 (1974) 97. But it will be clear, in referring to these articles, that I do so in large part only to disagree. Their author sees a far more rational assessment of the times by contemporaries than I can discern.

27 Ibid. 96.

28 Commod., *Carm.,* lines 808 f., 823 f., 845 f., etc.

29 The Sibyllines apart, see Genesis and Exodus Rabbah of the

late third cent., in *The Midrash,* Eng. trans. (Sancino Press, 1939) 1.279 and 3.88. The parallels of Commodian with the Sibyllines, quite obvious, are noted by Bousset 51 and L. Herrmann, *Latomus* 20 (1961) 314.

30 "Et cela est formel," says Herrmann 315. For various other reasons, he dates Commodian to 416–421 (p. 321); E. Faure, *RIDA* 11 (1964) 163 n. 31, prefers ca. 360; J.-P. Brisson, *Autonomisme et christianisme dans l'Afrique romaine . . .* (1958) 390 f., accepts P. Courcelle's preference for ca. 440. Various other writers choose the mid-third-cent., i.e. Decius to Gallienus: Mazzarino, *Trattato* 343 and 350, Bousset 50, Gagé 295, and Alföldy, *GRBS* 15 (1974) 95. *Non liquet.*

31 On Dio, see ibid. 92 f., though the passage (71.36.4) actually refers to life under Commodus. Herodian's words, 1.1.3, are οὐκ ἀτερπῆ τὴν γνῶσιν.

32 Ps.-Aristides, *Or.* 35. Proposed dating ranges from the 160s to the 260s, L. J. Swift, *GRBS* 7 (1967) 267–269. Swift, p. 270, with Groag, prefers 247. Philip's reign meets the consensus, Mazzarino, *Trattato* 406, and J. Moreau, *Scripta minora* (1964) 35 and 40, both scholars citing other names. The emperor described came to power not by inheritance but not by force either (ed. Keil 5, fitting Philip but not Macrinus or Gallienus); there was no civil war, though his predecessors had risen to the throne in the midst of rebellions (6 f., ruling out emperors before Septimius Severus, perhaps before Gordian); he wreaked no vengeance on his enemies (8–10, not Severus); he had held an office evidently civil, not military, before accession (13, suitable to Philip or Decius); he was a private citizen previously (26, not a Severan or Gallienus); "so great a man," τηλικοῦτος (22, not "such a young man," as Swift 273 would translate), but nevertheless preferred skill and cunning against barbarians (32, an apology for a bought peace?); yet he annihilated the Celts (35, ruling out Macrinus) and set in order the whole East, formerly in a state of upheaval (36, ruling out Gallienus, Aurelian, Diocletian, Jovian). These and other elements have been often analyzed; I just indicate some reasons of my own for subscribing to the most commonly accepted dating.

33   The problems are compactly clear in *CAH* 12 (1939) 88, where W. Ensslin accepts a dating to Philip but also accepts invasions "perhaps as early as 244" (p. 92; for the Carpi, see also E. Stein, *RE* 10.758, with slightly different chronology). Yet, representative of many scholars, Alföldy, *GRBS* 15 (1974) 94, accepts the oration—in *some* parts—as a good sign of a sense of general catastrophe.

34   By (among others) G. Pugliese Carratelli, *La parola del passato* 2 (1947) 63 n. 1; for a first- or second-cent. date, see D. A. Russell, *"Longinus," On the Sublime* (1964) xxv and xxix f., and Dodds 4.

35   P. Fay. 20 (222) = A. S. Hunt and C. C. Edgar, *Select Papyri* 2 (1934) 94 f. For dating, see Moreau 37 f.; for interpretation (from which I depart) see C. Préaux, *Chron. d'Egypte* 16 (1941) 126 ("le sentiment du déclin était vif")–131, and Alföldy, *GRBS* 15 (1974) 92 and 105, "what we now call 'crisis' was then clearly said in other words: . . . τὸ κλῖνον (thus the emperor Severus Alexander)."

36   Ps.-Aristides, *Or.* 35, ed. Dindorf 103 f.; Tac. *Ann.* 1.78,; Suet., *Vesp.* 16.1, *inopia, de qua testificatus sit initio statim principatus professus,* etc.; R. Mouterde and C. Mondésert, *Syria* 34 (1957) 281, Domitian declares "it is right to bring help to the provinces exhausted, hardly able to cope with their basic needs," and refers to his father's awareness of the necessity to grant relief; and SHA *Had.* 6.5, "he remitted the crown gold to Italy, lessened it in the provinces, and yet made much of explaining in detail the Treasury's financial straits." Cf. Dio 71.3.3, Marcus Aurelius.

37   T. C. Skeat and E. P. Wegener, *JEA* 21 (1935) 231–233 and 246.

38   Lines 70; 75 f.; 93 f., "When Arsinoe's size of population was once large, but is now going from bad to worse"; and 100–102. But the cause of the situation may be Philip's tax innovations, P. J. Parsons, *JRS* 57 (1967) 138; and the plaintiff's lawyer asserts that "the divine Decius will relieve the situation, ἐπανορθώσεται." The exchange recalls the prytanis' opening address to a meeting of an Egyptian town senate in 248 (P. Erlangen 23 no. 18). There are no liturgists to take

care of the gymnasium, "in the (severe) times and straits of affairs that you know prevail."

39 A. J. Festugière, *La révelation d'Hermès Trismégiste* 1 (1944) 5 and 12 f.; Dodds 80 f., 92 f., and 100 (quoting Festugière, "misery and mysticism are related facts").

40 H.-C. Puech, *Eranos Jb.* 20 (1951) 93, speaking of gnosticism; cf. Plot., *Enn.* 2.9.5, the Gnostics "do not value our earth but rather that new one that they say will be theirs, and that will remove to here." As to body hatred and sick souls, see Dodds 30 f. and 135.

41 Gnostic dualism typified: E. C. Blackman, *Marcion and His Influence* (1948) 85; Puech 88; and Dodds 17 f.

42 A. Calderini, *I Severi* . . . (1949) 386 f. and 407, comparing late-second and third-cent. religions to war psychoses; F. Cumont, *Mysteries of Mithra* (1956) 148, seeing in the "troublous times" from Marcus Aurelius on "one of the secrets of [Mithraism's] powers"; and H. Jonas, *Gnosis u. spätantike Geist*[3] 1 (1964) 58, referring to views of R. Reitzenstein and others that the horrors of the time engendered feelings of guilt, helplessness, hatred of this world, etc., expressed in religious movements. Still more clearly the same reasoning in Puech 93, seeing Gnostic constructs (Sophia, for example) as projections of the worshiper's tortures, sadness, etc.; and Dodds 3, 36, and 100, emphasizing material decline and distresses of the third cent., with its invasions, civil wars, plagues, and inflation, all as factors in determining the Zeitgeist. As to precrisis manifestations, "Moral and intellectual insecurity can anticipate its material counterpart," ibid. 4—an interpretation unintelligible to me.

43 Dodds 28, Marcus Aurelius to Fronto, Loeb ed. 1, p. 216.

44 Dodds 18; F. Sagnard, *La Gnose Valentinienne* . . . (1947) 95, on dating.

45 R. Delbrueck, *Die Münzbildnisse von Maximinus bis Carinus* (1940) 215 and pl. 7 no. 16; B. M. Felletti Maj, *Iconografia romana imperiale da Severo Alessandro a M. Aurelio Carino* (1958), pl. xxiv and xxiii no. 75.

46 Examples (mostly from Rome): Felletti Maj, pl. ix no. 29; A. Merlin and L. Poinssot, *Monuments Piot* 40 (1944), pl. xi,

but not Gordian I, rather a priest, according to R. Bianchi
Bandinelli, *Rome: The Late Empire* . . . (1971) 221 f., 433,
and pl. 204; D. Mustilli, *Il Museo Mussolini* (1939) 154 and
pl. xci no. 340, unknown of 200–250 but identified as Valerian
by G. Zinserling, *Klio* 41 (1963) 205–213; J. Frel and
E. Buckley, *Greek and Roman Portraits from the J. Paul
Getty Museum* (1973) 30 and pl. 43 (unknown of 240–250);
G. Kaschnitz-Weinberg, *Die Antike* 2 (1926), pl. 4 (unknown of 225–250) and 6 ("Decius"); V. S. M. Scrinari,
Catalogo delle sculture romane (1972) 69 and pl. 205 (unknown of 225–250); H. von Heintze, *RM* 63 (1956) 59 f.
and pl. 23–28 (allegedly Decius); G. Ricci, *Bull. comm.* 67
(1939) 83 (unknown of 240–249); B. Schweitzer, *Neder-
lands Kunsthistorisch Jaarboek* 5 (1954) 187 and Abb. 8b
(unknown of third cent.); L. Budde, *Jb. deutsch. arch. Inst.*
54 (1939) 249 f. and pl. 4, "Gallienic" unknown, but perhaps
earlier; C. C. Vermeule, *Dumb. Oaks Papers* 15 (1961),
pl. 24 (unknown of the 250s); and an Egyptian painting
of the mid-third century, in C. Albizzati, *RM* 29 (1914)
243 fig. 1. For discussion, see the works just cited and
H. P. L'Orange, *Studien zur Gesch. des spätantiken Porträts*
(1933) 1–5; idem, *Proc. 2nd Congr. Class. Stud.* (*Acta
Congressus Madvigiani*) 3 (1957) 36; and G. M. A. Hanfmann, *Observations on Roman Portraiture* (1953) 13 f.

47 Hanfmann 15.

48 For example, portraits of "Decius" (Heintze, pl. 23–28),
perhaps rather "Gallus" (Felletti Maj 202 f., citing also
L'Orange and others); of Gordian I, perhaps rather of Gallus
(H. Jucker, *Das Bildnis im Blätterkelch* . . . [1961] 267,
but cf. F. Poulsen, *JRS* 6 [1916] 52); of Maximinus, perhaps
rather Tetrarchic (J. Meischner, *Arch. Anz.* 1967, 36 no. 1
and 37 no. 4, but cf. R. Calza, *Iconografia romana imperiale
da Carausio a Giuliano* [1972] 123, citing also Poulsen
et al.); impressionistic, or perhaps rather Gallienic (Mustilli,
pl. xci no. 340, 15, but cf. Giuliano 125); and impressionistic
portraits still turning up in the fourth cent., Schweitzer 174.

49 Zinserling 201–203, on propaganda in selective style revivals;
L'Orange, *Studien* 3, on Flavian models; Schweitzer 182–

187, 183 fig. 4a-b, 187 fig. 8a-b, on the nostalgic return visible in comparison of impressionistic portraits with Republican; the comparison accepted, for a different interpretation, by Zinserling 196; and G. M. Richter, *JRS* 45 (1955), pl. vi no. 21, for a third/second cent. B.C. parallel to impressionism or verism.

50 Some examples: Budde 253, attributing a sarcophagus o this period, though the head portrayed there, in mood if not in the rendering of the hair, better recalls impressionistic examples; G. Bovini, *Monumenti antichi* 39 (1943) 225–228; J. M. C. Toynbee, *Roman Portrait Busts* (1953), nos. 56 and 58; "Volusianus," in Meischner 224 no. 6; A. Alföldi, *Studien zur Gesch. des Weltkrise des 3. Jahr. n. Chr.* (1967) 271 and pl. 71, 2; Felletti Maj, pl. xlii and pp. 137 f., and 140 f., Gallienus; Vermeule, pl. 1 and 28, unknown of 265–285; on coins, see Delbrueck, *Münzbildnisse* 220 and pl. 15 no. 45.

51 Proponents of a "Gallienic renaissance" visible in portraiture include Alföldi, *Studien* 278 f.; L'Orange, *Studien* 10 f.; and G. Mathew, *JRS* 33 (1943) 65 f.; but the skepticism of Gagé 274 and 311 n.19 concerning the role of neoplatonism seems justified; so also E. Manni, *L'imperio di Gallieno* (1949) 65, pointing to parallels between the emperor's "philosopher" image and that of Postumus' coinage; and S. Ferri, *La critica d'arte* 1 (1935–1936) 166–169, testing with negative results the supposed connections with Plotinus which are defended mainly for the fourth to sixth cent. by A. Grabar, *Cah. arch.* 1 (1945) 27 f., and flatly rejected for Gallienic art, ibid., 30.

52 J. D. Breckenridge, *Likeness. A Conceptual History of Ancient Portraiture* (1968) 214; Mathew 65–67, "a straining effort to recapture the . . . world view . . . of the Hadrianic age"; and Alföldi in the *CAH* 12 (1939) 557, "the changed mood which seeks to replace the dramatic and the emotional by solemn calm."

53 On the Athens head, see Mathew 68; Alföldi, *Studien* 272; Jucker 108–110; Bovini 304; Delbrück, *Antike Porträts* lii. Compare the confusion over the Miletopolis (now Berlin) head of the second cent. (as I think most likely), or of the 230s, 250s, or 260s: Alföldi, *Studien* 274; Jucker 110;

D. M. Brinkerhoff, *A Collection of Sculpture . . .* (1970) 14 n.43. On the similarities between later Severan and Gallienic sculpture, see Schweitzer 186; Toynbee, no. 56, referring by a slip to Delbrück, *Antike Porträts,* pl. 50 (actually pl. 51, and there dated a half century earlier than by Toynbee). For development of the style in the 250s, see Meischner 226–228, and for its continuation after Gallienus, compare the head in L. S. B. MacCoull, *Berytus* 17 (1967–1968) 71, called Gallienic, with that shown by Felleti Maj, pl. lviii, 203 and p. 282 (here by a slip referring to his own pl. lviii, 202). The latter head Felletti Maj and others take as Carinus, but it is variously dated to the mid-third cent. or to Probus; so MacCoull's portrait bust may similarly be earlier or later than the 260s.

54 Examples: Aurelian on coins, in G. Mazzini, *Monete imperiali romane* 4 (1957), pl. 46 no. 61; Carinus on coins, Vermeule, pl. 45; Tetrarchic cubism becoming evident in coins of Aurelian, with even earlier anticipations, H. A. Cahn, *Festschrift Karl Schefold* (1967) 92; a few less familiar examples in stone, e.g. Brinkerhoff 20 and pl. 23, and V. Müller, *Antike Plastik. Walter Amelung zum 60. Geburtstag* (1928) 152 f.; and the more obvious imperial portraits, e.g. in the Arch of Constantine, Calza, pl. xlvi no. 136.

55 L'Orange, *Studien* 30 f.; cf. Calza 123 f. and pl. lxi no. 193; and Kaschnitz-Weinberg, pl. 7.

56 J. Burckhardt, *Age of Constantine the Great,* trans. M. Hadas (1949) 219–222 and 243. On Burckhardt's views on the Zeitgeist, see E. H. Gombrich, *In Search of Cultural History* (1969) 16 and chap. 3 passim; on Gombrich's own views with which I am in sympathy, see ibid. chaps. 6–7.

CHAPTER 2

1 Firm. Matern., *Math.* 1.7 passim. For third-cent. historians— Dexippus and others, little more than names—see F. Millar, *JRS* 59 (1969) 15.

2 Paneg. vet. 12(2).11.6, all six names in four lines; cf. 18.3, citing Hortensius, Lucullus, Caesar, "classical" exempla

drawn from handbooks; W. Sydow, *Zur kunstgesch. des spätrömischen Porträts* . . . (1969) 49, on the Republicanism of the panegyrists; Ammianus' preference for historical parallels from the Republic, as seen by A. Demandt, *Zeitkritik u. Geschichtsbild im Werke Ammians* (1965) 85 and 113 f., and P.-M. Camus, *Ammien Marcellin* (1967) 106; Symm., *Or.* 3.7 passim (a. 369) for a similar concentration on the Republic; Jerome, *Ep.* 123.16, searching for parallels to barbarian penetrations into the empire and skipping past the 200s back to the fourth and third cents. B.C., like Vegetius, *Re milit.* 1 praef., 4.9 and 26 (to 390 B.C.), 4.20, etc.—all texts showing an equal taste for the very remote past. But the phenomenon was long ago seen and forcefully described by J. Burckhardt, *The Age of Constantine the Great*, trans. M. Hadas (1949) 217.

3 Plin., *Ep.* 6.21; cf. many other passages praising something or someone as *antiquus*, 1.14, 1.22, 2.9, 3.1, 5.1, 5.14, etc.; Nerva with similar views, 7.33; Dio Chrys., *Or.* 31.75, ed. Loeb, with reff. to other authors ad loc.; Tac., *Dial.* 31.

4 Herod. 1.2.3; L. Robert, *CRAI* 1970, 14; Plot., *Enn.* 2.9.10; *ILS* 1218; *CIL* 6.1741 (360s, *ad exemplum veterum . . . omnibus virtutibus semper illustris*); SHA *Valerian* 5.7, *moribus singularis, exemplum antiquitatis;* Symm., *Rel.* 10.1, *antiquae probitatis adsertor.*

5 *SIG*³ 797, on Caligula; Sen., *De clement.* 2.1.4; Calp. Sicul., *Ecl.* 1.47–88; E. Bickel, *RhM* 97 (1954) 194 f., and R. Verdière, *Eos* 56 (1966) 174, all on Nero; above, chap. 1, n.6, on Severus; Macrob., *Sat.* 5.16.7, the Golden Age is a cliché in his day. In an admittedly more conventional phraseology, even Philip's reign is seen as "most blessed," *ILS* 5785 and *OGIS* 519.

6 H. P. L'Orange, *Studi Aquileiesi . . . Brusin* (1953) 192.

7 Aurel. Vict., *De Caes.* 37.3; SHA *Probus* 23 f.; Eutrop., *Brev.* 9.17.3.

8 Paneg. vet. 5(9).18.5; cf. 11(3).23; for Constantine's golden and blessed age, Optatianus Porphyrius 7.24 f., *ILS* 5359 and 5518.

9 B. Gatz, *Weltalter, goldene Zeit u. sinnverwandte Vorstel-*

lungen (1967) 141 n.128, "eine politische 'aurea aetas' hat es nie gegeben"; E. A. Thompson, *The Historical Work of Ammianus Marcellinus* (1947) 132, Ammianus ascribes the age of iron "solely to psychological causes"; and L. J. Swift, *AJP* 89 (1968) 146, "for Lactantius, that history [of man's salvation] is essentially one of moral regeneration."

10 Lact., *Div. Inst.* 5.5–8 passim, 7.24.7.

11 A cliché, e.g. in Dio Chrys., *Or.* 3.5; Herod. 2.11.2 and 3.6.9; Menander, *Peri epideiktikon* 3.372, ed. Spengel; Paneg. vet. 2(10).5.3; 7(6).3.3; 9(12).9.4; 11(3).4.6; 12(2).10; Them., *Or.* 2.47; 9.145; Liban., *Or.* 18.174 f.; Amm. 17.1.2.

12 *FIRA*² 1.290 (a. 56), warning everyone "to abstain from so foul a kind of business" as tearing down buildings, "especially in this *saeculum* in which new ones should be rising and all things should be adorned with whatever may make the *felicitas orbis terrarum* shine brighter"; *SIG*³ 837 (127), encouraging building repairs; *SIG*³ 850 (145), Pius praises Ephesus' building program; Lucian, *Phalaris* 3; and H. Kloft, *Liberalitas Principis* . . . (1970) 115 f., with many texts. For actual building done or stimulated by the government, see MacMullen, *HSCP* 64 (1959) 208 f. and 219 f.

13 Euseb., *H.E.* 9.7.10 (Maximin); Paneg. vet. 2(10).7.7; 2(10).12.7; 3(11).9.2; 3(11).15.2–4; 4(8).2.2; 4(8).7.2 f.; and 4(8).15.1.

14 Paneg. vet. 3(11).13.1; 3(11).18.5, *felicitatem istam . . . pietate meruistis;* 10(4).16.2, *id (scil.* divine favor) *vita mereatur; OGIS* 569, "the reward most deserved by your way of life"; Aurel. Vict., *De Caes.* 42.24, the lives of good emperors insure blessedness; and Euseb., *H.E.* 9.7.11.

15 Paneg. vet. 2(10).11.3; 3(11).3.6, *Hercules perpetuus est virtutis adsertor . . . , in omni certamine conatus adiuvat iustiores;* Menander, ed. Spengel 377, "the rains come in good season and the fruits of the sea and abundant harvests, through the monarch's justice."

16 On *abundantia* and cornucopiae ending famine under Marcus Aurelius, see J. Vogt. *Die alexandrinischen Münzen* 1 (1912) 140; on Gallienus-Demeter, A. Alföldi, *Zeitschr. f. Numis-*

matik 38 (1928) 188 f.; on the four seasons, on coins from Hadrian on, see examples under Gallus, F. Gnecchi, *I medaglioni romani* (1912) 102 and pl. iii no. 6, and J. M. C. Toynbee, *Roman Medallions* (1944) 90; on a mosaic (second quarter of the fourth cent.), G.-C. Picard, *Karthago* 3 (1951–1952) 176, 179, 188.

17   *FIRA*² 1.421 f. (Pergamum, A.D. 74); J. Keil and G. Maresch, *JOAI* 45 (1960) 86 f., Ephesus honors a third-cent. gymnasiarch for improving the character of the young; *CIL* 13.1393, at Limoges, a second-cent. "instructor in literature and teacher of *mores*"; and a great deal of theoretical discussion, e.g. in Art., *Onirocriticon,* ed. Pack 2.69.195; Julian, *Ep.* 36.422; and Amm. 27.6.9.

18   Tac., *Dial.* 31; Paneg. vet. 5(9).14.3 (a. 297) and esp. 5(9).8.2, *"litterae* are the foundation of all vertues," etc.

19   Dio 52.21.3 f.; SHA *Alex. Sev.* 27.4 and 41.1 f., *Aurelian* 45.4–46.6, *Tac.* 11.6; and a wealth of evidence on the importance attached to plain dress, plain diet, etc., at all periods of the Empire. Cf. the well-known essay of Alföldi, cit. above, n.16, 156–164, on the disgrace of luxury.

20   Paneg. vet. 10(4).38.4; cf. 11(3).4.3, *emendatio morum;* Julian, *Or.* 2.88C, the good ruler suppresses "depraved manners, luxury, and licentiousness"; and Aurel. Vict., *De Caes.* 9.5, Vespasian "by the example of his life put an end to many vices."

21   Sydow 45, coin portraits from Constantine on, their message echoed in archaizing passages in literature, ibid. 45 n.16. On *disciplina* restored, see e.g. Fronto, Loeb ed. 2, pp. 148 and 192, on Verus' and Avidius Cassius' love of old-fashioned discipline; *CIL* 13.11831 (Sept. Severus); Eutrop., *Brev.* 9.14, Aurelian *disciplinae . . . militaris et morum dissolutorum . . . corrector;* Paneg. vet. 7(6).2.2, on Claudius; Amm. 18.6.1, on Ursicinus; and carried to a civilian context in *FIRA*² 2.560 (a. 295), consanguineous marriages being *contra disciplinam legesque Romanorum;* in Galerius' edict of 311, restoring public *disciplina* (ἐπιστήμη in the Greek version), Lact., *De mort. persecut.* 34.1, and Euseb., *H.E.*

8.17.6; and by Constantine and Licinius in 315, legalizing
Christianity "so that *disciplina* might not be corrupted,"
W. H. C. Frend, *Journ. Theol. Stud.* 25 (1974) 347.

22 *CJ* 8.22(23).3 (a. 239); cf. 5.17.3.2 (290) and 4.44.8 (293),
dolus ex calliditate atque insidiis emptoris; CT 14.3.1 (319),
haec astutia et detestabilia commenta.

23 S. Lauffer, *Diokletians Preisedikt* (1971) 90–92; cf. the
similar Tetrarchic "preaching" tone in *FIRA*[2] 1.456 f. and
2.559, though here benign; P. Cair. Isidor. 1 (297); and
FIRA[2] 2.580 f., Diocletian declares, *pertinaciam pravae
mentis nequissimorum hominum punire ingens nobis
studium,* etc.

24 For rhetoric in law, see below, p. 90; for a propagandizing,
emotional, hortatory tone in earlier, eastern texts, see e.g.
OGIS 515 (209–211), the decree of Mylasa excoriating "the
malice and villainy of a few people who assail and rob the
community," etc.; MacMullen, *Traditio* 18 (1962) 370 f.;
and the remarks of E. Paulovics, *Arch. Hungarica* 20 (1936)
47 n.33; for *utilitas publica* on Diocletian's coins, see
G. Mazzini, *Monete imperiali romane* 4 (1957) 278, and in
texts, P. Oxy. 1409 (278), lines 10, 19, and 21, in the prefcct's
letter, and A. Steinwenter, *Festschr. Paul Koschaker* 1
(1939) 91–94.

25 E. Vernay, *Etudes . . . Paul Fréderic Girard* (1913) 2.264;
cf. 263 on the "change in style in the imperial constitutions
of Diocletian and Constantine," and W. den Boer,
Mnemosyne 21 (1968) 268, speaking of Aurelius Victor as
typical of ancient historians in general: "moral criteria are
the only ones by which he will judge men's historical value."
For the same judgment passed specifically on Ammianus,
with discussion of his moralizing views on causation, see
Demandt 99–105.

26 SHA *Aurelian* 43.1; on *rerum copia* there, see Ps.-Sall., *Ep.
ad Caes.* 2.7.3 f. (dated by R. Syme, *Mus. Helv.* 15 [1958] 54,
to the mid-or-later second cent.), the greatest benefit will
accrue to the human race "through diminishing or . . . re-
moving the appetite for wealth. . . . Love of money sets at
nought all other talents, ruins kingdoms," etc.—comparing

Lact., *Divi. Inst.* 5.6.1, *omnium malorum fons cupiditas*, and
Amm. 22.4.3 f.

27 *CT* 7.20.2 (320); CIL, vol. 6, 1, p. 551 (a. 213), the priests
chant *felicissime! te salvo salvi et securi sumus,* etc.; on coins
of Nicaea declaring, Κομμόδου βασιλεύοντος ὁ κόσμος εὐτυχεῖ,
see H. Mattingly, *Roman Coins from the Earliest Times . . .*
(1928) 203.

28 *RIC* 4, 3 (1949) 151 f., on Gallus. To the other two examples
of a common practice, add the invention of *divi* for Carinus,
F. Taeger, *Charisma . . .* 2 (1960) 434 (though his other
instances, 434 n.262, seem not to the point).

29 *FHG* 4.197; *FGH* 2A, p. 460 (Dexippus).

30 For the emperor as *homunculus,* see *RIC* 4, 3 p. 16 and pl.
1, 2 (Gordian), or Gnecchi 2, pl. 63 nos. 3 f. (Marcus
Aurelius)—both coins celebrating Jupiter Conservator. For
the upturned gaze, see Alföldi 177, and H. P. L'Orange,
Apotheosis in Ancient Portraiture (1947) 63 (Domitian), 75
(Sept. Severus), and 88 (Gallienus in 260), and for Gallienus
again, R. Delbrueck, *Die Münzbildnisse von Maximinus bis
Carinus* (1940) 220 and pl. 15 no. 45.

31 A. U. Stylow, *Libertas u. Liberalitas . . .* (1972) 73, on
third-cent. *congiaria* coin scenes; cf. 184 n.28, the disappearance of the recipients complete by the 230s; but the symbolic
disproportion of figures in works of third- and fourth-cent.
art, to show degrees of importance, is well known.

32 W. Ensslin, *Gottkaiser u. Kaiser von Gottes Gnaden*
(Sitzungsber. Bay. Akad. Wiss., 1943, 6) 39, from Alexander
Severus on.

33 Taeger, *Charisma* 447; idem, *Saeculum* 7 (1956) 182 f.;
Ensslin 42–44; D. Fishwick, *JRS* 59 (1969) 87, on the worship of living emperors being "exclusively" of the third cent.,
esp. from Alexander Severus on. The divinity of the later
third-cent. emperors has obscurities, with resultant differences
in interpretation. See e.g. S. Calderone, in *Le culte des
souverains* (Entretiens Hardt 19, 1973) 217 f.; and from the
early fourth cent., a reversion to the emperor as ruler only by
divine favor can be discerned. But it is a mistake to look for
uniformity in all the evidence.

34 For a good survey of titulature—σωτήρ, φιλάνθρωπος, *parens, providens,* etc.—with bibliography, see J. Gaudemet, in *La monocratie* (Receuils de la Soc. Jean Bodin 20, 1970) 445 f.; for the fuller list of third-cent. imperial attributes, see Ensslin 40 f. Some 600 inscriptions in *ILS* give a convenient indication of what is found in all periods and what is found rarely or not at all before 200; note as new nos. 510, 533, 577–579, 589, 617 f., 648, 674, 677, 687, 690–692, 699, 731, 737, 739, 741 f., 750 f., and 765.

35 For *restitutor,* see the index to *ILS;* index V s.v., in *RIC* 5, 1 (1927) and 2 (1933), covering 253–305, *restitutor generis humani, orbis,* etc., in a new prominence and variety of issues; Ensslin 41; and J. Vogt, *Orbis Romanus* . . . (1929) 19 f.

36 Lact., *De mort. persecut.* 19.2.

37 P. Oslo 113 (346), a church deacon (!) "swears by the divine and holy Fortune of our all-conquering Lords."

38 H. W. Pleket, *HThR* 58 (1965) 332–334; and L. Robert, *REA* 62 (1960) 321 f.

39 Robert 320 f.; P. Lemerle, *BCH* 59 (1935) 145 f.; *AE* 1935, 53; 1962, 232, on *dendrophori Augustales;* L. Foucher, *Hadrumetum* (1964) 284 n.1179, and 182–196 passim, on the emperor's favoring Dionysiac worship; Pleket 336–345 passim, on Dionysiac *sebastophantes* in Asia and Bithynia up into Severan times; *ILS* 6242 and 6245, with H. Dessau's note ad loc., on the joining of imperial and Hercules cults at Tibur; and L. Cracco Ruggini, *Settimane di Studio del Centro italiano di studi sull'alto Medioevo* 18 (1971) 79 f., on connections of cult with *collegia,* ceasing inexplicably in the early fourth cent.

40 Suet., *Vesp.* 7.2; Tac., *Hist.* 4.81; cf. P. Fouad 8, as possible confirmation, and Jos., *B.J.* 4.622; compare a similar power attributed to Hadrian, SHA *Had.* 25.1–3.

41 *CIL* 8.18892, *Fortunae Augustae sacrum:* . . . *monitu eius* . . . ; *IGR* 1.41, obeisance to the emperor's tribunal heals a blind man, "for there were powers living in the time of our emperor Antoninus."

42 A. D. Nock, *Conversion* (1933) 85; J. Beaujeu, *La religion*

romaine à l'apogée de l'empire 1 (1955) 343. Cf. commemoration of a lightning bolt divinely offered in battle, on aurei of A.D. 171/172, ibid. 345.

43 Beaujeu 344; Nock 130.

44 Suet., *Vesp.* 7.1, with Serapis; SHA *Marc. Aurel.* 27.1, with Ceres, *Aurelian* 25.5, with Elagabalus; and more generally, MacMullen, *GRBS* 9 (1968) 83.

45 Ibid. 82 f. and 88 n.25.

46 Philostorgius, *H.E.* 2.9, ed. Bidez; *CT* 13.5.7.

47 MacMullen, *Enemies of the Roman Order* (1966) 121, 127 f., 157 f.; idem, *Riv. storica italiana* 84 (1972) 13 f.

48 T. Wiegand, *Abh. Preuss. Akad. Wiss.* 1924, 22 f.

49 J. Palm, *Rom, Römertum u. Imperium in der gr. Literatur* . . . (1959) 54–75, Galen, Lucian, and Aelius Aristides.

50 *CIL* 8.2170 (235); *MAMA* 8.424 (250); P. Oxy. 41, lines 2 f. and 21 (late-third/early-fourth cent.).

51 F. Paschoud, *Roma aeterna* (1967) 18; A. N. Sherwin-White, *The Roman Citizenship* (1939) 284.

52 Palm 83, on the split between the empire and barbarians; 82 and A. Alföldi, *RM* 49 (1934) 7–18, on the split between empire and Persians; Sherwin-White 284, collecting from the Latin panegyrists passages on the split, Gallia vs. Germani; 285, on rejoicing at sufferings of the latter, which is also noticeable from 250 on in pictures on coins, J. Babelon, *Studies Presented to D. M. Robinson* 2 (1953) 281 f.

53 B. Levick, *Roman Colonies in Southern Asia Minor* (1967) 142, with other types showing Roma on coinage struggling against a rising tide of Hellenic culture in the city.

54 *RIC* 5, 2 (1933) 496 and 512, RENOVAT ROM.

55 A. D. Nock, *HThR* 23 (1930) 258, *Roma aeterna* in coins and inscribed dedications of Alexander Severus through to the Tetrarchy. On *dea Roma* in Probus' and Tetrarchic coinage, see S. Mazzarino, *Trattato di storia romana* 2 (1956) 409.

56 Nock, *HThR* 23 (1930) 251 and 256; L. Homo, *Essai sur le règne de l'empereur Aurélien* (1904) 129 f., n.1, Aurelian's gold statue to the Genius, and the same on coins of Diocletian and later; M. Alföldi, *Constantinische Goldprägung*

(1963) 13, on Maximian's, Maxentius', and Constantine's coins with the wolf.

57   Toynbee, *Roman Medallions* 184; L. Barkoczi, *Acta antiqua* 13 (1965) 255; and much familiar discussion of the significance of "Jovius" as the regime's special characteristic.

58   For stressing of *leges, pietas,* and *disciplina Romana(e)*, in opposition to Christian, see *MAMA* 8.424, in W. H. C. Frend, *Martyrdom and Persecution in the Early Church* (1965) 406; *Passio Cypr.* 1.1 and 3 f. (a. 258); *FIRA²* 2.558, comparing p. 580, "Roman" opposed to Manichaean, and *CJ* 8.46(47).6 (a. 288), "Roman" opposed to "Greek"; Lact., *De mort. persecut.* 34.1; and Frend 478–480. It is not the old capital that the first Tetrarchs advertised—note how little favor it enjoyed among them, J. Polzer, *AJA* 77 (1973) 148 —but rather larger ideas of history and empire.

59   P. R. Franke, *Kleinasien zur Römerzeit* (1968) 18, on Asia Minor local coinage; MacMullen, *Enemies* 228–239.

60   *RIC* 4, 3 (1949) 113 and 117; Frend, *Martyrdom* 405.

61   *CIL* 3.12333 (with restorations), addressed to Aurelian, and embodying attributes specially characteristic of his reign, I. Calabi Limentani, *Epigrafia latina* (1968) 170; cf. also MacMullen, *Soldier and Civilian* . . . (1963) 177, on the phenomenon of "re-" in other contexts.

62   *ILS* 625 and 659; P. Merlat, *Répertoire des inscriptions* . . . *de Jupiter Dolichenus* (1951) 72 f., on "the first known pagan council" of the priests of all Pannonia, under Diocletian, praying *I. O. M. Dolicheno, pro salute dominorum Augustorum;* and a Sun-temple built in Italy on Diocletian's orders, in Nock, *Conversion* 292.

63   Lact., *De mort. persecut.* 11.7 (a. 302); A. Rehm, *Philologus* 93 (1938) 74 f., 78, 82 f.

64   Euseb., *H.E.* 9.7.7; R. Andreotti, *Studi di antichità classica offerti a E. Ciaceri* (1940) 2, on Postumus' advertisement of Hercules of Deuso and Magusa, a cult popular on the Rhine and Rhone; *CAH* 12.199, on celebration of Aziz on Gallus' coins, though the evidence is very slight; and the goddess Vagdavercustis native to the region around Cologne, upholding VIRTUS MILITUM on Laelianus' coins, in E. Krüger, *Germania* 22 (1938) 103 f.

65 Tac., *Hist.* 5.5; on the whole subject, MacMullen, *Journ. Theol. Stud.* 26 (1975) 405 f.

66 Lact., *Div. Inst.* 5.19.3; cf. 2.6.

67 Amm. 21.10.8, on Julian's propaganda letter to the senate, accusing Constantine of having departed from *mos antiquitus receptus.* Cf. Licinius in Euseb., *Vita Const.* 2.5; *FIRA*² 2.580 (a. 297), repudiating Manichaeans *qui novellas et inauditas sectas veterioribus religionibus obponunt;* and *CIL* 3.12132 (a. 311), rejecting Christians' "mischievous new cult," καὶ[νῇ θρησκείᾳ]

68 SHA *Elagabalus* 35.4, *aurei parens saeculi,* whatever value the source may have; cf. Sherwin-White, *Roman Citizenship* 283, on the genuineness of gratitude for a crisis surmounted, citing the Panegyrists; and the *Acta S. Tarachi* 9, in T. Ruinart, *Acta primorum martyrorum sincera*² (1713) 443 f., speaking of "the emperors who have secured profound peace for the world."

69 Lact., *De mort. persecut.* 34.1; Euseb., *H.E.* 9.2.1 f.; 9.4.1; 9.5.1 f.; 9.7.3; *IRG* 4.214; and many other texts are well known. For devices of propaganda, see good collections of evidence in J. Maurice, *Numismatique constantinienne* 3 (1912) ix f., xii f. (interesting city coin issues), and xvi–xx; and Frend, *Martyrdom* 497 f. and 506 f.

70 E. H. Swift, *AJA* 27 (1923) 299 f., on the "amazing speed" of portrait distribution attested in the 230s. I do not believe a clear case can be made for portrait busts conveying *in artistic form* the "image" (e.g. militaristic or classicizing) of the regime, though emperors of course did show themselves in significant costumes and poses. See the discussion above, chap. 1, and note the careless reuse of coin dies of some other emperor in the late third and fourth cents.: Maurice 72; P. Castelfranco, *La critica d'arte* 2 (1937) 12 f.; and C. C. Vermeule, *Num. Circular* 65 (1957) 2 and 6 n.34.

71 Herod. 3.9.12; 4.8.1; 7.2.8; Greg. Naz., *Contra Julianum* 80 (*PG* 35.695): ceremonial advertisement "so that veneration for themselves might be fuller and more perfect."

72 Amm. 16.12.70, Constantius' distortions slipped into the imperial records; and, on acceleration of the regnal years, A. Chastagnol, *Rev. num.* 9 (1967) 56 f. and 65; L. Laffran-

chi, *Riv. italiana di numismatica* 43 (1941) 131 f.; and *CAH* 12.91.

73 *RIC* 4, 3 (1949) 111, Decius' appeal to Illyrian armies and provinces; 5, 2 (1933) 278 and 593, Aurelian's and Julianus' appeals to Pannonia; 383 f., second- and third-cent. appeals to specific legions; P. L. Strack, *Untersuchungen zur röm. Reichsprägung* . . . 2 (1933) 142 n.314, Moesia Superior on coins of 239–254/255; P. Bastien, *Le monnayage en bronze de Postume* (1967) 61, regional compliments by Postumus; F. Redo, "Numismatical Sources of the Illyr Soldier Emperors' Religious Policy" (Diss. Arch.[2] 2, 1973) 65, 107, and 146–149, adaptation of differing mint issues to differing regions. As M. Hendy points out, *JRS* 62 (1972) 81 n.55, the most lively variations in type and legend are seen in precious metals—not, as he argues, because coin production had nothing to do with propaganda but because gold and silver went in salaries and donatives to the most vital support groups, military and civilian.

CHAPTER 3

1 Victorinus, *Opera,* ed. J. Haussleiter (*CSEL* 49, 1916) 42, *fiducia litterarum.* He writes in Diocletian's time.

2 Firm. Matern., *Math.* 3.5.37; 3.7.13; 3.9.10; 3.10.14—on *scribae* and *notarii* as well as more gifted *oratores;* Greg. Nyss., *Contra Eunomium* 1 (*PG* 45.264), a rise from farmer's son, by knowledge of shorthand and letters; and *Prosopog. of the Later Rom. Emp.* s.v. Datianus, citing Liban., *Or.* 42.24 f. and 62.10.

3 R. Münsterberg, *Num. Zeitschr.* 8 (1915) 123, rhetors in Greek cities of 230s and 240s; J. Keil and G. Maresch, *JOAI* 45 (1960) 93 f., an Ephesian *grammaticus* who is senator of the city and liturgy-exempt (early third cent.?).

4 *Memoirs of the Life of the Right Hon. Sir John Eardley-Wilmot* (1802) 45 (ed. 2, 1811, 98). He was Lord Chief Justice in England, dying in 1792. Cf. a Roman rhetor made governor of Spain under Constantine, Auson., *Prof.* 18.12 f.; Paneg. vet. 5(9).6.2, a *magister memoriae* while still a pro-

fessor of rhetoric; 5(9).5.4 (a. 298) and 7(6).23.1 (a. 310), palatine offices for persons trained in rhetoric; *RE* s.v. Annius Tiberianus, col. 766 f., a poet and scholar who rose through many high offices to praetorian praef. of the Gallic provinces in 336; a traveling panegyrist doubling as procurator and *curator civitatium* in the 330s, G. E. Browne, *Proc. XIV Int. Congr. of Papyrologists* . . . (1975) 30; *RE* s.v. Hermogenes (16), col. 864, serving as high legal adviser to Constantine during a lifetime of devotion to philosophy, poetry, and history (Himer., *Or.* 14.18); *ILS* 2941, orator and great-grandson of a famous orator, prefect of Rome in 305/306; and, for the periods before and after the crisis, floods of case histories for which there is no room here.

5 *CJ* 10.53.3 (Philip) strips poets of *immunitas*, but in P. Oxy. 2338 (late third cent.), with C. H. Roberts' commentary on p. 112, Upper Egyptian cities continued to exempt them from taxes right through the third century. Philosophers are (still?—cf. *Dig.* 50.5.8.4) exempt from *munera personalia* along with other learned professions (50.4.18.30, Arcadius Charisius; cf. *CT* 13.3.7 [a. 369]). *Grammatici* and *oratores* received exemption through public test of their skills in cities having endowed educational systems, *CJ* 10.53.2 (Gordian) and 4 (Diocletian, on *liberalium studiorum professores*); and Constantine confirmed exemptions to *grammatici* and *professores litterarum* (*CT* 13.3.1 [a. 321 or 324]) and extended to the latters' family exemption also (13.3.3 [333]), *quo facilius liberalibus studiis et memoratis artibus multos instituant*. See A. D. Nock, *Sallustius, Concerning the Gods and the Universe* (1926) xxiii f., and MacMullen, *Riv. storica italiana* 84 (1972) 11 f., on the decline in philosophy; on exemptions to teachers and students, W. Langhammer, *Die rechtliche u. soziale Stellung der Magistratus municipales* (1973) 68-72; V. Nutton, *JRS* 61 (1971) 52-56; C. Kunderewicz, *Rev. hist. de droit* 50 (1972) 575 f.; and esp. H. I. Marrou, *History of Education in Antiquity* (1956) 302-308.

6 F. Millar, *A Study of Cassius Dio* (1964) 118 and passim; R. Syme, *Ammianus and the Historia Augusta* (1968) 89.

7 See above, chap. 2, n.25, on moralizing in history; or, for

Aurelius Victor, the kind of self-satisfied idiocy displayed in the opposition between *boni* and *indocti, De Caes.* 9.12, or the shallow interpretation of 3.15. On Ammianus also, note E. A. Thompson, *The Historical Work of Ammianus Marcellinus* (1947) 4, "in his history he tends rather too often to judge a man's worth by the extent of his reading."

8 Aul. Gel. 19.13.1, a most revealing scene; but Fronto's letters to Marcus Aurelius are filled with the same sort of discussion, and Aul. Gel. 13.10.1–3 shows it again, in the writings of a great legist.

9 See e.g. R. Grosse, *Röm. Militärgesch.* (1920) 27 and n.6, on "the incredible inadequacy of the military terminology of the period"; and below, pp. 147 f. on administrative documents.

10 Lact., *Div. Inst.* 1.16.11 f.—not dissimilar in mode and level of reasoning from Tac., *Agr.* 21.2, on urbanization in Britain.

11 Rufus Ephesius, ed. C. Daremberg and C. E. Ruelle (1879) 225 f. and 292 (Flavian?); cf. Lebas-Wadd. 1336, a "doctor and *syngrapheus* and poet of works on medicine and philosophy," "the Homer of medical poetry."

12 Hygin. Grom., *De limit. const.,* ed. F. Blume et al. (1848) 185 f. (Verg., *Georg.* 1.233 f.) and 191 (Luc., *De bello civ.* 3.247).

13 Julian, *Ep.* 7.403D; *RE* s.v. Alypius 1 (Seeck, 1893) 1709. Similarly, Strabo 1.1.2 f. feels obliged to tie his work to literature, Homer and (1.1.16) "the poets," and describes the line of the Nile (17.1.2) in a bookish though intelligible way, as a backward *nu*. See Vegetius' battle formations described as letters of the alphabet, shaped like a *V* or an *I* or an *A* (*Re milit.* 3.19 f.).

14 Paneg. vet. 5(9).20.3 (a. 298).

15 The Peutinger Table presents the world as it was post-250, E. Manni, *L'impero di Gallieno* (1949) 30; H. Gross, *Zur Entstehungs-Gesch. der Tabula Peutingeriana* (1913) 107, giving a Diocletianic date; and A. and M. Levi, *Itineraria Picta* (1967) 172, suggesting a late Severan model, with redoing later (ca. 400?).

16 D. van Berchem, *L'armée de Dioclétien . . .* (1952) 52 and 69, date 280–290.

17 Gross 3; date, pre-Peutinger, pp. 13 and 31.

18 J. Rougé, ed., *Expositio totius mundi et gentium* (1966) 19 (dating probably to 359) and 76 f., on wild mislocation of places in Gaul, Asia Minor, Pannonia, Noricum, and Italy; 62, on the secs. 1–21, with Herodotean fantasies deriving from some lost mid-fourth-cent. work; compare Plut., *Thes.* 1.1, "geographers cram into the margin the parts of the world with which they have no real acquaintance, adding notes like 'Beyond here, waterless sands and wild beasts,' or 'Unexplored marshes and Scythian frost' and 'Sea of Ice.'"

19 Van Berchem 52 and 69.

20 R. K. Sherk, in *Aufstieg u. Niedergang der röm. Welt* 2, 1 (1974) 560, shows strategies being based on maps, citing Veget., *Re milit.* 3.6 (*itineraria,* some also *picta*), and Ambrose, *In Ps.* 118, *Sermo* 5.2 (*PL* 15.1251, *itineraria* supplied by the emperor with attendant *annonae* and *mansiones*).

21 Amm. 15.10.11; Herod. 1.6.6.

22 Plin., *N.H.* 3.17; D. Detlefsen, *Die Geographie Afrikas bei Plinius u. Mela* . . . (1908) 8–10.

23 E.g. Plin., *N.H.* 4.93 and 12.19, giving distances between points in the Euxine area and Ethiopia; Plut., *Moral.* 419E; R. Rebuffat, *Antiquités afr.* 1 (1967) 43 n.2; and Sherk 540–542.

24 Rebuffat 31–57 passim, esp. 43.

25 *Curatores* native to the city or region, in *RE* s.v. Curatores (E. Kornemann, 1900) 1808; *CIL* 3.2026, and 5.4368 and 5126; and see further J. H. D'Arms, in *The Ancient Historian* . . . (*Essays in Honour of C. E. Stevens*) (1975) 157.

26 H.-G. Pflaum, *Les procurateurs équestres* . . . (1950) 28, with other types of office mentioned there also.

27 M. G. Jarrett, *Historia* 12 (1963) 223; H.-G. Pflaum, *Les carrières procuratoriennes équestres* . . . 1 (1960) 4, 300, 656, and 716 (exceptions, 716, 720, and 901); and L. Harmand, *Le patronat sur les collectivités publiques* . . . (1957) 300–302, on native quaestors and legates.

28 A good example of regional expertise in R. Etienne, *Bordeaux antique* (1962) 124 f.; others in Pflaum, *Carrières* 35, 167, 172, 354, 436 f., and 646; G. Alföldy, *Noricum*

(1974) 160 f.; R. Sherk, *Historia* 20 (1971) 111–119, esp. 119; and S. J. De Laet, *Portorium* (1949) 218.

29 M. Mazza, *Lotte sociali e restaurazione autoritaria nel 3. secolo d. C.* (1970) 464–466; Pflaum, *Procurateurs,* passim.

30 Dio 71(72).31.1; cf. SHA *Pescen. Niger* 7.5 and *CT* 8.15.3 (365); but for an exception, see Harmand 301.

31 *Dig.* 1.22.3 (Macer). But still, the governor's councillors would insert themselves into the local aristocracy; see e.g. R. Etienne, *Latomus* 14 (1955) 258 f.

32 I find little evidence on the personnel of governors' councils: P. Fouad 21 (63); *CIL* 10.7852 (69); BGU 288 (Ant. Pius); J. F. Gilliam, *Zeitschr. für Papyrologie u. Epigraphik* 13 (1974) 149, on the career of a law-trained *assessor* at the Egyptian prefect's court in the fourth(?) cent.; and Greg. Thaumat., *Paneg. ad Orig.* 5.65, showing the drafting of a person to a governor's staff "for he was a lawyer." On the three earlier citations, see E. Balogh and H.-G. Pflaum, *Rev. hist. de droit* 30 (1952) 119–124.

33 For a good review of a well-known subject, see W. Eck, in *Aufstieg u. Niedergang der röm. Welt* 2, 1 (1974) 177 f. and 191–210.

34 Pflaum, *Procurateurs* 96.

35 See the discussion and references in B. Malcus, *Opuscula Romana* 7 (1969) 214–235; H. Petersen, *JRS* 45 (1955) 47–56; Pflaum, *Carrières* 923 f.; J. Fitz, *Acta antiqua* 11 (1963) 304–306; and Manni 55–58. For foreshadowings of Gallienus' changes, diminishing the senatorial role in military commands in the several preceding decades, see W. Eck, *Chiron* 4 (1974) 538.

36 Above, chap. 2, n.72; A. A. Boyce, *AJA* 53 (1949) 338–343, Sept. Severus' irregularly acknowledged acclamations, even on official inscriptions.

37 E. J. Bickerman, *Chronology of the Ancient World* (1967) 10, 48 f., and 89, on third- and fourth-cent. confusions.

38 Suet., *Galba* 5.2; A. Nagl, *Die Rechentafel der Alten* (1914) 37; H. Wussing, *Mathematik in der Antike*² (1965) 192; B. E. Thomasson, *Opuscula Romana* 3 (1961) 174–176; L. C. West and A. C. Johnson, *Currency in Roman and Byzantine*

Egypt (1944) 54–61; but the errors in papyri occur more in rounding off (trivial) or in multiplication and division. Cf. Marrou 402 n.10, finding it "very instructive that an educated man, an official, . . . did not know his 'times tables.'" Prof. O. M. Pearl very kindly informs me by letter that, from his experience, papyri maintain quite good overall standards of accuracy.

39   Prof. Pearl writes, "the cumbersome fractional series [used in land survey, assessment rolls, etc.] must have required the scribe to use tables, like our multiplication tables, to arrive at speedy summations. Even so, there is considerable evidence of difficulties experienced. . . . See, e.g., P. Bouriant 42." For the treatise on fractions, see Volusius Maecianus 1 and 64 (ed. P. E. Huschke, *Iurisprudentiae anteiustinianae quae supersunt*[6], 1908, pp. 409 and 416). For the writer's distinguished career in government under Ant. Pius, see W. Kunkel, *Introduction to Roman Legal and Constitutional History,* trans. J. M. Kelly (1966) 101 f.

40   Marrou 281 f. and 431 f. n.13, citing the express lack of support offered by government to the teaching of mathematics, in *CJ* 10.53.4 (Ant. Pius) and Diocletian's *Edict* 7.66 f.; cf. *FIRA*[2] 2.496, no exemptions to *geometrai;* and F. Jürss, *Klio* 43–45 (1965) 382 f., on the status of the exact sciences in the later empire.

41   On education of imperial slaves, see S. L. Mohler, *TAPA* 71 (1940) 263, 270–272, and 277; V. Väänänen et al., *Graffiti del Palatino* (1966), 56, 74, 115, and passim, on Palatine *paedagogium;* Pflaum, *Carrières* 592, on imperial slaves following procurators about from post to post. And note in Philo, *In Flaccum* 2 f., surprise and praise that the governor of Egypt in the 30s was not "a pupil" of his scribes, who had been "guides" and "teachers" to his predecessors.

42   No *immunitas* for *calculatores, CJ* 10.53.4 (Ant. Pius) or teachers of ABCs, *Dig.* 50.4.11.4 (Caracalla).

43   On the *grammateus,* see H. C. Youtie, *Chron. d'Egypte* 40 (1966) 132–135; idem, *GRBS* 12 (1971) 243; on decurions, *CJ* 10.31(32).6 (293); and on age-knowledge, A. Mocsy, *Acta antiqua* 14 (1966) 393–413 passim.

44   The ratio of public:private documents in 20-year periods varies between 2:1 and 3:1 up to A.D. 220; thereafter, between 3:2 or 3:3, up to A.D. 380. I draw on a random sampling of documents datable to a given 100-year period, more often to a 20-year period—in the former sense, 1,700 documents; in the chronologically more exact sense, 3,300 (of which the public ones total 2,550). Despite the size of the sampling, 5,000 documents in all, the data are subject to too many questions to support more than the broadest statements. But they receive some independent confirmation from P. Bureth, *Rev. hist. de droit* 46 (1968) 248–262, showing a precisely similar pattern of document frequency in the office of the Egyptian prefect: a sharp decline after 225 in edicts etc. from, and appeals etc. to, his office.

45   Tac., *Ann.* 1.11; *SEG* 9.8, cf. Dio 59.22.3; Plin., *N.H.* 3.18.28; Detlefsen 8 and 63 f. Ptolemy under Hadrian "was using a Latin list of *populi*," A. H. M. Jones, *Cities of the Eastern Roman Provinces*[2] (1971) 395—so they were evidently continued in circulation. *Dig.* 50.15.8 shows similar lists (of cities with *ius Italicum*) also available to Paulus.

46   T. Mommsen, *Röm. Staatsrecht*[3] 2 (1878) 1091 f.; *DE* s.v. Census (Kalopothakes, 1900) 176; *RE* s.v. Census (W. Kubitschek, 1899) 1919; F. Heichelheim, *ESAR* 4 (1938) 160 f.; C. Jullian, *ESAR* 3 (1937) 493 n.106; O. Hirschfeld, *Kaiserliche Verwaltungsbeamten*[2] (1905) 56–66; and Pflaum, *Carrières* 17 f.

47   On Hadrian, see Kalopothakes 176 and *ESAR* 3.493 n.106. Egypt remained on a 14-year cycle of the "house-to-house census" up to 258, the κατ' οἰκίαν ἀπογραφή. See A. C. Johnson, *ESAR* 2 (1936) 248, and S. L. Wallace, *Taxation in Egypt* (1938) 98, who adds that ἐπίκρισις ceased also after 250. J. Lallemand, *L'administration civile de l'Egypte* . . . (1964) 171 f., dates the cessation of the equivalent censusing of landed property to the 250s—so every kind of registration is unattested from Gallienus to Diocletian.

48   On Severus, see Hirschfeld 66, and Pflaum, *Carrières* 600 f.

49   *FIRA*[2] 2.504 (Caracalla), listing *qui studiorum causa Romae sunt*. On the alleged innovation of Marcus Aurelius for

births registration in Italy and the provinces (SHA *Marc. Aurel.* 9.7 f.; cf. Apul., *Apol.* 89.2 f.), see Hirschfeld 62; Mocsy 411–414; A. Steinwenter, *Beiträge zum öffentlichen Urkundenwesen der Römer* (1915) 6 and 41; F. Schulz, *JRS* 32 (1942) 80–82. Roman citizens had actually been registered from Augustus on, and Marcus only acted to bring illegitimate births under the same system. For pre-Marcus registrations, see e.g. Mocsy 412 f.; F. W. Kelsey, *TAPA* 54 (1923) 189; *FIRA*² 3.6 f. and 11. To illustrate the careful registration system for citizenship under Marcus, see W. Seston and M. Euzennat, *CRAI* 1961, 318, the *tabula Banasitana*. On veterans' registrations, see e.g. *CIL,* vol. 3, pp. 844 f., or A. Degrassi, *Scritti vari di antichità* 1 (1962) 32 f; on centenarians, *FGH* IIB, p. 1185, culled under Hadrian from census lists of Italy and five provinces and cities, cf. F. Jacoby's commentary ad loc., p. 847 f. On the total population of Egypt, see Johnson, *ESAR* 2.245, on Jos., *B.J.* 2.16.4, culling figures from tax lists.

50 *CIL,* vol. 3, p. 945, rental of a house in Alburnum in A.D. 59, terms covering *pro ea domu tributa; Dig.* 50.15.45 (Ulpian), on registration of one's slaves to include their *aetates et officia et artificia;* special *inquisitiones* of equestrian census, J. and L. Robert, *REG* 81 (1968) 524, citing Greek and Latin inscriptions, cf. Strabo 5.1.6 on Padua's *equites* "by recent census"; details of registration including qualification of "HS CCCLXXV" or the like, P. Mich., III, 166 f., with editors' note ad loc., p. 154, Schulz 59, and Pflaum, *Carrières* 232; App., *Syr.* 50, Syrian and Cilician taxes being 1 percent of one's τίμημα, and Tac., *Ann.* 13.51, on *naves* included in *census negotiatorum,* both texts suggesting assessments on movable property.

51 For the *forma,* see e.g. *CIL* 8.22787, cited by T. R. S. Broughton, *Romanization of Africa Proconsularis* (1929) 90 f.; A. Caillemer and R. Chevallier, *Annales. Econ. Soc. Civ.* 9 (1954) 446, on the maps lying behind centuriation. Centuriation is a subject developing so rapidly, one can hardly offer an up-to-date survey; but for a brief sketch by a master, see R. Chevallier, *Etudes rurales* 3 (1961) 65 f., and

a more recent and fuller treatment in O. A. W. Dilke, *Roman Land Surveyors* (1971) 134–138.

52 *RE* s.v. Archive (Dziatzko, 1896) 562; T. Mommsen, in F. Blume et al., *Die Schriften der röm. Feldmesser* 2 (1852) 152 f.; Hirschfeld 63 n.2 and 64; and Dilke 41–43 and 113 f. The dominant character of much surveying, to determine legal status, appears for instance in the mention of rights, *aes(timatio) iuris,* considered in a late Antonine survey, V. Velkov, *Acta antiqua* 13 (1965) 211 and 214.

53 The inscribed stone map of Arausio provides a fine illustration of the format; see Dilke 159–177. I take "Cadaster A" to be for purposes of fixing *ius* of big sections of territory, Cadasters B and C to fix individual plot boundaries and owners. Here and with certain texts of the Gromatici, the problem is to distinguish different phases of survey, so as not to require the burying of Rome in bronze maps.

54 *Dig.* 50.15.4.1.

55 For the system of deed deposit, see Cic., 2 *In Verr.* 3.120; *ILS* 5918a (114, Caere); Dio Chrys., *Or.* 31.51; C. J. Cadoux, *Ancient Smyrna* (1938) 197; R. H. Pierce, *Symb. Oslo.* 43 (1968) 70; and A. Büchler, *Economic Conditions of Judaea* . . . (1912) 41. P. Oxy. 2665 (305/306) and Mitteis, *Chrestomathie* no. 196 (309), show municipal property registries capable of certifying what if any property a local citizen owned.

56 The best evidence appears naturally in papyri of Roman Egypt. See Johnson, *ESAR* 2.248 f.; P. Mertens, *Les services de l'état civil et le controle de la population à Oxyrhynchus* . . . (1958) 10 f., 61 f.; and P. Oxy. 2928 f. But see *IGBulg.* 1:317 = *IGR* 1.769, where tradesmen in the third cent. are invited to register to do business in Mesembria (as in Ephesus, see next note), and the legal texts in Mocsy 415–417 and Schulz 81–87.

57 E. Weiss, *JOAI* 18 (1915), Beibl. col. 286 f. (second cent.), registration of the newborn, of residents, of victors in games, and of tradesmen of various trades (in monopolized occupations?); cf. G. Daux, *BCH* 50 (1926) 226 f., registration of property transfers for a fee, in second-cent. Thasos.

58 N. Lewis, *JEA* 23 (1937) 68 f. and 73, the Egyptian evidence providing motive and explanation for tax amnesties empirewide. See below, chap. 6, n.13.

59 Mommsen, in Blume 153 f.

60 Mertens 132, "the year 235 was exceptionally rich in controls"; Lewis 67 n.2, on depopulation of the Fayum from ca. 250 on, well documented by the sufferers themselves; Euseb., *H.E.* 7.21.9, cf. above, chap. 1, n.17, showing a citizen's familiarity with depopulation, as also in ca. 250, T. C. Skeat and E. P. Wegener, *JEA* 21 (1935) 231; and Pflaum, *Carrières* 931, local *a censibus* acting in concert with the persecutors.

61 Above, n.47.

62 See A. H. M. Jones, *Greek City* (1940) 239. The municipal τιμητής and πολειτογράφος correspond to the *duovir* (*quinquennalis*) in western cities. Municipal *tabularii* as liturgists first appear in the second half of the third cent., *RE* s.v. Tabularius (Sachers, 1932) 1971, citing *Dig.* 50.4.18.10 (Arcadius Charisius); cf. 50.4.1.2 (Hermogenianus), first mention of local census taking as a munus, and 50.4.18.6.

63 Cic., *Pro Archia* 8, and Suet., *Vesp.* 8.5, remind us of the perishability of records of any sort.

64 A. Déléage, *La capitation du Bas-Empire* (1945) 152, dates the earlier boundary inscriptions to 293 (cf. further, 156 f. and below, chap. 6, nn.59 and 64); but E. Erxleben, *Klio* 51 (1969) 312 f., would date the survey's beginning to 297. A. Piganiol, *Rev. hist.* 176 (1935) 4, cites PSI 285 to show a new survey begun in Egypt in 293 or 294 but interrupted by Achilleus' revolt. One censor's activities thereafter can be traced over a space of five years, P. Corn. 19, and discussion by W. L. Westermann and C. J. Kraemer ad loc., p. 104 (A.D. 297–302); Lallemand 172 n.4 draws attention to the renewal of property registration in 298, but population registration only from 309 onward. For a unique and purely local antecedent of Diocletian's survey, see J. Devreker, *Latomus* 30 (1971) 352 f. and 355. For Galerius' census, see Lact., *De mort. persecut.* 23 (306 or 307). On censusing in Gaul, see below, chap. 6 n.36.

65 See below, chap. 6, on *capiti censi* and connected terms; Euseb., *H.E.* 9.8.5 (ca. 312), on "the formerly populous registers of the rural population wiped almost clean" by plague and famine; *CT* 11.16.4 (328), directing governors in drawing up tax lists to "annex in ink the names of the tax-payers" with their own hand, against fraud; and in Egypt, personal registration from 309, Lallemand 172 n.4, and Déléage 44 and 107.

66 The introduction of the five-year census cycle, not to be con-fused with the fifteen-year indiction cycle from 313/314 on, dates to 297 but started actual operation a year later—accord-ing to N. Lewis, *JEA* 29 (1943) 73 n.2. But the evidence is confusing and may carry back to 287, according to Lallemand 170 f.

67 J. H. Oliver, trans., *Trans. Am. Philos. Soc.* 43, 4 (1953) 899, Aelius Aristides' *To Rome* 32 f., slightly condensed.

68 *RIC* 2 (1926) 229, mules serving the *cursus publicus* (a. 97); P. Oxy. 900 (322), donkeys from the ὀξὺς δρόμος! Cf. A. C. Johnson and L. C. West, *Byzantine Egypt: Economic Studies* (1949) 139; A. H. M. Jones, *Later Roman Empire* (1964) 403, and esp. X. Loriot, *Mél. . . . offerts à W. Seston* (1974) 306, on delays of many weeks or months in transmission of news around the empire. See further below, chap. 4, nn.40–42; but for exceptional speed in local communications, see T. C. Skeat, *Papyri from Panopolis* (1964) xx f.

69 Eunap., frg. 74, *FHG* 4.46, condensed; for the cutting of communications across the empire in time of civil wars or pretenders, see Euseb., *H.E.* 8.15.1.

CHAPTER 4

1 For *utilitas publica* conceived of in generally confined set-tings, see *Dig.* 16.3.1.4; 48.2.13; 50.12.13.1; *CJ* 6.54.2 (Marc. Aurel.); cf. *CJ* 12.62.3 (Diocl.); 1.40.4 (335); 12.57.2 (358); 10.32.31 (371); and A. Steinwenter, *Festschr. Paul Koschaker* 1 (1939) 93, noting "under the Dominate a sharp upswing of appeals to *utilitas publica*" from Diocletian on.

2 Of guards, the most important are the *protectores* appearing

first under Gallienus (*CIL* 11.1836): *RE* Suppl. 11 s.v.
(H.-J. Diesner, 1968) 1115 f. On curtains, see slave *velarii* in
e.g. *CIL* 6.9086; SHA *Alex. Sev.* 4.3; Athan., *Apol. ad Const.*
3; D. Levi, *Antioch Mosaic Pavements* (1947) 125; G.-C.
Picard, *Karthago* 3 (1951–1952) 177 f.; T. Klauser, *Jb. f.
Antike u. Christentum* 3 (1960) 140–142; and A. Alföldi,
RM 49 (1934) 34–37, the emperors behind curtains from
Tetrarchic times on. On the practice underlying the terms
secretum and *secretarium,* the latter first attested in Lactantius, see Euseb., *H.E.* 7.30.9; SHA *Marc. Aurel.* 10.6;
and MacMullen, *Traditio* 18 (1962) 376 n.45. On the ritual
underlying *silentiaria,* ibid., Alföldi 38, and A. Piganiol,
L'empire chrétien[2] (1972) 345, the council sessions as *silentia*
from Constantine on. On the ritual underlying the *consis-
torium,* see Alföldi 44 f., and *CT* 11.39.5 (362). On a spirit
of worship infecting even legal recourse to the throne, note
from mid-third century onward the description of the emperor *cognoscens sacras appellationes, CAH* 12.361 f.

3   Maecenas' words in Dio 52.15.2 confirm *Dig.* 1.3.31.

4   GAUDETE ROMANI on gold coins of 303, fruits of the
aurum coronarium, RIC 6 (1967) 312; τῶν γνησίων σιτικῶν,
P. Ryl. 341 (Sept. Sev.); payment of τὰς εὐσεβεῖς εἰσφορὰς,
P. Ryl. 617 (317), P. Cairo Preis. 4 (320), etc.; cf. ἱερᾶς
ἀννώνης (e.g. in Wilcken, *Ostr.* 1019, third cent.) . . . τῶν
γεννεότατων στρατιωτῶν (e.g. in PSI 683, a. 199, or P. Oxy.
1415, late third cent.).

5   R. M. Honig, *Humanitas u. Rhetorik* . . . (1960) passim,
e.g. p. 13, on the emperor's announcements aiming at "eine
Ethisierung des Herrscherbegriffs" and "Ethisierung des
Rechts" (p. 20); moralizing in later third- and fourth-century
imperial decrees, e.g. even in Diocletian's Price Edict, above
p. 29, and the similar text of 301 in K. T. Erim et al., *JRS*
61 (1971) 173, *iustum esse aequissimumque,* etc. See further
above, chap. 2, and below, n. 47.

6   M. Hadas, *Philol. Quarterly* 8 (1929) 385, quoting Pesik.
77a.

7   P. Romanelli, *Storia delle province romane dell'Africa* (1959)
462 (a. 243) and 475 (a. 256/257).

8   E. Kornemann, *Klio* 7 (1907) 278 and 288.

9   M. Crawford and J. M. Reynolds, *JRS* 65 (1975) 163 f.; P. Cair. Isidor. 1 (297).

10   W. Kunkel, *ZSS* 85 (1968) 323-325, after Hadrian, emperors heard evidence in public but deliberated in camera; for local judges, see the same practice under Diocletian, *Acta S. Eupli* 1 (G. Krüger, *Ausgewählte Märtyrerakten* [1965] 100 f.), under Constantine, *CT* 1.16.6 f. (331), and in the 380s, *Const. Apost.* 2.52.

11   *CT* 12.1.4 (317), only *primates* at curial meetings shall sit; MacMullen 435 f., on high manners in high society generally.

12   SHA *Alex. Sev.* 16.1; cf. 44.5, he subsidizes solicitors to take cases in the provinces.

13   H. I. Marrou, *History of Education in Antiquity* (1956) 290 f.; *Expositio tot. mundi* 25, Beirut, *inde viri docti in omnem orbem terrarum adsident iudicibus et scientes leges custodiunt provincias;* and Eunap., *Vit. soph.* 490, for the successful career of its graduates.

14   Gregorianus ca. 291, Hermogenianus ca. 295, according to H. F. Jolowicz, *Historical Introduction to the Study of Roman Law*[2] (1952) 482, and M. Amelotti, *Per l'interpretazione della legislazione privatistica di Diocleziano* (1960) 9; but B. Schmiedel, *Consuetudo im klass. u. nachklass. röm. Recht* (1966) 52, would set the Hermogenian Code in Diocletian's last years. For the *Coll. leg. Mos.*, cf. D. Sperber, *Israel Law Rev.* 8 (1973) 273 n.35. The *Sent. Pauli* according to the most recent opinion seems to originate under Diocletian, too: L. Wenger, *Die Quellen des röm. Rechts* (1953) 518 n.307, and E. Levy, *Mediaevalia et humanistica* 1 (1943) 22-24, with apparent confirmation in G. G. Archi, *Pauli Sententiarum Fragmentum Leidense* (1956) 57, the text dated to ca. 300 paleographically. A slightly later compilation is the Ulpian epitome (Schmiedel 53, Constantinian?).

15   Above, chap. 3, n.4; n.13, above.

16   Jolowicz 483 n.2, on the domination of Diocletian over legislation within the Tetrarchy; Liban., *Or.* 1.214, cf. 234, protesting at the flight to Latin; H. Cadell, *Münchener Beiträge zur Papyrusforschung* 66 (1974) 61 f., on Diocletian's Latinizing of the Greek East.

17 Jos., *A.J.* 19.291; *ILS* 6089. For general discussions, see F. von Schwind, *Zur Frage der Publikation im röm. Recht* (1940) passim, esp. 86 f. and 150 f.; U. Wilcken, *Hermes* 55 (1920) 35 f.; and L. Wenger, *Mél. H. Grégoire* (1951) 472–478.

18 S. Lauffer, *Diokletians Preisedikt* (1971) 14–39, publication in 43 locations; *FIRA*² 1.493–495 of a. 198–212 cites a *lex Hadriana, FIRA*² 1.491 f.; W. Williams, *JRS* 64 (1974) 90, Severan rescripts quoted in papyri by litigants decades later; a similar practice in P. Mich., IX, 529 (232–236), and other texts cited ad loc., p. 25, by E. M. Husselman; T. C. Skeat and E. P. Wegener, *JEA* 21 (1935) 232, an appellant of ca. 250 cites a law of Severus; P. Oxy. 899 (200), an appellant cites several decisions of the first and second cents.; P. Oxy. 2104 (241?) repeats *Dig.* 49.1.25, cf. P. M. Meyer, *Studi in onore di Pietro Bonfante* 2 (1930) 341; P. Fay. 10 (first half of third cent.) embodies *Dig.* 29.1.1, which in turn cites an edict of Trajan; C. J. Kraemer and N. Lewis, *TAPA* 68 (1937) 357 f., an appellant under Constantine cites *CJ* 7.39.2 and *CT* 4.11.2; F. M. Heichelheim and G. Schwarzenberger, *Symb. Oslo.* 25 (1947) 1, an edict of 320 is known in three inscriptions (Crete, Lycia, Italy) and in both Codes; and historians have access to laws, e.g. T. C. Skeat, *Brit. Mus. Quarterly* 18 (1953) 72, P. Lon. 878 = Euseb., *Vita Const.* 2.28, and Amm. 22.6.5 recalling *CT* 2.29.1 (362).

19 J. Keil and G. Maresch, *JOAI* 45 (1960), Beibl. 83 f., a text of the third or fourth cent.

20 Wenger, *Mél. Grégoire* 478–486, Caracalla as judge in Syria. Earlier texts usually cited to show the emperor's openness as judge include Dio 60.4.3, 65.10.5, 69.6.3, and 69.7.1.

21 M. de Dominicis, *Scritti Romanistici* (1970) 272 f., studies deputations and their effectiveness, e.g. *CT* 12.1.21 (331–336); cf. *CT* 7.20.2 (320), Constantine's meeting with a crowd of soldiers; 8.9.1 (335), his response *oblatis precibus;* and Euseb., *H.E.* 10.5.18 and other texts of his reign studied by W. Ensslin in *Studi in onore di A. Calderini e R. Paribeni* 1 (1956) 315. *CT* 8.15.1 is exceptional, showing Constantine as judge in the old style.

22 De Dominicis 271; *CJ* 9.47.12 (Diocl.) and 7.62.6.4 (294).

23 Ael. Arist., *To Rome* 32 f., and Plin., *Ep.* 6.31, are good evidence for the emperor's case load; for discussion of it, see W. Kunkel, *Introduction to Roman Legal and Constitutional History,* trans. J. M. Kelly (1966) 120 f., and P. Garnsey, *Social Status and Legal Privilege in the Roman Empire* (1970) 68 and 79–82.

24 Williams 92. The process is amply attested and discussed, e.g. by Williams, by Wilcken, *Hermes* 55 (1920) 8–37, on rescripts (a special variety of *subscriptiones*), and by A. Dell'Oro, *"Mandata" e "litterae"* . . . (1960) passim.

25 *CIL* 3.781 = *IGR* 1.598 (a. 201); Suet., *Claud.* 25.3.

26 Not all these offices were in operation at the same time, of course; but on their archives, see *FIRA²* 3.521 and 528 f.; Liban., *Or.* 14.53; A. Steinwenter, *Beiträge zum öffentlichen Urkundenwesen der Römer* (1915) 19 f.; and *RE* s.v. Tabularium (Sachers, 1932) 1967.

27 Professor Brunt has drawn my attention to this *conventus* record, P. Yale 61 (208–210), in J. F. Oates et al., *Am. Studies in Papyrology* 2 (1967) 188 f.

28 Lucian, *Apol.* 12, condensed; for date ca. 175, see C. Gallavotti, *Luciano* (1932) 184.

29 Steinwenter, *Beiträge* 6–13, 17 f. (there citing interesting texts on the openness of eastern and African court records), and 25 (there citing Caere's city records, cf. Sacher 1968). On public opinion about judges openly expressed, see *CT* 1.16.6 = *CJ* 1.40.3 (331).

30 *CT* 11.7.3 (320); MacMullen, *Roman Social Relations* (1974) 34–37.

31 In the time of persecutions, Cypr., *Ad Donat.* 10, Firm. Matern., *Math.* 3.11.7 and 13, and Iamblichus, in Eunap., *Vit. soph.* 461, suggest that not only Christians suffered from cruel judges; Lact., *Div. Inst.* 5.6.3 and *De ira dei* 23.13 f. depict rule as ultimately based only on fear and force, and Ammianus, after describing how Julian beheaded and burned people alive, goes on directly to call him *placabilis imperator et clemens* (21.12.20, cf. 22.3.11). Further examples in MacMullen, *Art Bull.* 46 (1964) 452, are to be balanced against Symm., *Rel.* 34.4, "Your Clemency . . . often aims serious

threats at Your subjects rather in Your zeal to spur them on than to hurt them."

32 Philostr., *Vita Apollon.* 5.36, to Vespasian, and Dio Chrys., *Or.* 1.5, to Trajan, both enunciating a cliché of speeches on kingship; Tac., *Hist.* 1.11, Egypt is *inscia legum, ignara magistratuum.*

33 Plin., *Ep.* 10.114, violations of the Lex Pompeia, and 10.115, Trajan's reply that past infractions should be ignored, recalling Claudius' decree on the Anauni, *FIRA²* 1.418 f. For the illegal lavishness of the gift of honorific citizenship, see e.g. *IG* 3, 1, 129 (ca. 250).

34 *ILS* 5947 (Sardinia in 67), esp. line 22; *CIL* 9.2438 (Saepinum, ca. 170). But cf. also Tac., *Ann.* 14.18 (Cyrene), and the second-cent. emperor who despairingly recalls that "the matter [here legislated against] has already been ruled on often by the governors, and nothing useful came of their judgement because people disobeyed," in G. E. Bean, *Anatolian Studies* 10 (1960) 71.

35 Earliest and clearest in Euseb., *H.E.* 5.1.47–50. See further S. Mazzarino, *Trattato di storia romana* (1956) 2.314–316, citing Hippol., *In Dan.* 4.18, and other instances; irregularities and inconsistencies in application of the first three edicts of A.D. 303 f., in V. C. De Clercq, *Ossius of Cordova* (1954) 131 and 143, and W. H. C. Frend, *Martyrdom and Persecution in the Early Church* (1965) 499 and 503.

36 MacMullen, *Soldier and Civilian* . . . (1963) 50 f. and 132 f., on inadequate police forces; G. E. M. de Ste. Croix, *Past and Present* 26 (1963) 35 f. nn.99–100, on *contumacia.*

37 P. Oxy. 2104 (241?) = P. Oxy. 3106 = *Dig.* 49.1.25 (Paulus).

38 *CT* 9.1.4 (325) and 12.12.4 (364), trans. C. Pharr. The problem here addressed was not solved, cf. *CJ* 7.62.20 (341) and 21 (355); *CT* 11.30.31 (363) and 12.12.12 (392).

39 P. Ryl. 617 (317) and editors' further reff., P. Ryl. vol. 4, p. 105.

40 *Legationes* in *CJ* 10.41.2 (Gordian) and 10.65.3 (Diocletian), cf. a *legatio* to Constantine requiring three years, in H. I. Bell et al., *The Abinnaeus Archive* . . . (1962) 11.

41 *FIRA²* 1.453.

42 *CT* 2.10.1–2; 10.1.3; and 11.30.8.

43 F. M. de Robertis, *Annali della Facoltà di Giurisprudenza, Bari* 4 (1941) 5 n.1, 23–28, and 39; C. Castello, *RIDA* 12 (1965) 243–245; and above, n.23.

44 T. Mommsen, *Röm. Strafrecht* (1899) 340, calls the essence of criminal law "legalized shapelessness"; on purely discretionary sentencing uncorrected till the third cent., see de Robertis 86 f.; on specific instances of this, above, n.35.

45 F. Schulz, *History of Roman Legal Science* (1946) 154 and 243 f.; G. Liberati, *BIDR* 71 (1968) 119 and 124. F. Wieacker is among those who correctly see the shift of interest to administrative law already under Septimius Severus, *Rev. hist. de droit* 49 (1971) 209 f.

46 For reff. to antiintellectualism, see above, chap. 2, n.47. For postclassical rejection of the complexity of law in its classical embodiment, see F. Wieacker, *Sitzungsber. Heidelberger Akad. Wiss.* 1955, 3, p. 11; idem, *Studi in onore di P. de Francisci* 3 (1956) 121; E. Levy, *West Roman Vulgar Law* . . . (1951) 6; G. Stühff, *Vulgarrecht in Kaiserrecht* . . . (1966) 116 f., detecting in law of the period "ein wissenschaftsfeindliche Einstellung."

47 Honig 40 sees traces of "chancery style" in statements of law under Diocletian but (elsewhere, passim) the developed examples emerge from Constantine on; further, Stühff 93 f., 109, and 119–128 (dating the change to Constantine, not Diocletian; similarly, Wieacker, *Sitz. Heidel. Akad.* 24 and 45 f., and Amelotti 18 f.). On the special character of the *a libellis* style, see e.g. A. Steinwenter, *ZSS* 65 (1947) 93; E. Volterra, *Mél. Henri Lévy-Bruhl* (1959) 325 f.; and Amelotti 21 f. On Diocletian's greater conservativeness in the realm of law, see Amelotti 61 f., Stühff 133, and G. Donatuti, *Studi Parmensi* 3 (1953) 207, 213 f., and 221.

48 *CT* 1.2.3, *stricti iuris ratio;* 1.4.1., *perpetuae prudentium contentiones.*

49 Levy, *Mediaevalia et humanistica* 1 (1943) 21 f.; Volterra 329; Wieacker, *Rev. hist. de droit* 49 (1971) 218 f.; idem, *Studi . . . Francisci* 3.132.

50 For the edict, see above, p. 29; for bureaucratese, MacMullen, *Traditio* 18 (1962) 369–373; and for examples of the

loss of precision and thus of meaning itself in legal documents, below, chap. 5, nn.84–87.

51   SHA *Macrinus* 13.1, *nefas esse dicens* [Macrinus] *leges videri Commodi et Caracalli et hominum imperitorum voluntates,* cited by A. M. Honoré, *Studia et documenta historiae et iuris* 28 (1962) 191; A. N. Sherwin-White, *Journ. Theol. Studies*² 3 (1952) 201, on lapsed edicts.

52   For imperial archives being consulted, see above, n.25; on the other side, see Dell'Oro 68, showing *mandata* easier to unearth than the law they interpreted; Schulz 154, imperial court records not collected or codified. On Trajan's dilemma, Pliny, *Ep.* 10.73. On gubernatorial archives, see *RE* s.v. Tabularium 1966; Steinwenter, *Beiträge* 6 f. and 16 f.; and some interesting pages and insights into the helter-skelter filing systems of both central and gubernatorial offices, and the consequences thereof, in G. Cencetti, *Studi . . . C. Manaresi* (1953) 154–156.

53   Plin., *Ep.* 10.114; von Schwind 74 f.; *Dig.* 18.1.71 (Marc. Aurel.): 42.5.37 and 22.1.1 pr. (Papinian); Gaius, in 13.4.3, 21.2.6, and *Inst.* 1.2.11; Ulpian, in *Dig.* 17.1.10.3 and 25.4.1.15, on *mos regionis* etc.; *CJ* 6.32.2 (256), decision *secundum leges moresque locorum;* Schmiedel (above, n.14) 36 f.; and G. I. Luzzato, *Scritti di diritto romano in onore di C. Ferrini* (1946) 284 f.

54   Plin., *Ep.* 10.114, 66, and 72. The danger of a rescript that might be interpreted beyond its intended scope is pointed out by Fronto to Antoninus Pius, cf. Garnsey 68.

55   Compare the degrees of purity of Roman law increasing as one moves toward Italy: in Dacia, E. Polay, *ZSS* 79 (1962) 51–85; in Pannonia, K. Visky, *Iura* 9 (1958) 99 f. and 13 (1962) 132; in the West generally, F. De Visscher, *Cah. d'hist. mondiale* 2 (1955) 804 f.; and in Italy, R. Taubenschlag, *Opera minora* (1959) 1.431 f.

56   On the singularity of provincial codes, see esp. Luzzato 266–285; also von Schwind 75 f., Taubenschlag 1.505–517, De Visscher 788 f., and L. Wenger, *RIDA* 3 (1949) 522–533. For full bibliography, esp. on the status of "Lokalrecht" after 212, see C. Sasse, *Die Constitutio Antoniniana* (1958) 134–143.

57   For instances of such irregular jurisdictions, see *Dig.* 43.8.2.4;
      IGR 1.598; Kraemer and Lewis 357; H.-G. Pflaum and
      G.-C. Picard, *Karthago* 2 (1951) 104; MacMullen, *Soldier
      and Civilian* 62 f., and *Roman Social Relations* 39 f.

58   A. Piganiol, *Journ. des Savants* 1946, 131.

59   *Dig.* 1.3.32 (Julianus—unless interpolated) and 1.3.35 (Her-
      mogenianus—condensed), in Stühff 43 f., and Constantinian
      texts, 69 f. The distance between "Vulgarrecht" and "Ge-
      wohnheitsreicht" in or underlying the view of *consuetudo*
      does not concern us here. On the two *Digest* texts, see also
      A. A. Schiller, *BIDR* 45 (1938) 352 f., and W. E. Brynteson,
      RIDA 12 (1965) 213–216; and further discussion of related
      points, Brynteson 218 f., esp. *Dig.* 1.3.38, Alex. Steverus *re-
      scripsit in ambiguitatibus quae ex legibus proficiscuntur con-
      suetudinem . . . vim leges optinere debere;* cf. Aul. Gel.
      12.13.5 and Tert., *De corona* 4, *consuetudo . . . etiam in
      civilibus rebus pro lege suscipitur, cum deficit lex,* and other
      texts cited by J. A. C. Thomas, *RIDA* 12 (1965) 480–482.
      For *mos* also as borrowing the respect paid to *consuetudo,*
      see E. Polay, *Differenzierung der Gesellschaftsnormen . . .*
      (1964) 93 f. For *longi temporis praescriptio,* see D. Nörr's
      book of that title (1969) 32 f., 54 f., and passim, the big rise
      in its importance beginning in the third cent.

60   Plin., *Ep.* 10.115; Tac., *Ann.* 14.18; *FIRA²* 1.443.

61   R. Mouterde and C. Mondésert, *Syria* 34 (1957) 281, and
      N. Lewis, *RIDA* 15 (1968) 139, with questionable interpre-
      tation; K. T. Erim and J. Reynolds, *JRS* 59 (1969) 56.

62   E.g. *CT* 5.20.1; 16.10.1; *CJ* 8.52.2; 6.9.8.

63   Donatuti 207, on the beginnings under Diocletian, and 210
      n.19 and 236, for *vetus* describing something only a decade
      or two earlier; Stühff 115 f., on such phrases as *vetus ius* in
      Constantine's laws; and Honig 134.

64   W. M. Calder, *CR* 40 (1926) 18, τὰ ἐξαίρετα in third-cent.
      inscriptions; cf. many similar euphemisms and jargon terms
      in MacMullen, *Traditio* 18 (1962) 366 f., and above, n.4.

65   Above, n.44; *CT* 11.7.3; 15.1.2; 1.16.3; 1.12.2; cf. 4.13.3
      (321), 9.37.1 (319), etc.

66   *CT* 1.16.7 (331, trans. C. Pharr); cf. 6 (331).

67   On corruption prevalent earlier, see MacMullen, *Soldier and*

Civilian 61 f. and 87 f.; idem, *Roman Social Relations* 113 f.; *AE* 1971, no. 464; and "festival money" (ἐνεορτάδια) in *ESAR* 4.893, and N. Lewis, *Greek Papyri in the Collection of New York University* . . . (1967) 28 no. 12 (θαλλεία). On the third cent., Hadas 373, on Palestine in ca. 200; *Dig.* 48.10.1.4 f., Egypt ca. 200; 48.10.25 and 32 f., forgery of *edicta* and *constitutiones;* Cypr., *Ad Donat.* 10, the judge *sententiam vendit* . . . *Nullus de legibus metus est* . . . *Quod potest redimi non timetur;* L. Robert, *Hellenica* 4 (1948) 108, noting a new vocabulary of praise from the third cent. on, and "this eulogy of justice and integrity in our honorific inscriptions for governors is the counterpart of the complaints and accusations heard from in our literary and legal texts, on the corruption of provincial tribunals"; *CJ* 7.64.7 (285), on *venales sententiae* of judges; and (up into the early fourth cent.), Firm. Matern., *Math.* 3.7.26.

68   Cypr., *Ad Donat.* 10.

69   *CT* 8.4.6.

70   E. Van't Dack, in *Aufstieg u. Niedergang der röm. Welt* 2, 1 (1974) 883; commentary to P. Oxy. 1476 (260), p. 233, cf. above, chap. 3, n.68.

71   Synesius, *Ep.* 148 (ed. R. Hercher, *Epistolographi graeci,* p. 732, a. 411).

72   Honoré 171 f. discusses the *CJ.* Except for the totals in 293–294 (more than twice as large as in A.D. 220–230, and reflecting the Gregorian codification), the *relative* proportions make sense, and the patterns of activity can be confirmed fairly well through the *CT:* e.g. the early 350s and later 370s yield few laws, but soon after Licinius' death or Valentinian's accession the number of constitutions climbs sharply.

73   Amelotti 31 f.

74   Anon., *De rebus bell.* 21.1, the coda to the whole treatise; for earlier complaints, see e.g. Lact., *Div. Inst.* 5.8.9, *tam multae et tam variae leges;* Eutrop., *Brev.* 10.8; and Amm. 22.10.7.

CHAPTER 5

1   Birthday celebrations of Constantinople: *Chron. pasch.* (Niebuhr), p. 529 f.; G. Pugliese, *Studi in onore di P. de Fran-*

cisci (1956) 3.375; and R. Janin, *Constantinople byzantine* (1950) 29 f. Coins proclaim its founding, A. Alföldi, *JRS* 37 (1947) 10. On Constantine's self-image as city founder (here, of Orcistus), see *FIRA*² 1.462. Cf. the similar tone in Diocletian's letter (here, to Tymandus), "it is in our very nature that the rank and number of cities should be increased throughout our universe . . . ," *FIRA*² 1.455. For his efforts on his own capital, not much less than Constantine's, see Amm. 22.9.3 and T. C. Skeat, *Papyri from Panopolis* (1964) 135.

2 On flimsy building, see Them., *Or.* 3, cited by Pugliese 376; on pillage of statues, etc., Pugliese 376; on the stripping of other cities (quoted), Hier., *Chron.* 181, cited by C. Kunderewicz, *Studi in onore di E. Volterra* 4 (1971) 141.

3 *Chron. pasch.* 1, p. 394 (*PG* 92.711); Eunap., *Vit. soph.* 462; Anon. Vales. 6.30; Soc., *H.E.* 1.35; *CT* 13.5.7 (334), exemptions to *navicularii* serving Cple.; 14.17.9 and 11, dole rights to palace guards if they built residences; and other texts in Pugliese 376–378.

4 Nero offered citizenship to persons with Latin rights who built in Rome, Gaius 1.34 (*FIRA*² 2.14 f.); but the first migration I know of dates to 202 (Pizos, *SIG*³ 880); thereafter, Tetrarchic, cf. *CJ* 10.1.4 (Diocletian), *metoeci qui iussu principis in aliam civitatem translati sunt;* Paneg. vet. 4(8).21.1 (a. 297), Diocletian's "recent" moving of *incolae* from Asia to Thrace's desert areas; 8(5).4.4, *metoeci undique transferendi* to Autun; 5(9).4.3, *ex amplissimis ordinibus provinciarum incolae novi* moved to Autun by Constantius; and Amm. 28.1.5, Diocletian moves Carpi to Sopianae in Pannonia. For pillage of building materials forbidden, see *CJ* 8.10.6 (321); *CT* 9.17.2 (349, referring back to 333); 15.1.1 (357). For reuse of material in city walls, see F. Millar, *JRS* 59 (1969) 27, Athens in the 270s; H. Bloch, *I bolli laterizi* . . . (1938) 313, Rome at the same date, the brickyards being inoperative; and below, chap. 8 n.27. But Constantine in Rome as in Cple. pillaged freely for new building, cf. A. Chastagnol, *Fastes de la préfecture urbaine de Rome* (1962) 31 f. and 85, and officials and private citizens like-

wise violated the law. For reused statues, a phenomenon rare before 250, see G. Alföldy, *Flamines prov. Hisp. Citerioris* (1973) 16 n. 54, and H. Blanck, *Wiederverwendung alter Statuen* . . . (1969) 105, instancing Constantine's arch and other monuments; for reuse of old milestones, see I. König, *Meilensteine der Gallia Narbonensis* (1970) 118.

5 *CT* 13.41. (334) and 2 (337); cf. 15.1.2, enjoining urban renewal in Africa, and 10.19.1 (320), throwing open the African marble quarries to anyone who will work them.

6 Paneg. vet. 5(9).4.3; cf. 5.1; 4(8).21.2; 7(6).22.4; 8(5).1.1 f. —all on Autun restored by Constantius and later also by Constantine.

7 In Italy, besides Rome, see *AE* 1939, no. 151, an aqueduct feeding eight Campanian cities (317–324); in Asia, the rebuilt basilica at Nicomedia, *Expositio tot. mundi,* ed. Rougé 286; in Africa, see above, n.5.

8 Dio 52.30.1 on embellishment of the capital; on the value of κατάπληξις, see MacMullen, *Art Bull.* 46 (1964) 440 f.; on the ruler as city builder, above, chap. 2 n.12, and A. Mocsy, *Acta antiqua* 10 (1962) 379–381.

9 Above, n.3, on the *annona* to Cple.; but cf. also state allowances for participants in *ludi* in the early fourth cent., Euseb., *Mart. Pal.* 8.2.3, and upkeep of imperial studs of racehorses, MacMullen, *CQ* 12 (1962) 277 f., and P. Mich., IX, 548 (298), "fiscal horses" in Alexandria. For annona to Athens, Julian, *Or.* 1.8D; to Antioch, Soz., *H.E.* 3.7; and to Puteoli, Symm., *Rel.* 40.

10 SHA *Aurel.* 35.2 and 48.4, continued by Constantine, *CT* 14.4.1 (334); for oil "in freight to the market of the *populus Romanus,*" see *Dig.* 50.6.6(5).6 (Marc. Aurel.).

11 For the Alexandrian dole, see Euseb., *H.E.* 7.21.9 (261), and V. Martin and D. van Berchem, *Rev. de philol.* 6 (1942) 21, operating under Constantius II; for Hermopolis and Oxyrhynchus, see J.R. Rea, to P. Oxy., vol. 40 (1972), pp. 1 f., and on Antinoopolis from the 160s, p. 9 n.1.

12 R. F. Hoddinott, *Early Byz. Churches in Macedonia* . . . (1963) 73.

13 For imperial engineering works in aid of marine or riverine

transport, see Strabo 3.1.9 (Spain, Republic); Dio 61.30.6 (Germany, a. 47); Tac., *Ann.* 16.23 (Ephesus, Nero); *ILS* 298 (Italy, 114/115); Plin., *Ep.* 6.31 (Italy, Trajan); P. J. Sijpesteijn, *Aegyptus* 43 (1963) 71 f. (Egypt, Trajan); *SIG*³ 839 (Ephesus, Hadrian); G. Alföldy, *Noricum* (1974) 181 (second half of third cent.); J. Le Gall, *Le Tibre* . . . (1952) 312 f. (Italy, 286–293); *Expositio tot. mundi* 28 (Orontes, Constantius II; cf. Rougé ad loc. for other reff.); *CT* 10.23.1 (Orontes, 369/370); *MGH* 1.296 (Egypt, 367–70). For imperial bridge building, see e.g. Dio 63.13.6, 71.3.1; and P. R. Franke, *Kleinasien zur Römerzeit* (1968) 15, Mopsus in 255/256.

14 MacMullen, *Athenaeum* 54 (1976) 27–33.

15 Lact., *De mort. persecut.* 7.3 (290s). For an attempt at a headcount of the civil service, see MacMullen, *HSCP* 68 (1964) 307.

16 For the severity of third-cent. tax demands, see P. Oxy. 2789; D. Sperber, *RIDA* 19 (1972) 41–42 n.30, ca. 250–270; Herod. 7.3.3., a. 237; for the advice to the ruler, see Menander in *Rhetores graeci,* ed. L. Spengel (1856) 3.375, though very much a cliché, compare e.g. Dio Chrys., *Or.* 4.91–100. For complaints of taxation at other periods, see the reff. below, chap. 6 nn.11 f. The temporary combining of the posts *a libellis* and *a censibus* seems to indicate, too, that the bulk of the central government's correspondence had always had to do with tax appeals. See *DE* s.v. Libellus (G. Samonati, 1962) 822. For the date of the combining, in ca. 140, see H.-G. Pflaum, *Les carrières procuratoriennes équestres* . . . (1960) 1.256.

17 Chap. 6, n.13, below; on auctions, see SHA *Marc. Aurel.* 17.4, *Pertinax* 7.8; Zon. 12.1; Dio 74.5.4 and 79.12.5.

18 *Dig.* 50.16.27 (Ulpian); Herod. 3.13.4; Dio 52.28.1, 52.29.2, 78(77).10.4; Lact., *De mort. persecut.* 7.2 f. and 5; anon., *De rebus bell.* 5.1; SHA *Alex. Sev.* 53.9, *Probus* 23.2 f.; Amm. 30.8.8; and so to the statement, "the Treasury will be empty because of Roman soldiers' wages," in an apocalyptic vision of ca. 400 (fourth to fifth centuries). The text is in F. Wilhelm, *Deutsche Legenden* . . . (1907) 41*, dated by J.

Quasten, *Patrology* (1950) 1.149, and by the *Lexikon für Theologie und Kirche* 1 (1957) 702. On military expenses, see further, below, nn.22 f. Passages from Tacitus and Dio, to show the army payroll less than half the budget, cited by T. Pekary, *Historia* 8 (1959) 472, and M. Mazza, *Lotte sociali a restaurazione autoritaria nel 3. secolo* (1970) 441, seem to me rhetorical exaggerations, quite valueless. I agree rather with Heichelheim and Frank, quoted ibid., pp. 440 f.

19   Most recent is the discussion by R. Develin, *Latomus* 30 (1971) 688–695, with bibliog.

20   D. van Berchem, *Mém. Soc. Nat. des Antiquaires de France*[8] 10 (1937) 125 f.; A. H. M. Jones, *Econ. Hist. Rev.* 5 (1953) 306; and Mazza 420 f.

21   Develin 693, on Herod. 3.8.5. C. R. Whittaker in the Loeb ed., ad loc., compares σιτηρέσιον meaning the whole of the *stipendium* at 2.11.5, 4.4.7, and 6.8.8. J.-P. Callu, *La politique monétaire des empereurs romains de 238 à 311* (1969) 310, takes the word in the same inclusive sense—similar to τροφή in Dio 78(79).34.3, according to Brunt and others. See Develin 693, though he himself translates the word narrowly, not broadly. P. Lips. 84 (Diocl.) records a payment "for σιτηρέσιον to the office of prefect," showing the system of payments in kind to the civil service. For the value of the cash part of army rewards, the stipendium and donatives together "difficult to calculate," see Jones 305 and Callu 311 f. (his calculations of donatives per annum having only "une valeur indicative").

22   Greg. Naz., *Or.* 19.14. For Severus, see Dio 75.3.3; thereafter, ibid. 78(77).9.1; Herod. 7.3.3; Julian, *Or.* 1.21B and 34B; *Ep.* 73.428D; Liban., *Or.* 18.282; anon., *De rebus bell.* 1.1 (twisting the connection into a vicious circle, *profusa largitio semina magis excitet proeliorum*); and Theod., *H.E.* 5.19, who brings us to Theodosius' war taxes.

23   G. Biraghi, *La parola del passato* 6 (1951) 265–270.

24   Van Berchem, *Mém* . . . (1937) cit., pp. 138–141 and passim; MacMullen, *Soldier and Civilian* . . . (1963) 59–62; and a string of texts showing the effect of troop transfers, e.g. *OGIS* 665 (Libyan actions of the 40s); *SEG* 1.276 (Trajan's

wars); A. von Premerstein, *Klio* 12 (1912) 165 f., a special
war tax to meet the Bastarnian threat ca. 170; P. Yale Inv.
296 (216/217), Philadelphia paying a tax of "the supplies
and items prepared for dispatch to Syria to the most noble
armies of our emperor Caracalla," in his campaign against
Artabanus (my thanks to Prof. N. Lewis for help with the
text); and G. E. Bean and T. B. Mitford, *Denkschr. Oesterr.
Akad. Wiss.* 102 (1970) 41, supplies by a liturgist to eastern
campaigns of 233 and 243. Note finally the quarrels of African cities over their boundaries, subject to *vecturae aut copiae
devehendae, Controv. agr.* 45, ed. Thulin.

25   Herod. 6.3.2.

26   On the *horreum,* see *AA* 1968, 566 f.; cf. MacMullen, *Athenaeum* 54 (1976) 28 n.26, on the new or renovated palace,
and 36 n.43, on *horrea* in other capitals.

27   Aurel. Vict., *De Caes.* 39.31; compare *Expositio tot. mundi*
32 (on Antioch) and 58 (on Gaul), "an abundance of everything but at high prices, due to the emperor's presence." On
the taxation of north Italy, see E. Faure, *RIDA* 11 (1964)
155, and L. Cracco Ruggini, *Riv. storica italiana* 76 (1964)
265, who sees the disruptions as economically stimulating.

28   MacMullen, *Athenaeum* 54 (1976) 34–36. Many papyri record such costs for major visits, e.g. P. Goth. 3 (in *ESAR*
2.631), of Caracalla, or Skeat xxv f., of Diocletian.

29   The elaborate network of necessary *mansiones, mutationes,
horrea,* etc.—for a mere governor and provincial garrison—is
well attested by P. Salama, *Les voies romaines de l'Afrique
du Nord* (1951) 84.

30   To A. U. Stylow, *Libertas u. Liberalitas* . . . (1972) 76 and
187 nn.54 f., add *RIC* 5, 2 (1933) 513 and 516, coins of
Carausius.

31   T. Pekary, *Pro Vindonissa* 1966, 5–8. For the phenomenon
more generally producing in all areas "a currency concentration along the glacis of the empire," see Callu 166.

32   M. F. Hendy, *Num. Chron.* 12 (1972) 118; idem, *JRS* 62
(1972) 77 and 81.

33   C. Bosch, *Arch. Anz.* 1931, 426–428 and passim; A. R. Bellinger, *Syrian Tetradrachms of Caracalla and Macrinus*

(1940) 6 f. and 12–15; MacMullen, *Soldier and Civilian* 93 f.; T. B. Jones, *Proc. Am. Philos. Soc.* 107 (1963) 326; and Mazza 447 f.

34 "In this period [the mid-third cent.] the foundation of mints was without exception designed to provide pay for the troops," as A. Alföldi points out in *CAH* 12.177; for anniversary issues, see T. B. Jones 333 on large issues in 202–205; for donatives, Alföldi, *CAH* 12.20, noting that "the large gold pieces of Gallienus, with the legend 'ob fidem reservatam,' express only too clearly the purpose for which they were issued"; D. Barag, *Int. Num. Convention, Jerusalem . . . 1963* (1967) 119–122, tracing waves of activity of Syrian issues in the first and second cents.; Pekary, *Historia* 8 (1959) 456, connecting specially large emissions with the civil wars of the 190s; F. Redo, "Numismatical Sources of the Illyr Soldier Emperors . . . " (*Diss. Arch.*² 2, Budapest, 1973) 77 f., on "the close connection with the emperor's [Probus'] whereabouts and festive occasions. It is especially characteristic of the smaller mints, the production of which is almost exclusively limited to the occasion when the emperor stays somewhere near the mint."

35 Debasement of silver coinage has often been described, e.g. by F. Heichelheim, *Klio* 26 (1932) 97 f.; G. Mickwitz, *Geld u. Wirtschaft im röm. Reich . . .* (1932) 19 f.; A. C. Johnson, *Egypt and the Roman Empire* (1951) 4 f. and 29 f.; J. Guey, *Rev. num.* 4 (1962) 80 f.; R. A. G. Carson, ibid. 7 (1965) 226 f.; idem, *Int. Num. Convention . . . 1963* (1967) 233. The equivalence of the antoninianus to two, not one-and-a-half, denarii has often been contested, but only the 2d.-value makes sense and gains increasing scholarly acceptance. See Mazza 365, Callu 197, C. H. V. Sutherland, *JRS* 51 (1961) 95, and A. H. M. Jones, *The Roman Economy* (1974) 194 n.19.

36 Inflation up to 250 produced an apparently even, gradual doubling of prices. Data of course are few. Most can be found in the *ESAR* passim, esp. Johnson, *ESAR* 2.147 f., 230 f., 279 f., 303, for Egypt, adding idem, *Aegyptus* 32 (1952) 70, and H. C. Youtie, *TAPA* 76 (1945) 145; for Palestine,

D. Sperber, *Archiv Orientalni* 34 (1966) 57–66. But some data are tricky or prove nothing, e.g. prices of slaves and wine; see W. L. Westermann, *Slave Systems of Greek and Roman Antiquity* (1955) 101, and L. Casson, *TAPA* 70 (1939) 7 f. and 15. For the steadiness of the rise where it is best tested, in Egypt, see e.g. Johnson, *Egypt and the Roman Empire* 26–29 and 40. Mickwitz 39 and 48, and Heichelheim 102–106 see a special upswing empirewide under Commodus, but this view, accepted by Carson and Mazza, is rightly rejected by A. Passerini, *Studi in onore di G. Luzzato* (1949) 6–12, by Pekary, *Historia* 8 (1959) 445 f., and by Guey 80 f. In Egypt in the later 240s prices can be seen taking a somewhat sharper rise. It accelerates tremendously from about 275, leveling off until the 290s.

37   Besides the well-known Neronian denarius which inspired imitation even by Constantine, note the revival of the antoninianus in 238, or the earlier perpetuation of Philip Philadelphus' silver by Pompey and then by Caesar: A. R. Bellinger, *Excavations at Dura-Europus, Final Report* 6 (1949) 202.

38   Carson, *Int. Num. Conv. 1963* 233, and Guey 89 f.

39   Johnson, *Egypt and the Roman Empire* 42–44, on the connection between excessive minting and large price rises in 260–275; Callu 188 f. and 403.

40   Callu 198 n.1, the number of coin types more than doubles beginning with Valerian and rises much higher in subsequent reigns; 403, on issues of 265–274. For the connection between mint activity and changes in weight and purity, see Pekary, *Historia* 8 (1959) 456 f., on Severus' mints in 194/195 producing ten times the number of types annually that Antoninus Pius had produced; Mazza 384–388, surveying the still more rapid absorption of better coins by mints of the 240s to 260s, and the corresponding outflood of worse coins; and Callu 257–276 passim, in more detail, and p. 237, where he shows how numbers of mints (two to three, up to Valerian) increased sharply to nine between 269 and 274. Perhaps most telling is the estimate of Callu, in *Aufstieg und Niedergang der röm. Welt* 2, 2 (1975) 604, that between 238

and 274 "le volume des frappes se soit multiplié environ par 7, la période cruciale se situant entre 266 et 274."

41 Callu, *Politique* 243 points out how mints—Milan, Rome, Trier, etc.—produced silver of rising and falling weights sometimes 50 percent different from each other at a given moment (see also Mickwitz 58 f.). Similarly the gold piece from mid-third cent. for decades varied wildly in weight though not in purity. See M. Bernhart, *Handbuch zur Münzkunde der röm. Kaiserzeit* (1926) 19; Carson, *Rev. num.* 7 (1965) 230; D. Sperber, *JRS* 56 (1966) 192 f., attempting to fix the value of aurei in denarii at different points, Decius-Diocletian; and J. P. C. Kent, *Num. Chron.* 13 (1973) 64 f. For deterioration of third-cent. coins as works of art, see e.g. S. Skowronek, *On the Problems of the Alexandrian Mint* (1967) 17.

42 Zos. 1.61.3; Mickwitz 59–63; Mazza 380 f., 390–396, and 400 f.; A. H. M. Jones, *Econ. Hist. Rev.* 5 (1953) 297 f.; idem, *Roman Economy* 196; Carson, *Rev. num.* 7 (1965) 231 f. and 236; Sutherland 95 f.; and Callu, *Politique* 323–329 and 340. On the good appearance of the aurelianianus, H. A. Cahn, *Gestalt u. Gesch. Festschr. K. Schefold* (1967) 92. D. Kiénast, *Chiron* 4 (1974) 547 f., raises serious doubts about the Zosimus text, but his attempt to show that Aurelian's "XXI" and similar coin marks were for the internal use of the mints, not showing any retariffing, does not persuade me (pp. 550–555).

43 Bosch 431 f.; T. B. Jones 309–312 and 325.

44 On countermarks, rare before the third cent., see Bosch 437 f.; Heichelheim, *ESAR* 4.219 f.; H. Hamburger, *'Atiqot* 1 (1955) 117 f.; Callu, *Politique* 15–19, 69, 77, 93 f., and 109 f.; idem, *Atti del Congresso int. di numismatica . . . 1961* (1965) 2.368 f.; E. W. Klimowsky, *Int. Num. Convention . . . 1963* (1967) 134; Carson, ibid. 240 f.; O. Morkholm, ibid. 247; and T. B. Jones 309, 317 f., 325, and 335–344.

45 On western local silver and bronze, where the evidence suggests that a very wide variety of weights quite uncontrolled proved nevertheless quite acceptable on the market, see

D. W. MacDowall, *Schweizer Münzblätter* 15 (1965) 92,
first-cent. Rhineland anticipations of the third-cent. phenomenon; M. R. Alföldi, *Chiron* 1 (1971) 351–363, on coins cast,
not struck, in the second- and third-cent. Danube and African provinces as well as Gaul; Alföldy, *Noricum* (1974) 178–
180, on the dearth of coins in Noricum; for Gaul and Britain,
see P. Le Gentilhomme, *Gallia* 5 (1947) 332 f.; P. V. Hill,
Barbarous Radiates (Num. Notes and Monographs, 1949) 2
and 15 f.; H. Parriat, *Assoc. G. Budé, Actes du Congrès
1958* (1960) 322 f.; J.-B. Giard, *Bull. Soc. Nat. Antiquaires
de France* (1963) 128–135; G. C. Boon, *Scientific American*
231 (1974) 126–129; and Callu, *Politique* 305–308. On retariffing, see T. V. Buttrey, *Mus. Notes* 18 (1972) 47–50, on
reengraved or overstruck sesterces, and Carson, *Int. Num.
Conv. 1963* 236, on Victorinus' countermarked ("V") coins.

46   For counterfeiting after the 280s in the Danube area, see
Callu, *Politique* 303 n.1; P. Bastien, *Le monnayage de Mag-
nence* (1964) 103 f.; and such texts as *CT* 9.21.1 f. (319–)
and 9.22.1 (317, 343), and the anon. *De rebus bell.* 3.1.

47   On the retariffing of Aurelian's radiates, see F. Ehrendorfer,
Num. Zeitschr. 71 (1946) 105; A. H. M. Jones, *Roman
Economy* 196 and 200; L.Cracco Ruggini, *Rend. Accad. Naz.
dei Lincei* 16 (1961) 308; E. Frézouls, *Mél. . . . offerts à J.
Carcopino* (1966) 382 f.; and Callu, *Politique* 369. On the
date of the silver reform (probably 294, at that time also
extended to Egypt), see Callu, *Politique* 372; Sutherland, *JRS*
51 (1961) 97; and Hendy, *JRS* 62 (1972) 77.

48   In the latter part of 301, the Edict on Prices said how many
denarii went to a pound of gold: in its Elatea publication
(Phocis), 50,000, but at Aezani (Phrygia), 72,000. The readings seem certain: for the first, see J. Bingen, *Chron. d'Egypte*
80 (1965) 431 f., and F. M. Heichelheim, *JRS* 55 (1965)
251; for the second, p. 57 and pl. 14 in R. and F. Naumann,
Der Rundbau in Aezani (1973), comparing also the government price of 60,000 in Egypt in Feb 300, P. Beatty Panop.
2.216 (with my thanks to Dr. C. E. King for first calling the
Naumann book to my attention). M. Crawford, in *Aufstieg
u. Niedergang der röm. Welt* 2, 2 (1975) 580 and 593, sim-

ply rejects all readings out of hand, so as to retain an other-wise invalidated reconstruction of Diocletian's currency changes. But engravers' errors are not inconceivable. Cf. in the Elatea text, 12,000 for "drawn-out gold," where the alpha over the mu should surely be a zeta (i.e., 72,000, as at Aezani—thereby making nonsense of the Elatea 50,000). An announcement complementary to the Edict on Prices has been seen as fixing a pound of silver at 9,600 denarii, by K. T. Erim et al., *JRS* 61 (1971) 173. But cf. the very real questions raised by Callu, *Bull. Soc. Francaise de numisma-tique* 27 (1972) 292, and the silver pound at Aezani, 6,000 denarii (Naumann 57). Denarii (whatever actual coin or multiple the texts refer to, endlessly disputed) nevertheless changed value often, almost always upward in this general period—as is best seen in papyri. This leads to the view that all coins in fact exchanged according to market realities. See Mickwitz, *Geld v. Wirtschaft* 68 f. and A. H. M. Jones, *Roman Economy* 77 and 204. Reality did not prevent pe-riodic fiats, that this or that coin (some retariffed by coun-termarks, e.g., by Licinius) henceforth equaled such-and-such a number of other coins. See the coins and early fourth-cent. papyri discussed by Mickwitz, *Geld v. Wirtschaft* 104 f.; A. Segrè, *Byzantion* 15 (1940–1941) 252 and 255; Callu, *Atti del Congresso int. di numismatica . . . 1961* 2.374; and A. H. M. Jones, *Roman Economy* 226. But reality has likewise not prevented periodic modern attempts, as vain as Diocletian's, to infer some table of rates among coins. Basic is the value of the follis, 12,500 denarii (P. Beatty Panop. 2.302 f.), about which many of the questions, if not the fundamental challenge, raised by Cracco Ruggini, *Rend.* cit., pp. 306–319, remain still to be answered.

49 On the psychology of new-seeming coins, see Mickwitz, *Geld v. Wirtschaft* 59 and Cahn 93; on deflationary changes, see comments on P. Ryl. 607 by most scholars cited in the fore-going few notes, esp. Erim 176 and Callu, *Politique* 403 f.

50 On inflation in 301 f., see Mickwitz, *Geld v. Wirtschaft* 98–102; A. C. Johnson, *JJP* 4 (1950) 156; Frézouls 380–385 and 391 f.; and Callu, *Politique* 397 f.

51 Mickwitz, *Geld v. Wirtschaft* 82 f. (and resulting rise in price of gold, 101 f.); J. L. Teall, *Dumb. Oaks Papers* 21 (1967) 24; C. Dupont, *La réglementation économique dans les constitutions de Constantin* (1963) 178; Segrè 250 and Cracco Ruggini, *Rend.* cit., p. 311, on the price of gold in denarii in Egypt; ibid. 314 on Constantine's enormous increases in quantities of bronze in circulation; A. H. M. Jones, *Roman Economy* 212, on Egyptian wheat and gold prices.

52 On the 1:10 ratio, Erim 175; on the 1:18 ratio, Mickwitz, *Geld v. Wirtschaft* 56 and 99, Bastien 89, Callu, *Politique* 241 f., and J. W. E. Pearce, *RIC* 9 (1951) xxviii.

53 Arguing for weight changes by policy are Mazza 315–317, drawing e.g. on Mickwitz, *Geld v. Wirtschaft* 9 f. and 32 f.; Mickwitz, *Annales. Econ., Soc., Civ.* 6 (1934) 240 f.; disagreeing are M. H. Crawford, ibid. 26 (1971) 1232 f., and A. H. M. Jones, *Roman Economy* 74.

54 *CJ* 4.62.2 (198–211), *vectigalia nova nec decreto civitatium institui possunt,* backed up by a number of instances where such financial measures were cleared through the emperor or his agents; *Dig.* 46.3.102 pr. (Scaevola), *pecunia, qua illa res publica utebatur, quasi aerosa iussu praesidis sublata est,* comparing imperial licensing of city coinages, L. Robert, *Hellenica* 11–12 (1960) 59; but municipal silver (not bronze) was extremely rare by this date and was no major force even in the first cent.; and Dio 52.30.9, advocating suppressing city issues, implies they were in his day ordinarily undisturbed—as their behavior certainly suggests. That it was illegal to reject imperial coinage is seen in Epict., *Diss.* 3.3.3; Paul, *Sent.* 5.25.1a = *FIRA*² 2.410; P. Oxy. 1411 (260), the strategos tells money changers to return to work and not refuse imperial coinage; and *CT* 9.22.1 (317, 343). See further *IGR* 4.352 = *ESAR* 4.892 f. (Hadrian to Pergamum) and *OGIS* 515 = 4.895 f. (Sept. Severus to Mylasa), the latter with commentary by Mazza 350 f. and 702 n.309 and Pekary, *Historia* 8 (1959) 464 f. But I see in both inscriptions attempts not to control coin ratios but merely to secure a convenience to the cities by legitimating and defending a monopoly that black-marketeers threatened.

55 *Dig.* 13.4.3 (Gaius).

56 Callu, *Atti del Congr. int. num.* . . . *1961,* 2.370; Pekary, *Historia* 8 (1959) 460; P. Oxy. 1414 (270–275), a new contract is needed due to only a year's change in price of labor and raw materials.

57 *CIG* 2826 (Aphrodisias, third cent.); P. Lon. 1243 (227); and from mid-third cent. in papyri an increasing number of ref., listed in the editors' commentary to P. Oxy. 1411 (260); Mickwitz, *Geld v. Wirtschaft* 52 and 118; Callu, *Politique* 186 f.

58 The term *follis* to mean a coin is first met with in P. Beatty *Panop.* 2.302 (300); next in 308/309, T. Pekary, *Schweizer Münzblätter* 12 (1962) 46. "Myriad" becomes common as a unit of reckoning only after 212, see e.g. Mickwitz, *Geld v. Wirtschaft* 85 n.22, inscriptions of the early fourth cent., and Callu, *Atti* cit., 2.374.

59 Johnson, *Egypt and the Roman Empire* 58, on the theoretical weight of bronze; S. Safrai, *Int. Num. Convention* . . . *1963* (1967) 256, quoting a third-cent. text.

60 Mickwitz, *Geld v. Wirtschaft* 122, 125, and 129.

61 R. Rémondon, *Rev. de philol.* 32 (1958) 244–258.

62 On the continued use of coinage, esp. in fourth-cent. texts, see Mickwitz, *Geld v. Wirtschaft* 120–122, 127, 136 f., and 156–162; J. G. Milne, *Aegyptus* 32 (1952) 146 f., on the predominance of bronze in rural areas.

63 E. Manni, *L'impero di Gallieno* (1949) 4 f.; Mazza 416–418; and S. Mazzarino, *Aspetti sociale del quarto secolo* (1951) 114. Against these advocates of the view that inflation actually favored the *latifondiste,* the point is sometimes made that inflation also favors the debtor class, who pay back less value than they borrow.

64 Johnson, *JJP* 4 (1950) 158.

65 C. H. Kraeling, *Ptolemais* (1962) 20 f.

66 On urban prosperity, see L. Leschi, *Djemila, antique Cuicul* (1953) 13; B. H. Warmington, *North African Provinces from Diocletian to the Vandal Conquest* (1954) 30 f.; P. Romanelli, *Storia delle province romane dell'Africa* (1959) 506 f.; and P.-A. Février, *Cah. arch.* 14 (1964) 46 f. Add,

that Mauretania enjoyed its Golden Age in the period Gordian-Gallienus, W. H. C. Frend, *Donatist Church* (1952) 44. On export and influence of mosaicists, see A. Carandini, *Dialoghi di archeologia* 1 (1967) 107, 110, and 118 n.49; P. Romanelli, in *La mosaique gréco-romaine* (Colloques internationaux du CNRS, 1963) (1965) 279; and R. Bianchi Bandinelli, *Rome: The Late Empire* . . . (1971) 273. On the development of pottery industry from centers in Proconsularis, J. Hayes, *Late Roman Pottery* (1972) 296 and 423.

67   S. Frere, *Antiquity* 38 (1964) 108 and 110; idem, *Britannia* . . . (1967) 249 and 281 f.

68   N. Jacobone, *Un'antica e grande città dell'Apulia: Canusium* (1925) 149; F. M. de Robertis, *La produzione agricola in Italia* . . . (1948) 8 n.1 and 12.

69   Above, n.6; F. Lot, *Recherches sur la population* . . . 1 (1945) 33; P.-A. Février, *Le développement urbain en Provence* . . . (1964) 42 and 46; L. A. Constans, *Arles* (1928) 54; C. Jullian, *Histoire de la Gaule* 7 (1926) 117 n.1; A. Grenier, *Habitations gauloises et villas latines dans la cité des Mediomatrices* (1906) 118 and 179–181; idem, *Manuel d'archéologie gallo-romaine* 2 (1934) 864 and 936; G. Faider-Feytmanns and J. Hubaux, in *Mél. . . . H. Grégoire* 2 (1950) 254. As shown by E. Thevenot, *Rev. arch. de l'Est* 3 (1952) 121 f., the shrunken circuits of walled cities constituted a fortress, not the whole, with always reviving suburbs outside them, e.g. at Autun and Paris. Toulouse's vast circuit of walls dates to the second cent., according to M. Labrousse, *Mél. . . . offerts à W. Seston* (1974) 266.

70   B. Levick, *Roman Colonies* . . . (1967) 102; A. M. Mansel, *AA* 1959, 365–395, 402; G. Kleiner, *Ruinen von Milet* (1968) 46.

71   Alföldy, *Noricum* 207; on Pannonia's wealth as attested mostly in the archaeological record, see V. Lanyi, *Acta arch.* 24 (1972) 136, tracing inflow of currency from Bithynian mints under Constantine, and on gold hoards, J. M. C. Toynbee, *Roman Medallions* 117. On Sirmium's blooming under Diocletian and later, see V. Popovic, *Sirmium* 1 (1971) 129; and M. Parovic-Pesikan, ibid., 2 (1971) 44. On another city, see *Intercisa* 2 (1957) 31, 97, 181, 197, 529, and 535 f.; on

Pannonian villas, see E. B. Thomas, *Röm. Villen in Pannonien* (1964) passim, esp. 128 and 382, and M. Biro, *Acta arch.* 26 (1974) 52 f. On Galerius' vast drainage and land-reclamation project in Pannonia, see K. Sagi, ibid., 1 (1951) 87 f., and A. Mocsy, *Pannonia and Upper Moesia* (1974) 272. On Serdica, see P. Lemerle, *Philippes et la Macédoine orientale* (1945) 70; T. Ivanov and S. Bobčev, *Serdica* 1 (1964) 68; and I. Venedikov, in V. Besevliev and J. Irmscher, *Antike u. Mittelalter in Bulgarien* (1960) 162. On Silistra, V. Velkov, ibid., 215. On Nicopolis, T. Ivanov, ibid., 281. On Philippopolis, L. Botusarova, in resumé in the *Zentral-blatt der bulgarischen wissenschaftlichen Literatur* 5 (1962) 39 and 6 (1963). On Diocletianopolis, K. Madzarov, ibid., 8 (1965) 42. On the Thracian countryside, V. Velkov, *Byzan-tinobulgarica* 1 (1962) 35 f. On the lower Danube and Black Sea cities (Histria, Tomi, and Cellatis), see H. Nubar, *Dacia*² 7 (1963) 242 and 253 f.; E. Condurachi, ibid., 1 (1957) 247 and 8 (1964) 25 f.; V. Canarache, *Studii clasice* 3 (1961) 227, and V. Velkov, ibid., 245.

72 E.g. Plin., *Ep.* 6.19; Plut., *Moral.* 406B.

73 Suet., *Julius Caes.* 54.2, *Aug.* 41.1, and other passages cited in C. Nicolet's excellent essay, *Annales. Econ., Soc., Civ.* 26 (1971) 1205 n.2, 1213, 1217 f., 1220 f., and 1225; also J. Guey, *Mél. . . . J. Carcopino* (1966) 472 f.

74 E.g. Cic., *De domo sua* 14, and below, n.82.

75 Philostr., *Vit. soph.* 613; *Dig.* 50.11.2 (Callistratus, quoting Plato, *Rep.* 371); and *CT* 11.10.1 (369).

76 For calculations of the profitability of provinces, see Strabo 2.5.8 and 4.5.3, and esp. App., *Praef.* 7, carrying the story up to the mid-second cent.; for emperors—Augustus but not Tiberius, Caligula in his good years only, Hadrian, An-toninus Pius, and Alexander Severus—knowing the accounts of the empire, see Tac., *Ann.* 1.11; Dio 53.30.2; 56.33.2; 59.9.4; Suet., *Calig.* 16.1; SHA *Had.* 20.11; *Ant. Pius* 7.8; *Alex. Sev.* 21.6 f.; cf. Valentinian's claim, *FIRA*² 1.512, for one area only, and indirect confirmation of earlier account-ings in Vell. Paterculus 2.39.1 and 3; Suet., *Vesp.* 16.3; and App., *Praef.* 15, an interesting item which I owe to the kind-ness of Dr. A. J. Graham. No doubt Nerva's Select Com-

mittee would have such documents before it: Plin., *Paneg.* 62.2, *Ep.* 2.1.9; and Biraghi 257 f.

77   The nearest we have to economic treatises are Dio 52 passim and the anon. *De rebus bell.* 2–4 and passim. Apropos the latter, A. H. M. Jones rightly says that the economic knowledge of the ancients was "crude," *Roman Economy* 74. Cf. similar judgments on the Roman understanding of coinage in M. Grant, *Roman Anniversary Issues* (1950) xviii, and M. Crawford, *JRS* 60 (1970) 46.

78   S. Lauffer, *Diokletians Preisedikt* (1971) provides the best edition; for date, see J. Lafaurie, *CRAI* 1965, 198; for attendant documents, Erim et al., art. cit., and M. Crawford and J. M. Reynolds, *JRS* 65 (1975) 160 f.

79   Erim 175; J. Rougé, *Expositio totius mundiet gentium* (1966) 371.

80   Lauffer 191 f. on prices of gold, etc., and 58–60, on the oath in a formula, P. Ant. 1.38, PSI 202, and P. Oxy. 85, up to 338; MacMullen, *Aegyptus* 41 (1961) 3–5, on the observance of Edict prices, e.g. in P. Cair. Isidor. 54 (314); see also Callu, *Politique* 407; and as to the Edict being still a living inscription in 310 in Cyrenaica, see Erim and Reynolds, *JRS* 60 (1970) 140, on *damnatio memoriae* of Maximian.

81   Above, nn. 27 f., on the economic effects of court and army. The Edict by its preface strongly suggests that it was elicited by complaints from billeting areas. On inflation and state spending seen together, see Lact., *De mort. persecut.* 7.5 f.

82   In defense of free buying and selling, see *Dig.* 18.1.71 (Marc. Aurel.) and *CT* 13.6.7 (375); against *dardanarii, Dig.* 47.11.6 (Ulpian), bidding the governor intervene, and 48.12.2pr. (Ulpian), specifically on a *lex Iulia de annona.* For instances of the emperor intervening to keep staples' prices low, see e.g. in Rome, Tac., *Ann.* 2.87 (Tiberius); *Dig.* 1.12.1.11 (Ulpian); and *CT* 14.19 (398); in Pergamum, *ESAR* 4.893 (Hadrian); in Athens, *IG²*, II-III, 1118 (209/210); in Antioch, by Domitian, D. Magie, *Roman Rule in Asia Minor* . . . (1950) 581 and 1443 f.; in Oxyrhynchus in 246, P. Oxy. 3048; in the empire generally, M. Rostovtzeff, *Social and Economic History of the Roman Empire²* (1956) 370 and

n.21, giving several reff. up to Marcus Aurelius; and on coins, advertisement of emergency relief to cities in time of shortage, e.g. B. V. Head, *Historia numorum*[2] (1911) 733, 782, and 798, and H. P. Kohns, *Bonner Historia-Augusta-Colloquium 1964/1965* (1966) 111 n.51. For a possible ceiling on prices, see Mazza 329 f. on SHA *Commod.* 14.3 and the obscure *forma censoria* registering the price of a slave (*CIL* 8.23956, surely not a ceiling price, however, but assessed value for taxation, cf. *Dig.* 50.15.4.1 and 5). *Dig.* 50.13.1.1 (Ulpian) says, *praeses provinciae de mercedibus ius dicere solet;* and P. Lugduno-Batava, XIII, 9 (under Constantine) shows the governor declaring that interest rates shall not exceed 12 percent.

83   On state-city relations, besides Pliny and other "state mayors" (above, chap. 3 nn. 25 f.), note *CIL* 8.7059, and H.-G. Pflaum, *Les carrières procuratoriennes équestres* (1960) 379 and 383 n.27; *DE* s.v. Calendarium (B. Kuebler, 1900) 27, on state-appointed city accountants; *Dig.* 50.12.14 (Trajan), 50.12.13 (Marc. Aurel.), and 22.1.33 and 50.12.1 (Ulpian), on the governor's right to press for payment of debts and promises to cities; *CIL* 8.26528b (168) and *Dig.* 30.73, on the rights of cities and *vici* to inherit; and Dio 52.30.3 and *Dig.* 1.16.7.1, 50.10.6, and 1.18.7, on municipal building projects as rightly subject to imperial control.

84   *Dig.* 50.11.1 (Modestinus), *IGR* 4.1381 (253/268), and other texts in MacMullen, *Phoenix* 24 (1970) 334.

85   MacMullen, *Soldier and Civilian* 59 n.27; R. Andreotti, *RIDA* 16 (1969) 215; and F. Millar, *JRS* 59 (1969) 25.

86   J. Rougé, *Recherches sur l'organisation du commerce maritime* . . . (1966) 438 f., on such texts as *Dig.* 39.4.11 (Paulus) and *Expositio tot. mundi* 22; and on the generally fiscal nature of the toll system, S. J. De Laet, *Portorium* (1949) 449 f.

87   *CJ* 4.63.2 (374?).

88   Callu, *Politique* 416 f., A. H. M. Jones, *Roman Economy* 203, and Mickwitz, *Geld v. Wirtschaft* 99, on such early fourth-cent. papyri as P. Oxy. 1430 (324), 1524, 1653 (306), 2106, P. Merton 31 (307), P. Thead. 33 (311/312), PSI 310

(307), and P. Ryl. 616, the price of a gold pound varying from 90,000 up to 300,000. For the process of gold-bullion purchase in the first quarter of the fourth cent., see J. R. Rea, *Chron. d'Egypte* 49 (1974) 163–169, redating PSI 310, a reference I owe to the kindness of Dr. C. E. King.

89   Julian, *Or.* 7.228B and *Caes.* 335B; Liban., *Or.* 30.6 and 46.22; Zos. 2.38.2 f.; Euseb., *In laud. Const.* 7.13 and 8.3 (*PG* 20.1357 and 1360) and *Vita Const.* 3.54; and matching texts on his liberality, Julian, *Or.* 1.8B; *Epit. de Caes.* 41.16; Zos. 2.38.1; Euseb., *Vita Const.* 3.1 and 4.1; anon., *De rebus bell.* 2.1; Amm. 16.8.12. On the two taxes to raise gold, see chap. 6 n.70; but add the fines exacted in gold bullion, CJ 1.22.3 (313), or solidi, *CJ* 6.1.5 (319), and rental on crown land, *CT* 11.16.1 (318; 319) and 12.6.2 (325), all three cited by Dupont 179.

90   For gold prices, see above, nn.41, 48, and 88. Compare P. Giess. 47, dated 115 by J. Schwartz, *Chron. d'Egypte* 28 (1962) 345, where a citizen says, "the [bullion, here silver] prices at Coptos change daily, as you know," with P. Oxy. 1223 (late fourth cent.) showing that not bullion but the coin itself (here, the solidus) "has come down." For the period when gold coins took on their new character as a commodity, the early 260s, see Kent 65.

91   Gold is more favored by third-cent. traders, Safrai 255 f. and Rougé, *Recherches* 455; but coins are simultaneously treated as objects, esp. or jewelry, Toynbee, *Medallions* 118 f., or are weighed on receipt by the state, *CT* 12.7.1 (325). For levying of ἄσημος or its use to pay troops, above, n.89, and Callu, *Politique* 297; ibid., 297 n.3, on plate in hoards; on gold torques and other precious objects as essentially (and regularly expected) items of pay to officers and dignitaries, see C. E. Van Sickle, *AC* 23 (1954) 48–59, and MacMullen, *Latomus* 21 (1962) 159–163, the surviving articles datable to Diocletian and later.

92   *CIL* 13.3162 (238) II, lines 15 f., for an officer; *CT* 13.5.7 (334), for *navicularii*.

93   For civil officials receiving *annonae* (by whatever term, Greek or Latin), see above, n.6, and *CT* 8.5.3 (326) and 8.1.3

(333). Evidence is puzzlingly sparse but, on the predominance of annona, just adequate. For annonae for the army, see above, n.21, *CT* 7.4.1 (325), and 7.22.2 (326). Troopers' uniforms and arms were worth about 6 sol. in 396 but were a nonrecurring item. See my "Manufactures for the State in the Later Roman Empire" (diss., Harvard, 1956) 35, A. H. M. Jones subsequently arriving at just the same figure, *Roman Economy* 209. At a slightly later date, annona came to 4–5 sol., R. Grosse, *Röm. Militärgesch.* . . . (1920) 246. Annona therefore greatly outweighed equipment, once the latter had been supplied. Different proportions would apply in 301: about 45,000d. for equipment on entry to the service (MacMullen, diss. cit. 35), but perhaps an eighth of that in value of wheat, wine, and *laridum* per year. Explanation for the difference may lie in the *stipendium* still paid in 301 but in 396 long since given up, cf. van Berchem, *Mém.* cit. (above, n.20), 130. The stipendium indeed appears in P. Oxy. 1047, but the text is datable only "fourth cent." and is useless for annual salaries, since we do not know how many installments were paid per year.

94   Salary for the *magister memoriae,* Paneg. vet. 5(9).11.2; Mickwitz, *Geld v. Wirtschaft* 176 n.1, finding the literal meaning *trecenarius* "völlig unmöglich," though A. H. M. Jones, *Roman Economy* 210, and Mazzarino 164 accept it. The latter assumes 1 lb.AV = 10,000d., whereas Jones assumes 50,000d., and I leave the figure at between 50,000 and 90,000 (cf. above, n.48), with the second-cent. wheat *modius* at 3HS. Van Sickle 52 would avoid all difficulties by supposing that "one hundred sesterces continued to equal an aureus," i.e. a *trecenarius* would be paid 30,000 aurei in gold. But for this there is no evidence.

95   MacMullen, *Aegyptus* 42 (1962) 99, on frequency of *adaeratio* in papyri; *CT* 7.4.1 (325) and later laws, in Mickwitz, *Geld v. Wirtschaft* 165–171, and Mazzarino 20 and 54 and Mazza 352–355. Dupont 181–185 gives a balanced discussion. An earlier statement by Sept. Severus forbidding adaeratio shows in its wording that it was a ban often announced, W. L. Westermann and A. A. Schiller, *Apokrimata* (1954)

32; but, despite many inferences that have been drawn from the text about the currency at the time, I think it only shows the government wanting to insure that taxpayers of grain shouldered transport costs of that article, not of a little bag of money, to delivery points.

96 Above, chap. 4, n.69, with nn.67 f. also; for the system after Constantine, see MacMullen, *Traditio* 18 (1962) 366 f. Note especially the "perquisites" openly secured to minor bureaucrats by Hadrian, *CIL* 6.971, and later, *Dig.* 31.1.22.

97 Under Constantine: Chastagnol 99, on the new rank of *comites;* W. Ensslin, *Mél. . . . J. Bidez* (1934) 361, on the new *patricii;* idem, *RE* s.v. Palatini (1943) 2544, on new *palatini; CT* 13.5.16 (380), Constantine makes *navicularii* equestrians; *CT* 6.38 (317), on trafficking in the perfectissimate; and in the Church, Soz., *H.E.* 1.24 and H.U. Instinsky, *Bischofsstuhl u. Kaiserthron* (1955) 84.

CHAPTER 6

1 Above, chap. 5, n.76.
2 Greg. Naz., *Or.* 19.14.
3 *Dig.* 13.7.43.1 (Scaevola, fl. ca. 173); U. Wilcken, *Grundzüge u. Chrestomathie der Papyruskunde* 1 (1912) 360 f.; idem, *Gr. Ostraka* 273 (185), cash payments "on the annona account," on which see S. L. Wallace, *Taxation in Egypt . . .* (1938) 23. S. Daris, *Il lessico latino . . .* (1971), gives no dated occurrence of annona before PSI 683 (199), though there are various "late second cent." examples, e.g. Wilcken, *Ostraka* 1479. But on the "Severan" receipts used by D. van Berchem, *Mém. Soc. Nat. Antiquaries de France* 80 (1937) 136, see the new dating to the 160s and 170s by C. Préaux, *Chron. d'Egypte* 26 (1951) 127–151, accepted by M. Mazza, *Lotte sociali e restaurazione autoritaria nel 3. secolo* (1970) 426 (= ed. 2, 1973, 379), and R. Develin, *Latomus* 30 (1971) 693. The annona militaris was a supertax, see J. Lesquier, *L'armée romaine en Egypte* (1918) 352–368; Wallace 339; and van Berchem 147.

4 Van Berchem 168 f., pressing the evidence rather hard; A. Mocsy, *Germania* 44 (1966) 323. *Horrea* are found widely

scattered: van Berchem 182 f.; P. Salama, *Les voies romaines de l'Afrique* (1951) 44; G. Jeanton, *BCTH* 1920, 158, fortified, like some that Salama mentions; and F. Stähelin, *Die Schweiz in römischer Zeit*³ (1948) 427 f., well-protected locations for horrea at Vindonissa and elsewhere.

5 See e.g. *Dig.* 50.8.12(9).2(5), Marcus Aurelius' rescript; 49.5.7 (Paulus), annona contrasted with *frumentum in usum militum;* 50.4.1.2 (Hermogenianus), annona is still for the city. But 26.7.32.6 (Modestinus), *onera annonarum et contributionum temporariarum,* probably refers to the *a. militaris* (van Berchem 165).

6 E.g. *CJ* 4.65.14 (259); P. Oxy. 1415 (Diocletian) and P. Beatty Panop. 1.53 f. (Diocletian); and note the confusion implied in P. Oxy. 1419 (265), where the "annona for the legionaries" is counted among the πολιτικά, contrasted with P. Wis. Sijpesteijn 32 (305), where the annona is distinguished from δημόσια τελέσματα καὶ παντοίαι ἐπιβολαί (the latter words recalling the *temporaria* of *Dig.* 50.4.1.2).

7 Annona levied on land: van Berchem 135, citing Aurel. Vict., *De Caes.* 33.13, *actuarii . . . genus hominum . . . fortunis aratorum infestum;* further, van Berchem 165, with other texts.

8 *Ibid.* 165; cf. 154 f., receipts every year from 213 to 217; and the city noble who oversaw annona deliveries from Cilicia to Syria thrice in a decade, in G. E. Bean and T. B. Mitford, *Denkschr. Oesterr. Akad.* 102 (1970) 41. For the variety of articles levied under the annona, P. Tebt. 404 (late third cent.) serves as a good example.

9 Van Berchem 135 (*actuarii*), 145 (equestrian *praepositi annonae* from 178 on), and 189 f. (powers of praetorian prefects enhanced).

10 Mocsy 315–321; MacMullen, *Soldier and Civilian . . .* (1963) 61 f.

11 A sampling of the evidence is sufficient: *IGR* 4.259; Philostr., *Vita Apollon.* 5.36; Commod., *Carm.* 890.

12 H. Henne, *Aegyptus* 13 (1933) 389 f.; MacMullen, *Roman Social Relations* (1974) 34; Basil, *Ep.* 85; P. Oxy. 708 (188) and 1194 (ca. 265).

13 On remission of taxes, local or general, see e.g. Tac., *Ann.*

12.63; SHA *Had*. 6.5, 7.6, *Marc. Aurel*. 23.3; Dio 72.32.2, and G. Alföldy, *Archivo esp. de arq*. 43 (1970) 172 f., under Marcus; and Aurel. Vict., *De Caes*. 37.7, Aurelian.

14 Capitation or poll tax, and annona or land tax, in D. Sperber, *AC* 38 (1969) 165 n.9; M. Hadas, *Philol. Quarterly* 8 (1929) 384; A. Déléage, *La capitation du Bas-Empire* (1945) 151; *RE* s.v. Tributum (W. Schwahn, 1939) 47, taxes on livestock, trades, etc.

15 Tert., *Apol*. 13.6; Plut., *Caes*. 5.5.; Stat., *Silv*. 3.3.90; Just., *Apol*. 1.17; Hygin. 205, ed. Blume et al., on the *octonarii* (one eighth of the harvest?).

16 E. Fabricius and C. Schuchardt, *Inschr. von Pergamon* (1890) 84, is pre-Roman. For the later Republic, see T. R. S. Brough-ton, *ESAR* 4 (1938) 563 f. Basic was th φόρος, the land tax, several times mentioned, Dio 42.6.3, App., *B.C*. 5.4, and Plut., *Caes*. 48.1; also in the Empire, Philostr., *Vit. soph*. 548, and Hygin. 206, implying assessment *ad modum uber-tatis. Pace* Broughton 565 and P. A. Brunt in A. H. M. Jones, *The Roman Economy* (1974) 182, there seems to be no rea-son to call this a tithe. Its form and yield are unknown, though there is evidence of a fixed annual money tax on land, in the earlier Principate. See P. Hermann and K. Z. Polatkan, *Sitz. ber. Oesterr. Akad. der Wiss*. 265, 1 (1969) 10, 23, and 26.

17 App., *Syr*. 50; Brunt, in Jones 164 f.; Cic., *Att*. 5.16.2.

18 Brunt, in Jones 182, citing Dio Chrys., *Or*. 38.26.

19 Hygin. 205, *arvi primi, arvi secundi, prati, silvae glandiferae, silvae vulgaris, pascuae . . . , per singula iugera;* date, under Trajan, O. A. W. Dilke, *Roman Land Surveyors* (1971) 228. Cf. the prescribed survey formula in *Dig*. 50.15.4 (Ulpian).

20 Hygin. 205.

21 Professor Brunt very kindly refers me to a number of testi-monies to taxes falling on persons: Tac., *Ann*. 12.34; *IG* 12, 5.724 and 946; *IGR* 4.181; and Dio 62.3. Add two further references to ἐπικεφάλαιον in L. Robert, *La Carie* (1954) 2.174 f.

22 *Dig*. 50.15.4.5 and *CIL* 8.23956. *Pace* Brunt (p. 164), neither text relates to the *tributum soli*. For Egypt, see Wallace 111.

23 F. Millar, *The Roman Empire and Its Neighbors* (1967) 90: the tax raised from 5 percent to 10 percent by Caracalla, reduced to 5 percent by Macrinus.

24 Ibid. 91: 5 percent, raised by Caracalla, lowered by Macrinus, and last attested ca. 240.

25 S. J. De Laet, *Portorium* (1949) passim, the most usual rate being 2 to 2½ percent.

26 P. Oxy. 1441, with comment by Wallace 282. It was levied on land, in Egypt.

27 E.g. *Dig.* 33.2.28 (Paulus), *temporaria indictio.*

28 *Dig.* 50.15.5. For *tributum* as the general word, cf. Tac., *Ann.* 13.51, indicating some property tax, *ne censibus negotiatorum naves inscriberentur tributumque pro illis penderent;* Gaius, *Inst.* 2.21, on *stipendium* vs. *tributum;* F. Grelle, *Stipendium vel Tributum* (1963) 16 f.; Schwahn 11 f.

29 *De condicione agr.* 74 (Thulin), quoted in Grelle 45, where disputes arise *propter exigenda tributa de possessione;* Philostr., *Vita Apollon.* 5.36, taxes are in money.

30 Jones 83 offers no support for his statement that the "main tax," i.e. as he sees it, the *tributum soli,* "seems to have produced over 90 per cent of the revenue," nor does De Laet 448, for the opposed view that tolls equaled or surpassed the yield of all tributa; F. Heichelheim (*ESAR* 4.242) is equally vague in assessing the annona militaris as "the most important tax levied in the Roman Empire," in the second half of the third cent.

31 Tax rises: A. C. Johnson, *ESAR* 2.538 and 532; A. Piganiol, *Rev. hist.* 176 (1935) 7, showing the twelve-drachma tax increased two hundredfold in the early 300s; P. J. Parsons, *JRS* 57 (1967) 140, on Philip's program, with P. Oxy. 3046–3050; on the *epibole* and land taxes, Johnson, *Aegyptus* 32 (1952) 69–72.

32 Sperber, *AC* 38 (1969) 165–167, A.D. 220–290s.

33 Amm. 30.8.8; but from Commodus on, stories (no doubt true, but hard to evaluate in firm outline) tell of the senatorial class falling victim to grasping rulers, e.g. Caracalla, Dio 77 (78).9.3.

34 *CJ* 10.16.3 (249), *non personis sed rebus indici solent.*

35 E. Faure, *Varia. Etudes de droit romain* 4 (1961) 4, is among those who date the oration to 312; so also E. Galletier in his edition of the Panegyrists, vol. 2, p. 78—though other scholars suggest 311, ibid. and Déléage 208.

36 Paneg. vet. 8(5).5.4 f., *novi census acerbitas,* dated to 298 by Galletier, 83 n.2, on grounds not conclusive.

37 Paneg. vet. 8(5).6.1, *agrorum modum* balancing *hominum numerum;* so I do not see the need of taking *modum* as a technical term of land evaluation rather than as it is used in *Dig.* 50.15.5 (Papinian), tax payments *pro modo praediorum.*

38 Paneg. vet. 8(5).13.1, 11.1, and 12.3.

39 Demographic implications are inconclusively discussed by Déléage 210 f.; Faure 78–89; and A. Cerati, *Caractère annonaire et assiette de l'impôt foncier au Bas Empire* (1968) 538. See below, n.76.

40 Amm. 16.5.14, A.D. 355, 25 *aurei* per *caput* which he reduced to 7. I accept the usual emendation of *capitula,* cf. S. Mazzarino, *Aspetti sociali del quarto secolo* (1951) 401.

41 Amm. 16.5.15 and 17.3.1 (*tributum*); 17.3.2, the continuation of the *tributum* story, uses *capitatio,* like 17.3.4, where this word underlies *commeatuum necessarii apparatus.*

42 C. Dupont, *La réglementation économique dans les constitutions de Constantin* (1963) 66, on *CT* 11.3.1 (313; 319), 3.1.2 (337), etc.

43 As argued by Faure 95, from specification of vineyards; and specification of *segnitia* of the land implies untilled land as a distinct category, too.

44 E. Erxleben, *Klio* 51 (1969) 314, sees reason to date one of the nine inscriptions to 307/308–311/313; A. H. M. Jones, *JRS* 43 (1953) 49, suggests the late third/early fourth cent., on the basis of circular conjecture. Other scholars (e.g. Cerati 395) settle for the fourth cent. without closer definition.

45 *IG* 12, 3, 180, line 7, where Hiller von Gaertringen takes the kappa to mean 20, but scholars subsequently are agreed on reading "head," e.g., Jones 54 and Déléage 188. Jones reads an entry, "So-and-So, living in his own house (declares) myself, aged 20, total, 1," as showing that one man = one

caput; but by his reasoning we would have likewise to accept one pig = one caput, which is absurd. See J. Keil and A. von Premerstein, *Bericht über eine dritte Reise in Lydien* . . . (1914) 68, col. II, line 18.

46 Cerati 405.

47 Especially by Déléage 164-193 and Cerati 385-409, whose viewpoints are complementary.

48 *FIRA*² 1.511 f.; R. Heberdey, *JOAI* 9 (1906) 188 n.7.

49 Déléage 182.

50 *CT* 11.1.13 (366) and 1.15.10 (379), the annona is equivalent to "the tax"; C. Suamagne, *Karthago* 1 (1950) 130 and 151; Cerati 90 n.2 and 91 n.1.

51 Saumagne 141 f.

52 Separate "head" registering in *CT* 13.5.12 (369), 13.4.4 (374); Déléage 227 and 231; Cerati 371 n.20.

53 A. E. R. Boak to P. Cair. Isidor, p. 25; Déléage 46 f. and 104; Piganiol 7. The latest payment for ἐπικεφάλαιον that I find is P. Oxy. 2579 (313?), other papyri being datable only to the fourth cent. as a whole.

54 Discussion by Dupont 63; Déléage 112 f., whose argument for a date before 377 seems questionable.

55 Some differentiated registration was familiar, e.g. in P. Bouriant 42 (167) and Piganiol 4 on PSI 285 (294); but the new system was much more detailed: Boak, P. Cair. Isidor., p. 26; Déléage 54 and 106 (the elaborate differentiation seems to wither away under Constantine—cf. Cerati 368 f. and Faure 108 n.273).

56 The simplification that did away with usiac, catoecic, and hieratic land was not completed until late under Constantine or Constantius, A. C. Johnson and L. C. West, *Byzantine Egypt. Economic Studies* (1949) 15 f., 19 f., 40, 72 ("probably eliminated under Constantine"), and 94; Johnson, *Aegyptus* 32 (1952) 72; Déléage 63.

57 A. C. Johnson, *Egypt and the Roman Empire* (1951) 112.

58 B. R. Rees et al., on P. Merton 88, p. 135 (for the three groups, compare *CT* 11.12.2 [362], *annona, species ceterae, largitiones*); Cerati 219; Déléage 73-76. The largest item is the *annona civica,* next the *militaris* (ibid. 76), which was

for a time (ca. 287–297) reconstituted as the ἐπιγραφή (Johnson, *Egypt and the Roman Empire* 48, 75, and 111; cf. P. Oxy. 259, etc.). But the annona militaris was (excluding special extraordinary levies) only a part of the general land tax. See P. Heinach 56 (early fourth cent.), Cerati 207, and Déléage 28. Its payments may specify, for instance, εἰς εὐθηνίαν τῶν στρατιωτῶν (P. Cairo Goodspeed 11, P. Oslo 70, P. Lon. 1245, etc.), payable in vinegar, wine, clothing, cash, or whatever, as forming part παντοίων εὐθηνιακῶν εἰδῶν.

59 New survey measures are referred to not only by Aristius Optatus in 297 (P. Cair. Isidor. 1) but in papyri of the early 300s: Déléage 44 f. and Piganiol 4.

60 Dupont 79 f.; Déléage 145; Cerati 417; F. Lot, *Nouvelles recherches sur l'impôt foncier* . . . (1955) 19; and A. E. R. Boak to P. Cair. Isidor., p. 25.

61 The Table of Brigetio of 310 or 311 (*FIRA*² 1.457) and *CT* 7.20.4 (325) have been often discussed: by Dupont 66–81, Déléage 24 f., Cerati 334 f., 357 f., and 495 f. *Pace* Jones 230 and n.8, the laws cover (7.20.4, explicitly) all veterans everywhere.

62 Note also in *CT* 7.20.4 the reference to *peculium* (the army equivalent of *patrimonium,* as rightly pointed out by Déléage 27 and Cerati 358 n.2) and the choice of the word *annona,* the land tax, to mean (as I take it) *capitatio.*

63 E.g. *CT* 11.7.2 (319), 5.17.1 (332), 11.1.14 (336; 372; 374), 11.1.26 (399). It followed naturally that a man paid less on deserted fields than on those where he had tenants. Cf. *CJ* 11.52(51) (393), *sublato . . . humanae capitationis censu, iugatio tantum terrena solvatur; Nov. Theod.* 22.12 (443), the siliqua tax *lucrativis iugationibus tantum, non humaneis vel animalibus censibus . . . iubemus indici.*

64 Lact., *De mort. persecut.* 7.3 (on Diocletian's oppression of coloni) and 23 (Galerius, usually dated to 307).

65 Paneg. vet. 8(5).12.3; *CT* 11.13.1 (383), cf. 10.25.1 (406); and cities and their territories are taxed as totals of people, including capita no longer extant. Cf. Cerati 533 and *CT* 15.1.33.

66 *CT* 11.12.2 (362), *annonarius titulus, verum etiam species ceteraeque atque largitionales.*

67 *CT* 7.20.2 (320) and 16.2.15 (359) must be read carefully. *Pensitatio* in both (the latter text helping to make clear the former) does not mean *capitatio*. By exception, minor tax officials received immunity from capitatio "if they had any property"—implying they had little. As *condicionales* they clearly counted among the humbler classes. *CT* 6.35.2 (319) belongs to the same category of carefully defined, incomplete exemption from all except those taxes falling on lands. See further *CT* 5.13.4 (364; 368), etc.

68 De Laet 461–471.

69 *CT* 13.10.2 (311; 313) extends exemption under Constantine from Oriens to Lycia and Pamphylia; cf. Soz., *H.E.* 5.4.5, cited by M. Forlin Patrucco, *Athenaeum* 51 (1973) 296. Exemption was also granted (from crown gold payments?) to widows' and virgins' *capitatio plebeia, CT* 13.10.4 (368; 370).

70 The lustral tax fell on the *matricula negotiatorum* (*CT* 16.2.15, 359/360), afflicting even a cobbler. See Liban., *Or.* 46.22, cited by A. Chastagnol, *Bonner Historia-Augusta-Colloquium 1964/1965* (1966) 47. Teachers of painting were thus exempted *sui capitis censione, CT* 13.4.4 (374), i.e. "from tax registration for their persons." The same usage of *caput* meets us in *Dig.* 50.4.18.8 (Diocletian), *exactores pecuniae pro capitibus.*

71 *CT* 11.12.1 (340).

72 *CT* 5.13.2 (341), meaning something like "square footage."

73 *CJ* 4.49.9 (293), speaking of the *capitatio* of a *praedium;* below, n.84.

74 Apparently by the 350s, Saumagne 165 on *CT* 13.5.14 (371 —miscited as 13.1.54); 16.2.15 (359), *clerici* exempted from taxes falling on *iuga.*

75 *CT* 11.20.6 (430); for the variety of terminology, cf. the *millena, iulia,* etc., of other provinces, and the *sortes* of *CT* 11.1.15 (369) and perhaps of 11.23.1 (361), recalling *kleroi = iuga* of Julian, *Misop.* 370D.

76 Julian, *Misop.* 370D, offers great Antioch relief on 3,000 *kleroi,* Constantine offers the far smaller Autun relief on 7,000 *capita.* The latter, however, bear the same tax burden as *kleroi = iuga* (e.g. *CT* 7.6.3 [377]). If Julian's benefi-

cence is not to be derisory, the Syrian tax unit must therefore contain more land than the Gallic. Déléage 220 and 231 shows the north Italian unit (*iugum, CT* 11.12.1 [340]) to be perhaps half the size of the African, twice the size of the Syrian of Diocletian's time, and (p. 161) four times the size found in fifth-cent. Cyrrhus. I therefore cannot accept various attempts to find one single physical size for the *iugum* = *caput* (the attempts are surveyed by Faure 95 n.240).

77   *CT* 13.10.2 (311; 313; referring to a measure of Diocletian), 13.1.11 (379), 7.6.3 (377), 6.2.14 (384), 13.11.2 (386), 11.1.29 (401).

78   Cerati 501 n.1; *CT* 13.4.4 (374), cf. Cerati 32 n.1; *CT* 6.3.4 (397). Hence *tributarius* = taxpayer, in *CT* 5.11.9 (364/365); cf. Amm. 31.14.1. Dupont 65 instances *CT* 11.1.2 (313) and 2.30.1 (315), but both texts concern *possessiones* and therefore may be dealing only with a land tax.

79   *CT* 11.1.3 (336), 7.9.4 (416); cf. Lact., *De mort. persecut.* 7.2.

80   Above, n.42; *CT* 7.13.6 (370); Dupont 66 on *CT* 11.3.1 (313; 319)—hence *censualis professio,* Amm. 19.11.3.

81   *CT* 11.16.8 (357); 15.1.18 (374); 10.20.8 (374); 11.16.13 (383); 5.13.4 = *CJ* 11.66.2, dated to 368 by Cerati 546 n.1.

82   *CJ* 11.55.1 (290), *capitatio* and *annona congrua; CT* 12.1.8 (323), comparing 11.30.12 (323); 11.1.13 (366); 1.12.7 (400), distinguishing annona from superindictions; and Lact., *De mort. persecut.* 31.3. Dupont 63 and 66, Déléage 29, and Cerati 77 all see the annona as the main element of taxation.

83   C. Pharr, *The Theodosian Code* (1952) 170 n.19, on *CT* 7.13.6 (370), clinched by reference to 7.20.4 (325) and 8.1.3 (333); 11.12.2 (362); Faure 150 n.338; Déléage 28; Dupont 61; and Cerati 428, 438, 444 (where *capitatio* is seen as the overall imposing of taxation, i.e. very close to my "taxability").

84   *CT* 7.13.7 (375), *capitatio* = *iugatio; tributa* = *annona* in *CT* 11.1.16 (367), by comparison with 11.1.15; *canon* = *annona,* 11.2.4 (384); *capitatio aut canon,* i.e. *capitatio* = *canon,* in 5.13.4, dated to ca. 368 by Cerati 546 n.1.

85   *Tributum* distinct from *canon, CT* 5.14.30 (386); *indictio*

as a mere *augmentum,* Saumagne 134; *census* distinct from *annona, FIRA*² 1.457; *capitatio* includes *annona, CT* 7.4.11 (364); 11.12.2 (362); 11.1.15 (366); *capitatio* distinct from *iugatio, CJ* 11.52 (393); *annona* distinct from money taxes, *Dig.* 50.4.18.8 (Diocletian); *canon* distinct from *annona, CT* 13.5.14 (371, but referring to an enactment of the 350s); *tributa* distinct from *vestium auri argentique debitum,* 11.9.2 (337); and *capitatio* as *caput* in the sense merely of one's head tax, 7.13.6 (370).

86　*Caput* as tax liability on one's person, excluding property, in *CT* 6.35.3 (319 or 352, mentioning slaves); 11.3.2 (327, slaves); 7.20.4 (325); 7.13.6 (370, mentioning *tirones vagi,* surely landless); and W. Goffart, *Caput and Colonate . . .* (1974), chap. 4, though I would not agree with him at all points. On *caput* as rations, see P. Oxy. 43 (295) IV, lines 9 f.; on *annona* as rations, ibid., line 16, and Firm. Matern., *Math.* 3.6.3. On both words together, see Déléage 150.

87　*CT* 11.16.4 (328), 11.1.27 (400); and compare the undefined εὔποροι of P. Oxy. 2104 (early fourth cent.), lines 19 f.

88　Julian, *Or.* 1.34B, *Ep.* 73.428D, Amm. 16.5.14—all in the 350s; Euseb., *Vita Const.* 4.2, and above, n.35; and compare the 50 percent cut in the annona in 367, Them., *Or.* 8.113; *CT* 13.11.2 (386, a reduction of some 50 percent) and 7.4.32 (412), showing certain major tax units increased in their burdens by 50 percent and on up to 90 percent.

89　Cruel exactions: *CT* 11.7.3 (320); 7 (337; 346; 353); Lact., *De mort. persecut.* 23; Zos. 2.38.1; *extraordinaria* are common, e.g. in *CT* 11.1.5 (339), insisting that *this* tax is *not* irregular.

90　Cerati 207; *CT* 10.20.8 (374); 13.5.14 (371).

91　*CJ* 10.62.3, to the governor to Phoenicia in 292/293, similar to the use of *capitularii* to provide men (or mounts?) for cavalry troops, *CT* 6.35.3.2 (319).

92　*CT* 11.16.4 (328).

93　On money as needed by the tax system, see above, nn.40, 58, 70; for Constantine's openness to cash transactions if they were in gold, see e.g. *CT* 12.6.2 (325), taxes on one's *fundi* may be made in *auri pondus.* The recovery from the brink of a natural economy has been often discussed, esp. in studies of the history of adaeratio. See above, p 127.

94 Trans. A. E. R. Boak, P. Cair. Isidor. 1, p. 29, condensed.

95 Faure, *RIDA* 11 (1964) 157–175, favors a Diocletianic date.

96 The word *capitatio* appears in *CJ* 11.55.1 (290) and 4.49.9 (293); and *protostasia* (above, n.91) requires capitatio, as W. Seston points out, *Dioclétien et la Tétrarchie* (1946) 262. He proposes 286 as the date in which capitatio was first applied (p. 281).

CHAPTER 7

1 On herds, see Firm. Matern., *Math.* 3.6.3, and MacMullen, *CQ* 12 (1962) 277.

2 On quarries, see *Dig.* 39.4.13; but *CT* 10.19.1 (320) shows quarries everywhere neglected by free entrepreneurs—though on forced labor in them, see below, n.4. On brickyards, see MacMullen 280 f.; A. Milosevic, *Sirmium* 1 (1971) 97, imperial kilns active under Hadrian in Mursa; of the same date, imperial kilns in Raetia and elsewhere, in G. Spitzlberger, *Saalburg Jb.* 25 (1968) 97. In Rome the kilns were cold by the 270s but revived briefly under Diocletian, H. Bloch, *I bolli laterizi* (1947) 313 f.

3 A. Persson, *Staat u. Manufaktur im röm. Reiche* (1923) 53, on *CIL* 3.536; Euseb., *H.E.* 7.32, dye workers at Tyre under Diocletian; and *CJ* 11.7.2 (317) and *CT* 1.32.1 (333), without specification of place. *Baphia* are many in the *Not. Dig.* later, e.g. *Oc.* 11.65–73.

4 Women condemned to *salinae, Dig.* 49.15.6 (Pomponius) and P. Ryl. 92 (late second or third cent.); but there were also free guilds that bid to exploit salt mines, *Dig.* 3.4.1pr.; on forced labor in mines, see e.g. Stud. Pal. 20.76 (Diocl.), for Egypt; Hippol., *Philos.* (ed. Wendland) 9.12.9, for Sardinia; Euseb., *Mart. Pal.* 11.6, for Cilicia; etc.

5 Condemnation to work on imperial horse farms, in Euseb., *Mart. Pal.* 12; to a Roman *pistrinum,* Hippol., *Philos.* 9.12.4 and *CT* 9.40.3 (314); cf. P. Thead. 36, IV (327), liturgists sent to bakeries in Alexandria; to unspecified "public works,"

Euseb., *Vita Const.* 2.20 and *CJ* 9.47.3 and 5; and work in *Caesarianae possessiones* in Italy, Cypr., Ep. 80.1.

6 Wall-building corvées, P. Leit. 9, at Palmyra; Malal., *Chron.* 12, p. 299 (Dindorf).

7 *Liber pont.* (ed. Duchesne) 1.164, a. 309, condemnation *in catabulum* means "to heavy transport service" (?); P. Thead. 16 (307), with P. Jouguet's comments.

8 Egypt's liturgies to quarries, in F. Oertel, *Die Liturgie* (1917) 83 f., and A. C. Johnson and L. C. West, *Byzantine Egypt: Economic Studies* (1949) 331 n.85, adding P. Rainer 290 = SB 2267 (ca. 300).

9 MacMullen, *Soldier and Civilian* . . . (1963) 33 f.

10 On the δημόσιος ἱματισμός, see BGU 1564 (138), for delivery to Cappadocia; BGU 1572 (139); P. Ryl. 189 (128); P. Oxy. 2230 (after 119), possibly for delivery to troops in Judaea. Compare the leather sent to Vindonissa from Italy or still further away, in A. Gansser-Burckhardt, *Das Leder u. seine Verarbeitung* . . . (1942) 99 and 102–104. On leather collected as a tax, see Tac., *Ann.* 4.72, PSI 465, and BGU 655.

11 Texts are numerous. See e.g. Persson 29 and 32; A. Déléage, *La capitation du Bas-Empire* (1945) 77 and 87; J. Lallemand, *L'administration civile de l'Egypt* . . . (1964) 193 f. and 197 f. Possible early references may be found in P. Oxy. 1414 (270–275), BGU 620 (third cent.), O. Mich. 59 (late third cent.), and P. Michaelidae 21 (285). Thereafter, instances become numerous, see MacMullen, *Aegyptus* 38 (1958) 186. Besides the basic items of taxation, the πάλλιον, χλαμύς and στιχάριον, which were also requisitioned still in the fourth cent., P. Ant. 39 and P. Ross.-Georg., V, 61, there are other items in PSI 886 and P. Ross.-Georg., V, 61, recto frg. B.

12 Tow (raw linen, cf. Diocletian's *Edict* 26.1a; intended for soldiers, ibid. 26.28 f.) is one of the items under the anabolic tax ascribed in Aurelian, SHA *Aurel.* 45. On the date and history of this tax, see MacMullen, *Aegyptus* 38 (1958) 196–198; but new texts correct certain points raised there concerning *adaeratio*. See P. Wis. Sijpesteijn 28 (321), and comment ad loc., pp. 100 f.

13 PSI 779 (third cent.) and P. Wis. Sijpesteijn 28 (321).

14 For payment in fractions of garments, see P. Oxy. 1905, dated between 311 and 365 by Déléage 73; P. Oxy. 1448 (ca. 318); P. Lon. 1259 verso (early fourth cent.); and *CT* 7.6.3 (377).

15 I here slightly alter a suggestion of J. P. Wild, *Latomus* 26 (1967) 655. The στίχη ἰνδικτιονάλια of the *Edict* 19.1–2 certainly shows that clothing items were levied by a tax.

16 P. Oxy. 2230 (after 119); BGU 1572 (139); P. Oxy. 2340 (192); BGU 927 (third cent.); P. Hibeh 219 (309); and P. Ryl. 654 (fourth cent.).

17 For quality control of tax receipts, see P. Ant. 40 (early fourth cent.); P. Lon. 1659 and P. Oxy. 1428, both fourth cent.; and *CT* 8.5.33 (374).

18 Wild 655 suggests that citizens are buying garments to present to the state; alternatively, the price may be set so as to regulate *adaeratio*.

19 *CT* 11.9.1 (323) and 2 (337); 12.6.4 (365); 7.6.3 (377); and above, n. 14.

20 BGU 21 (340), III, lines 4–6 and 17 f.; PSI 781 (341), ἐσθῆτος τιρώνων; *CT* 7.6.5 (423).

21 *CJ* 10.48(47).7, addressed to a vicar of Africa of 338/339, says *negotiantes vestiarii linteones purpurarii et parthicarii, qui devotioni nostrae deserviunt*, are to be exempt from *munera, secundum veterem consuetudinem*; Soz., *H.E.* 5.15 (*PG* 67.1256 f.), mentions evidently free woolen weavers in Cyzicus under Julian, with quotas "according to the decree of earlier emperors." For later texts, see Wild 656. In *CT* 11.1.24 (395), Carthaginian weavers were paid for what they delivered.

22 Lact., *De mort. persecut.* 21.4; Euseb., *H.E.* 7.32.3; *Vita Const.* 2.20 and 34, *Mart. Pal.* 2.20 and 36; Soz., *H.E.* 1.8; *CJ* 11.7.2 (317); *CT* 4.6.3.5 (336); J. P. Waltzing, *Etude historique sur les corporations professionnelles chez les Romains* (1896) 2.233; Persson 71 on the significance of "Jovian" as part of the name of the factory at Spalato; and Wild 651. Later, slaves are attested in weaving factories, e.g. *CT* 10.20.2 (357/358).

23 MacMullen, *AJA* 64 (1960) 29, adding now P. Beatty Panop.

1, lines 213–216 and 341–346 (298), the governor of the Thebaid ordering smiths to be forcibly sought out and sent to him for work in *fabricae*. Other relatively early texts on *fabrica* workers are Athan., *Hist. Arianorum* 18; *CT* 12.1.37 (344); and Amm. 31.6.2. For the factory at Marcianopolis, see now J. and L. Robert, *REG* 79 (1966) 395. On the activity of the army earlier in producing arms, see MacMullen, *Soldier and Civilian* 24–26; on supply of ore and fuel, ibid. 26, and P. Amh. 138 (326), coal levied as a tax.

24 MacMullen, *AJA* 64 (1960) 26; *CIL* 6.8648, *opifices;* H. Gummerus, *Klio* 14 (1915) 174, *corinthiarii; CT* 12.1.37 (344), *argentarii.*

25 *CT* 10.20.1 (317), to the Bithynians, perhaps therefore intended for mints of Nicomedia set up by Diocletian. But Soz., *H.E.* 5.15, mentions a body of minters at Cyzicus.

26 On forcible moving around of labor, see anon., *De rebus bell.* 3.2; Paneg. vet. 4(8).21.2, 5(9).4.2; and above, n.23.

27 On scarcity of artisans, see *CJ* 6.1.5 (319), *liberti artifices* in cities; *CT* 13.4.1 (334) and 2 (337), cf. 3 (344). On "continued legislation," I quote my diss. cit. (chap. 5, n.93, above), p.175, where I also gather material on the lack of apprentice traditions in the later Principate and Dominate (p. 165 nn. 58–60).

28 E. Tengström, *Bread for the People* . . . (1974) is the latest treatment, concentrating on the period after 350, but with great clarity and a good bibliography.

29 Tac., *Ann.* 13.51; Suet., *Claud.* 18 f.

30 Waltzing 2.399–402.

31 *Dig.* 50.6.6(5).12 f. (Callistratus), on which see Waltzing 2.49 f. and F. M. de Robertis, *Storia delle corporazioni* . . . *nel mondo romano* (1971) 2.121.

32 On the point at which *navicularii* status became compulsory, see Stoeckle, *RE* s.v. Navicularii (1935) 1916, offering dates under Alex. Severus and Aurelian, with no adequate evidence; J. Rougé, *Recherches sur l'organisation du commerce maritime* . . . (1966) 254 and 477, leans toward a date under Constantine. But *CT* 8.4.11 says certain officials are exempt from the *functio navicularia* by *privilegia* extended by

Diocletian, and *CT* 13.5.1 (314) takes for granted the status of *navicularius originalis.* Constantine would by then have had only a little more than a year to set up the new system. *CT* 13.5.3 ties property to the status and is dated to 314, with good reason, by L. Cracco Ruggini, *Settimano di Studi del Centro ital. di studi sull'alto Medioevo* 18 (1971) 155 n.189.

33 On the freedom enjoyed by *navicularii,* see some of their number not tied to *annona,* Rougé 240, 262, and 432; on payments for their services, *CT* 13.5.7 (334), Waltzing 3.527, and Rougé 467; on free time for nonstate voyages, Rougé 480.

34 For the *munus* of ship building or supplying, see *Dig.* 49.18.5, *navium fabrica,* quoting Sept. Severus; 50.4.18.29 (Arcad. Charisius); *FIRA²* 2.266 f. (Ulpian); P. Beatty Panop. 2.211–214 (300); for the registered (not literally fixed) number of *navicularii,* see *CT* 13.5.14 (371) and, if one may argue from analogy, P. Oxy. 1029, *Dig.* 27.1.46, and Frg. vat. 233 (Ulpian), *numerus pistorum,* and *FIRA²* 1.445 (205), the *numerus* of *centonarii* whose names then follow on the inscription. For the property of a ship owner seized for debts to the *annona* bureau, see BGU 8 (ca. 250) = *ESAR* 2.423 f. (but the state debtors of any trade might have their estates confiscated).

35 On *pistores'* exemptions, see Frg. vat. 223 and 234 f., and Gaius, *Inst.* 1.34. On strikes, see MacMullen, *Class. Journ.* 58 (1963) 270 f.

36 *FIRA²* 2.267 (Ulpian), a *munus* to a *pistrinum;* P. Beatty Panop. 1, lines 188 f. (298), bakers rounded up for a procurator of Lower Thebaid; *CT* 9.40.3 (319), condemnation to *pistrina,* and 14.3.12, Constantine arranges for *pistores* to be sent every *lustrum* to the capital from Africa.

37 *Centonarii* of Solva, *FIRA²* 1.445 (205); for state-appointed guild accountants, see a few second cent. examples in D. Magie, *Roman Rule in Asia Minor* (1950) 1.598 and 616. But members' estates would be easily known also from local tax rolls.

38 *CT* 14.8.1, on the date of which, see Cracco Ruggini 144

n.174, and C. Dupont, *La réglementation économique dans les constitutions de Constantin* (1963) 120; *CT* 10.20.1 (317), and 14.4.1 (334).

39 Compare such fourth-cent. inscriptions as *CIL* 9.2998 and 14.3649, NN *cum filiis*, etc., and R. Ambrosini, *Bull. comm.* 67 (1939) 92, *fabri* and their *filii*, with trade continuity in Cypr., *Ep.* 67.6.2, *Dig.* 50.6.6(5).4, and MacMullen, *Roman Social Relations* (1974) 97 f.

40 BGU 1087, Arsinoe in 276, cf. U. Wilcken, *Archiv f. Papyrusforschung* 5 (1913) 273; *civitas Figlinas* outside Rome, in L. Duchesne, *Liber pontificalis*² (1955) 197; MacMullen, *Roman Social Relations* 69–71 and appendix A.

41 For much continued free enterprise, see the good pages in Rougé 478 f. and 484; also MacMullen, *JRS* 54 (1964) 51 f.

42 Waltzing 1.55 nn.1 f., and *CIL* 3.6077.

43 Above, chap. 5, n.96; A. Marchi, *Archivio giuridico* 76 (1906) 299, 304, and 317; and T. Mommsen, *Röm. Staatsrecht* 3, 1 (1887) 450 and n.3.

44 *CT* 7.22.3 (331)—but A. H. M. Jones, *Later Roman Empire* 3 (1964) 175, finds this constraint later operating only on *cohortales*.

45 P. Iand. 68, lines 25 f.

46 For the πόρος attached to liturgies, see N. Lewis, *Inventory of Compulsory Services in Ptolemaic and Roman Egypt* (Am. Stud. in Pap. 3, 1968), passim; earlier, perhaps more accessible, examples in M. San Nicolo, *Agyptisches Vereinswesen*² . . . (1972) 2.25. U. Wilcken, *Chrest.*, p. 467, points out that πόρος means income, not value of estate.

47 *RE* s.v. Tabularius (Franke, 1932) 1970, citing *CJ* 7.9.3.1 (290/291).

48 *Dig.* 50.1.30 (Ulpian); D. Sperber, *AC* 38 (1969) 165 n.9, a mid-third cent. text.

49 *Dig.* 49.14.3.6 (Hadrian).

50 E.g. *Dig.* 26.7.32.6; 50.4.18.19 f. and 26, *decaprotia et icosiprotia;* 50.6.6(5).1; *CJ* 10.40.6 (Diocl.) and 11.30.4 (Diocl.).

51 *Dig.* 50.2.1 (Ulpian); *CJ* 10.62.1 (198–211); 10.44(43).1 (Alex. Severus); 7.64.3 (Gordian); 7.66.4 (238); 10.32.3

(285); 4.13.3 (294); A. Büchler, *Political and Social Leaders of . . . Sepphoris* (1909) 40; and P. Garnsey, in *Aufstieg u. Niedergang der röm. Welt* 2, 1 (1974) 233.

52   Expulsion from decurionate as a penalty under the Severi: A. H. M. Jones, *The Greek City* (1940) 343, and *CJ* 2.11.3 (197); subsequently, *CJ* 9.45.2 (Gordian), and note also 10.32.3 (285), the decurionate sought out.

53   W. Langhammer, *Die rechtliche u. soziale Stellung der Magistratus . . .* (1973) 193 f., on *spurii* and *liberti* from ca. 200 on; on illiterate decurions, see *CJ* 10.32.6 (293); on holdings of less than 25 *iugera*, *CT* 12.1.33 (342); on the decurionate as beneath dishonor, *CJ* 10.59(57) .(Diocl.) and 9.22.21 (316).

54   On minors as decurions, see e.g. *CJ* 4.13.3 (294); 4.26.1 (196); 10.39.3 (Philip); 10.62.1 (198–211); Garnsey 230; and Langhammer 229. N. Lewis, in his comment to P. Leit. 8, p. 21, gathers many reff. to papyri. On the decurionate by birth, see O. Seeck, *Gesch. des Untergangs der antiken Welt* (1901) 2.317, and R. Ganghoffer, *L'évolution des institutions municipales . . . au Bas-Empire* (1963) 56 and 61, on *CT* 12.1.5 (317) and 12 (325). The notion of *origo* (but not enforced) of course goes far back in law, e.g. *CJ* 10.39(38).1 (Caracalla—double obligations to two cities, cf. *Dig.* 50.1.29, Gaius, and *CJ* 8.47.7, Diocletian). But when Diocletian, *CJ* 10.39(38).4, declares no one can change his *origo,* the word has implications that give his statement the effect of conscription to service.

55   On spontaneous heritability of decurion status, note the term πατρόβουλοι, from 250 on, *IG* 12, 5, 141, and I. Levy, *Rev. de philol.* 26 (1902) 272 f. and 276 f.; more generally, MacMullen, *Roman Social Relations* 101; and on the *munus* of census taking, above, chap. 3, n.62.

56   For the decemprimate in Egypt, see Oertel 211 f.; E. G. Turner, *JEA* 22 (1936) 14 (from which I quote the apt phrase "finance committee," as does Jones, *Greek City* 139) and 8–19 passim. Jones 327 notes the disappearance of *decaproti* in the early fourth cent. and finds "no mention [of them] in the Codes," p. 333. But *decemprimi* continue in the

codes, e.g. *CT* 9.35.2 (376); cf. Langhammer 254, who rightly takes them as the Latin equivalent of *decaproti,* as likewise of *principales,* common in the Codes, e.g. *CT* 11.16.4 (328) and many later texts, and Firm. Matern., *Math.* 3.10.9, *civitatum principes aut decemprimi.* On the Top Ten generally, see Turner 12–15; F. Grelle, *Stipendium vel Tributum* . . . (1963) 56–62; and G. Liberati, *Bull. Ist. diritto romano* 71 (1968) 121 f., showing the institution becoming a *munus mixtum* in the 230s; but (p. 261) only *patrimonii* in *CJ* 10.42(41).8 (Diocl.). Jones, *JRS* 21 (1931) 271–273, shows similar committees appearing in certain eastern villages from mid-third cent.

57 M. Nuyens, *RIDA* 5 (1958) 521–533; Grelle 60–64, 82, and 84–102; and M. Mazza, *Lotte sociali e restaurazione autoritaria nel 3. secolo* (1970) 500–503.

58 Langhammer 251 and 263; D. van Berchem, *L'armée de Dioclétien* . . . 76; and above, chap. 6, n.67.

59 Forcible recall of decurions, *Dig.* 50.1.15.2 (Papinian), 50.2.1 (Ulpian), 50.5.7 (Papinian); and so into harsher times, e.g. *CT* 12.1.13 (326).

60 On *cessio bonorum,* see A. K. Bowman, *Town Councils of Roman Egypt* (1971) 112, from Alex. Severus on; *CJ* 10.67(65).1 (Cara.); 7.71.1 (223) to 5 (Diocl.); on nomination, Jones, *Greek City* 186–188, and Langhammer 41, 215, and 232 f.

61 P. Oxy. 2407, trans. J. W. B. Barns; for date and place, see N. Lewis, *Archiv f. Papyrusforschung* 21 (1971) 83 n.2.

62 On the tax *primipili,* see *CJ* 7.73.1; 12.62(63).4; 8.14(15).4; and 4.31.11 and 4.9.1. See also above, chap. 5, n.10. On the phrase *obnoxius necessitati,* see e.g. *CJ* 8.14.4 (283), *CT* 8.4.7 (361), etc.

63 Above, chap. 6, nn.90–92.

64 Exemption from *munera personalia* (rarely, *patrimonii*) as a part of the wage packet of civil servants and soldiers is a well-known feature of the Dominate. See e.g. *CJ* 10.48.2 (Diocl.) and 12.28.1 (314).

65 On peasants' threats to flee, see N. Lewis, *Greek Papyri in the Collection of New York University, I* . . . (1967) 3, no.

19 (316–320); idem, *RIDA* 15 (1968) 141; P. Oxy. 705 (202); P. Wis. Sijpesteijn 32 (305); *SIG*³ 888, lines 29 f.; *CIL* 8.14428; and D. Sperber, *RIDA* 19 (1972) 41 f. n.30. On *anachoresis* as endemic across the centuries of Roman rule in Egypt, see U. Wilcken, *Grundzüge u. Chrestomathie der Papyruskunde* 1 (1912) 325, and Lewis, *JEA* 23 (1937) 67. On recognition that land must never be left idle, see e.g. Dio Chrys., *Or.* 7.108; Dio 52.28.3 f.; *IGLS* 1998 (Domitian); *Dig.* 50.11.2 (Callistratus); *CT* 11.16.4 (328); and on legislation to secure this, see *CJ* 11.55(54).1 (Diocl.), protecting the *rustica plebs* from transport corvées; 4.61.5 (321), exempting farm tools from tolls; and below, n.87.

66 Suet., *Domit.* 7.2, giving the reason as shortage of grain; Philostr., *Vit. soph.* 520, with a different explantion; SHA *Prob.* 18.8; Eutrop., *Brev.* 9.17.2; *Chron. pasch.* 217.2 (*PG* 92.602); L. C. West, *Imperial Roman Spain . . .* (1929) 18, on *CIL* 2.2029; J. Schwartz, *Chron. d'Egypte* 37 (1962) 357 f., and H. Maehler (1968) in commentary to BGU 2060, on Hadrian's measures against viticulture in Egypt; and SHA *Aurel.* 48.2, on measures to plant vacant Italian land with vines. Cf. two somewhat doubtful controls of stock slaughtering: SHA *Alex. Sev.* 22.7 f., and I. Opelt, *Historia* 20 (1971) 764 f.

67 Government drainage projects: *AE* 1934, 40, under Commodus in Africa; in Pannonia, above, chap. 5, n.71.

68 P. Giess. 4–7 (117); W. L. Westermann, *JEA* 11 (1925) 173 f.

69 L. Leschi, *BCTH* 1944, 326–331; G. C. Picard, *Castellum Dimmidi* (1947) 112; P.-A. Février, *Cah. arch.* 14 (1964) 38 f.; idem, *Cah. de Tunisie* 15 (1967) 60–63; Mazza 223; and W. Held, *Klio* 53 (1971) 253.

70 See reff. gathered in MacMullen, *AC* 32 (1963) 554; for specific reff. to farming done by barbarian settlers, see Paneg. vet. 4(8).9.3, 7(6).6.2; Amm. 28.5.15; Them., *Or.* 16.257 f. (Dindorf); and Paneg. vet. 12(2).22.3.

71 On *epibole,* among many texts, note P. Oxy. 899 (200), referring to decisions by emperors back as far as Galba; A. C. Johnson, *Aegyptus* 32 (1952) 62–67; and A. H. M. Jones,

JRS 43 (1953) 59, assessing *epibole* as "a quite common procedure [but] on a small scale." On a similar device, see S. L. Wallace, *Taxation in Egypt* (1938) 21, and H. Poethke, *Epimerismos* (1969), passim. On a tax measure of 297 and later, designed to encourage the category of "seed land," see N. Lewis, *JEA* 29 (1943) 73.

72 On Africa, see *FIRA*² 1.491–497; R. His, *Die Domänen der röm. Kaiserzeit* (1896) 14 f.; M. Rostowzew, *Studien zur Gesch. des röm. Kolonates* (1910) 336 and 352; Février, *Cah. arch.* 14 (1964) 38–40; Mazza 223; Dupont 37; and N. Brockmeyer, *Arbeitsorganisation . . . des röm. Reiches* (1968) 412 f. Note how the first-cent. Lex Manciana covered reclamation of *subseciva* and *incultum, CIL* 8.25902, I 8 f., III 3 f., and IV 10. On the Thisbe inscription, see *SIG*³ 884 = H. Pleket, *Texts on the Economic History of the Greek World* (1964) 71 f.; Mazza 222; and Brockmeyer 234. Despite Rostowzew 304 and 311, there is no good evidence of serfdom on imperial estates in Asia Minor, which is also rendered unlikely by "the urbanization of the agricultural domains" in the period 200–450. See J. Strubbe, *Ancient Society* 6 (1975) 249. On Pertinax' law, see Herod. 2.4.6, including βασιλέως κτῆμα for reclamation; but C. R. Whittaker has pointed out in a lecture (1974) that Italian land was tax exempt in any case and that Herodian must be confused about a measure meant only to apply to crown lands. For other views, see Mazza 223.

73 *CJ* 11.59(58).1, *civitatum ordines pro desertis possessionibus iusserit* [Aurelian] *conveniri, et pro his fundis, qui invenire dominos non potuerunt quos praeceperamus* [We, Constantine], *earundem possessionum triennii immunitate percepta, de sollemnibus satisfacere;* but, failing decurions able to do this, the whole territory of the city shall corporately bear the load; and *Dig.* 50.4.18.27 (Arcadius Charisius), *qui annonam exigentes* [as a *munus*] *desertorum praediorum damna sustineant.*

74 On corporate responsibility to farm, see e.g. P. Teb. 288 (226); P. Gen. 42 (224); Oertel 97; Wilcken, *Grundzüge* 1.292 f.; San Nicolo² 1.165; and Wallace 21.

75   A. Segrè, *Traditio* 5 (1947) 103; A. C. Johnson and L. C. West, *Byzantine Egypt: Economic Studies* (1949) 34 f.; and above, chap. 6, n.56.

76   It is plausibly argued that, where imperial *coloni* are subject to municipal *munera,* it must be as holders of tracts of their own land. For men in such dual roles, see *Dig.* 50.6.6(5).11 (Callistratus); 50.1.38.1 (Papirius Justus, referring to a decision of Marcus Aurelius); *CJ* 5.62.8 (225); 11.68(67).1 (325); *Nov. Theod.* 5.1.1; *CT* 11.1.4 (337); 12.1.33 (342); *CJ* 11.75(74).1 (343); *CT* 5.19.1 (365); etc.; and the conclusion drawn by Dupont 32 f. For the explicit duality of the role being legal and possible, see *CJ* 5.62.8 (225), unless a gloss, *coloni, id est conductores, praediorum ad fiscum pertinentium* . . . , just like 4.65.27 (294), where *coloni* are *conductores* of a private *praedium.* The device of *adiectio* in general, and a great deal of evidence from Egypt in particular, provide still further illustration of a common practice.

77   *Dig.* 49.14.3.6 (Hadrian), *conductores vectigalium publicorum et agrorum* must not be forced to renew contracts, despite the common *mos;* cf. *CJ* 4.65.11 (244), *invitos conductores* (of private lands) *tempora locationis impleta non esse retinendos,* and *Dig.* 19.2.14 (Ulpian), *coloni*'s contracts on private land renew themselves by tacit consent, *nudo consensu convalescunt.*

78   *Dig.* 19.2.24.2 (Paul), a *dominus* can sue a *colonus* who leaves before the end of the lease; 19.2.13.11 (Ulpian) and 20.1.21 (Ulpian), *coloni* deposit a *pignus,* e.g. a slave, for fulfilling the term of their *conductio;* P. Gen. 42 (224), cited by Lewis, *JEA* 23 (1937) 73, δημόσιοι γεωργοί do the same.

79   On *reliqua colonorum,* see e.g. *Dig.* 33.7.20.3, 33.7.27.1–2; on the *fiscus* or *tributa* as first creditor on any estate, *Dig.* 49.14.46.3 (Ulpian); *CJ* 4.46.1 (Cara.); and 7.73.3 (213).

80   BGU 7, the strategos' orders regarding γεωργοί of a certain πεδίον who are sought by the village *decaproti.*

81   *CT* 10.8.1 (313), 11.3.2 (327); and on both texts, Dupont 20 and 29.

82   Instances in *Dig.* 33.7.12.3 (Ulpian), a slave *qui quasi colonus in agro erat; CJ* 4.10.11 (294); Held 249; and Brockmeyer,

Historia 20 (1971) 739. On p. 737, Brockmeyer accepts Paul, *Sent.* 3.6.48, as genuine, where the colonus counts explicitly in the *instrumentum fundi* and might be sold or bequeathed with it. The text is accepted by Held 249 also but convincingly rejected by Seeck, *Gesch.* 1.579, as interpolated.

83 *Dig.* 26.7.32.6 (Modestinus), *ipsi domini praediorum, non conductores, onera annonarum et contributionum temporariarum sustinere; CT* 11.7.2 (319); *IG* 12, 3, 343 and 12, 2, 79; and above, chap. 6 passim, e.g. n.63. *CJ* 8.51(52).1, already in 224 mentioning an *adscripticia tua,* is "certainly interpolated," say de Dominicis, *Scritti Romanistici* (1970) 12, and Seeck 1.579. As for landlords later continuing to pay taxes on their *coloni,* see *CT* 11.1.7 (361) and 14 (366; 377). But it is only *capitatio* and only the landless that are meant. See *CJ* 11.53(52).1 (371) and 11.52(51).1 (393), where capitatio (= *tributarius nexus* or *tributaria sors*) is distinguished from *iugatio,* the latter paid by and for each landowner himself.

84 *Dig.* 50.15.4.8, *si quis inquilinum *vel colonum** (interpolated, says Seeck 1.579; cf. also Levy-Ravel, *Index interpolationum*) *non fuerit professus, vinculis censualibus tenetur.*

85 *Dig.* 30.112, *praediis quibus adhaerent.* The text has many commentators, e.g. recently M. Jacota, *Etudes offerts à J. Maqueron* (1970) 380 f. In *Dig.* 43.32.1 (Ulpian), a lodger, *inquilinus,* must not leave a house he rents before the term is up—suggesting possible restraints on the rural equivalent. Elsewhere, inquilini appear rather rarely and obscurely but very similar to *coloni.* They are *sui iuris* like coloni, Gaius, *Inst.* 4.153; *possessio* may be asserted through but not by *coloni et inquilini aut servi, Dig.* 41.2.25.1, cf. 43.26.6.2; they may even be called *coloni inquilini* (not resident but day laborers from the next village?—*FIRA*² 1.489), barely distinct in rights from coloni, cf. e.g. C. Saumagne, *Byzantion* 12 (1937) 490; Brockmeyer, *Arbeitsorganisation* 216; and the next two notes.

86 *IGR* 4.598 (Philip), πάροικοι καὶ γεωργοί in Arague; *IG* 12, 3, 343, line 18, πάροικοι taken as *coloni* by Déléage, *La capitation du Bas-Empire* (1945) 175 f., and Jones, *JRS* 43

(1953) 53; *IG* 12, 2, 79b, line 5, γεωργός taken as *colonus* by *Déléage* 179 and Jones, loc. cit. *Dig.* 50.16.239.2 (Pomponius, toward the mid-second cent.), *incola = πάροικος*, to which one might add that *incola* and *inquilinus* have the same meaning in Latin generally.

87   *CJ* 3.38.11 and *CT* 2.25.1, to the *rationalis* of Corsica, Sicily, and Sardinia. As to the lumping together of these labor categories, compare *CJ* 11.48(47).6 (366), 11.53(52) (371), 11.48(47).13 (400), where Saumagne 502 would unconvincingly see a difference between *inquilini* and *coloni*. Brockmeyer is more persuasive, *Arbeitsorganisation* 285, speaking of "the obliteration of boundaries, from the third century on, between the various groups of dependent rural labor (slave, day laborers, *adscripticii, inquilini, coloni,* immigrants, etc.)."

88   *CJ* 11.68(67).2, with many commentators, e.g. Dupont 34.

89   G. Pugliese, *Studi in onore di P. de Francisci* (1956) 3.381–386; Dupont 40–42, 48 nn.47 f., and 50; and such texts as *CT* 15.3.1 (319), 11.19.1 (321), 11.1.4 (337), and *CJ* 11.63.1 (319).

90   Above, chap. 4, n.48.

91   N. D. Fustel de Coulanges, *Recherches sur quelques problèmes d'histoire* (1885) 75–86, and so in various authors up to Jones, *Later Roman Empire* 796. Fustel argued only from likelihood, while Jones 1326 f. can cite papyri that show only the continuation of much earlier measures to seat people in their ἰδία or *origo* (P. Thead. 16 f. and P. Cair. Isidor. 126 and 128, on which see the editors ad loc., p. 396). In Egypt, as Jones acknowledges also (*The Roman Economy* [1974] 298 f.), short-term leases continued in the 300s, and registration through one's village, not one's landlord. For the dating of the colonate to Diocletian there seems thus to be no hard evidence.

92   Above, n.76.

93   See e.g. L. Harmand, *Libanius. Discours sur les patronages* (1955) 130 f., quoting F. de Zulueta, *De patrociniis vicorum* (Oxford Studies in Social and Legal History I, 1909) 14 f.; *CT* 5.19.1 (365).

94   Palestine, in Harmand, *Libanius. Discours* 129 and 136, and

de Zulueta 16; Illyricum and Thrace, ibid.; cf. E. Faure, *Etudes de droit romain* 4 (1961) 128 f. n.306.

95 On heritability among decurions and soldiers, see above, nn.54 f., and *CT* 7.22.1 f. (313–); for *coloni*, *CJ* 11.68.3 (366?). On *CT* 5.17.1, W. Goffart, *Caput and Colonate* . . . (1974) 74f., has argued most recently that the *colonus* was tied only to his city or village, not to his master's lands, i.e. *origo* in the text was not one's tenancy and coloni were therefore not yet tied to a master and his estate. However, origo did mean "registration for taxation," and landlords did pay taxes incurred through having registered but landless tenants (above, n.83); so Goffart seems to be in error here. Further, he believes (p. 81) that tenants after 332 retained the right to move away at the end of a contract. They would be "bound" only in the sense of a *lustrum*. While this cannot be disproved, still, the often-discussed pressures on *coloni* to renew leases would operate to tie them down for life; and it is hard to imagine more restraint showed to the freedom of peasants than to soldiers and decurions. The ultimate change shows in a bound condition defined by birth, not contract—as was true by 371.

96 *CJ* 4.65.8 (231), rentals according to *mos regionis; Dig.* 26.7.32.6 (Modestinus), tax responsibility according to *consuetudo; CIL* 8.25902, II, lines 18 f.; BGU 2063 (second cent.), details of a lease should be decided ἐξ ἔθους; *CJ* 11.63(62).1 (319), tenants' rights are ruled by *solemnitas;* 11.50.1 (325); 11.48.5 (366), *consuetudo praedii.* Cf. common-law title to land established by occupancy for 10 years, *CT* 4.11.1; for 20 years, *CT* 5.15.15; or for 40 years, *CT* 4.11.2 and C. J. Kraemer and N. Lewis, *TAPA* 68 (1937) 358 f.

CHAPTER 8

1 On idealization of the peasant, see MacMullen, *Roman Social Relations* (1974) 29 f.; on peasants making the best soldiers, see Max. Tyr., *Diss. XXIV (XXX)*, and Veget., *De re milit.* 1.3.

2 The *ius liberorum* was for citizens only, G. Stühff, *Vulgar-*

recht im Kaiserrecht . . . (1966) 47. It gave exemption from
munera personalia, Dig. 50.2.6.5 (Papinian); 50.4.3.6 and 12
(Ulpian); *CJ* 10.32.9 (294); 10.52(51).3.1 (Philip), 5 (Diocl.),
and 6 (Const.); 10.69(67).1 (Gordian); P. Oxy. 1467 (263);
and *RE* s.v. Ius liberorum (Steinwenter, 1919) 1283; on
fraudulent attempts to claim such exemptions, see *CT*
12.17.1 (324); exemption from the decurionate, 12.1.55
(363). On Augustus' laws, see the antecedent thought in
Cic., *Leg.* 3.3.7, against *caelibes;* and Dio 54.16.1; 56.2–9;
Aul. Gell. 2.15.3; and Suet., *Aug.* 34.1; for an edict of
Marcus Aurelius urging procreation, see Fronto, *De orat.* 12
(Naber, p. 161).

3   On dowries, see *Dig.* 23.3.2 (Paul) and 42.5.18 (Paul); 47.11.4
(Marcian), Severus' law against abortion; and K. Hopkins,
Comp. Studies in Society and Hist. 8 (1965) 126 and 141.

4   *ESAR* 2.252, cf. *Dig.* 34.1.14.1, on Hadrian's alimentary law.
On the *alimenta* there is much written, e.g. P. Veyne, in *Les
empereurs romains d'Espagne* (1965) 164 and 169; P. Garnsey, *Historia* 17 (1968) 367; cf. V. A. Sirago, *L'Italia agraria
sotto Traiano* (1958) 15, on depopulation in Italy in the first
cent., leading to the state alimenta; on the latter's last signs,
see W. Langhammer, *Die rechtliche u. soziale Stellung
der Magistratus municipales* . . . (1973) 187—but cf. *CT*
11.27.1 (315; 329) to 2 (322), a state dole for parents too
poor to feed children.

5   Plin., *N.H.* 7.36.122, *Ep.* 4.15, cf. 7.32; and Epict., *Diss.*
3.7.26.

6   Plin., *Paneg.* 28.4 f., *subsidium bellorum;* Dio 79.22.5 (Bois-
sevain 3.428 with notes); the same reasoning in App., *B.C.*
1.1.9 and 11, and 1.4.27; in Dio 56.2.1 and 7; 56.4.2 and 4;
56.5.3; and in Paneg. vet. 6(7).2.4.

7   Paneg. vet. 4(8).9.4 (297); 7(6).6.2, to Const.; Amm. 19.11.7
(359); 31.4.4 (376); and Paneg. vet. 12(2).22.3—all these referring explicitly to *dilectus, tirocinia, vel sim.* On the phenomenon of barbarian settlements of increasing significance
in the later Empire, see above, chap. 7, n.70. For some antici-
pation, see Ps.-Sall., *Ep. II ad Caes.* (ed. E. Ernout, p. 12,

proposing a second-cent. date), recommending that Caesar make use of barbarians.

8   On the plague, see J. Fitz, *Ingenuus et Régalien* (1966) 25 f.; for its possible effects, see R. J. and M. L. Littmann, *AJP* 94 (1973) 243 f., esp. 255, arguing for a death toll of 7–10 millions in the plague of ca. 165–189.

9   Above, n. 7.

10 *Dig.* 27.1.6.8 shows Ant. Pius agreeing to a grant of immunity from conscription made by Hadrian; but 49.16.4.10 (Arrius Menander) shows volunteers generally adequate in ca. 200; for rare conscription needed, see *DE* s.v. Dilectus (1910) 1785, adding *CIL* 13.6763 (242); Tac., *Ann.* 14.18.1; Fronto, Ep. 4.12.2 (ca. 162); F. Grelle, *Labeo* 10 (1964) 9; and the undated (I think, third cent.) municipal recruiter in Thrace, J. and L. Robert, *REG* 73 (1960) 171.

11 *Dig.* 50.4.18.3 (Arcadius Charisius), a *munus personae*. Cf. *CT* 6.35.3.5(2) (319 or 352). The obligation may nevertheless be the *protostasia,* a *munus patrimonii* in *CJ* 10.62(60).3 (292/293) and 10.42(41).8 (Diocl.); cf. above, chap. 6, n.91. Grelle 14 says "it is difficult to determine how the burden was apportioned" in Diocletian's day, but from 335 (*CT* 11.16.6) it was levied according to *capita/iuga*. G. Gigli advanced a somewhat different reconstruction earlier, *Rend. Accad. naz. dei Lincei* 2 (1947) 274 f., and before him, E. Sander, *Hermes* 75 (1940) 192–194. How this developing system is related to "recruit money" is not clear: see M. I. Rostovtzeff, *JRS* 8 (1918) 27, a third-cent. inscription which W. Kubitschek calls without explanation "Severan," *RE* s.v. Temonarius (1934) 465; P. Oxy. 1905 (for date, A. Déléage, *La capitation du Bas-Empire* [1945] 73); P. Ant. 33 (346?); O. Tait 2064 and 2066 (fourth cent.); and A. E. R. Boak and H. C. Youtie, *Archive of Aurelius Isidorus* (1960) 273 f.

12 On "army families," see MacMullen, *Soldier and Civilian* . . . (1963) 100–103, and G. Forni, in *Aufstieg u. Niedergang der röm. Welt* 2, 1 (1974) 389 f., esp. on birth and enlistment *castris;* on laws, see H. Nesselhauf, *Historia* 8

(1959) 439 f., dealing with sons of auxiliaries in A.D. 140 ff. The view that heritability of enlistment existed under Sept. Severus can be traced back from Gigli to E. Stein to Rostovtzeff, and so to two texts—the SHA and *OGIS* 511—that cannot be used to prove the case at all.

13 *CT* 7.22.1, where it is clear that the obligation is not a new one; 7.20.2.7(2) (320); 12.1.10 (325); 7.22.2 (326); etc. For enforcement, see Sulp. Sev., *Vita S. Martini* 2.5, conscription ca. 331, but with historical errors in the next few lines that show it to be a poor source; and Greg. Naz., *Ep.* 225. The *Vita S. Pachomii* shows conscription in the 320s by Constantine's bare order, no system implied.

14 J. Szilagyi, *Acta ant.* 2 (1954) 194 n.444, offers an estimate of 400,000 under Aurelian, after an actual diminution in the decades earlier. In the early fifth cent. (pp. 195 and 203) he would estimate the army at about 500,000. A. H. M. Jones, *Later Roman Empire* (1964) 60, imagines a doubling of Severus' army by some point under Diocletian (therefore, to ca. 600,000), though R. Grosse, *Röm. Militärgesch. von Gallienus* . . . (1920) 253, and D. Hoffmann, *Das spätröm. Bewegungsheer* . . . (1969) 1.2, would suggest a figure around 400,000. A. Segrè, *Byzantion* 16 (1942–1943) 431–433, would accept this latter and, with Grosse, conjectures 500,000 under Constantine. All these conjectures seem to me idle. Hoffman 1.187 and 199, and 2.76, is himself rightly suspicious of the figures in Zosimus, on which modern calculations are largely based, and Lydus is much too late to be trusted. On the other hand, the testimony to some army increase of unknown amount under Diocletian is better; see Hoffmann 1.188 and 216, Grosse 58, and D. van Berchem, *L'armée de Dioclétien* . . . (1952) 115.

15 Hoffmann 2.76.

16 E. Birley, *Epigraphische Studien* 8 (1969) 65–67.

17 R. Saxer, *Untersuchungen zu den Vexillationen des röm. Kaiserheeres* . . . (1967) 118–120, on Marcus' use of detachments; 121 f., on early third-cent. use; *DE* s.v. Cuneus 1319, *cunei Frisiorum* under Alex. Severus, Philip, etc.; M. Amit, *La parola del passato* 20 (1965) 219 f., on marches of

232–234; and S. Mazzarino, *Trattato di storia romana* (1956) 2.334 f. and, p. 405, the "Goths and German tribes" brought by Gordian against Shapur.

18 On *protectores,* see A. Schenk von Stauffenberg, *Das Imperium u. die Völkerwanderung* [1948] 17 and 214 n.24, and 217 n.29, emending Cedrenus' statement. Stauffenberg also postulates German ideas behind the *protectores;* but there were precedent Germans in Caracalla's palace—leading Grosse 14 to conjecture that protectores began then. Still, the first epigraphic evidence is indeed Gallienic (ibid.). Grosse 16 accepts Cedrenus. On commanders like Aureolus, see ibid., 18, Mazzarino 360, Hoffmann 1.248, and A. Alföldi, *Zeitschr. für Numismatik* 37 (1927) 199; ibid., 211, on coins. Fitz 67 dates the first actions of the cavalry army to 258 and cites Milan as its headquarters (cf. also Hoffmann 1.247), the cavalry along with the vexillations accounting for the transfer there of the mint in 258 or 259 (Fitz 69 f.). For Gallienus' *stablesiani* recruited from governors' *stratores,* see M. L. Speidel, *Chiron* 4 (1974) 541–546.

19 A. Alföldi, *Studien zur Gesch. der Weltkrise des 3. Jahrhunderts* (1967) 6 f., 14, 370, and 408; and Hoffmann 1.247.

20 Alföldi, *Studien* 14; on the significance of the unit title *Illyriciani* and of the Illyrian provinces in the fourth-cent. army, see Grosse 19; T. Mommsen, *Gesammelte Schriften* (1910) 6.238; van Berchem 81; and Hoffmann 1.149 and 255.

21 Arguing for Diocletian's role as founder of the *comitatus* (with Constantine as expander on the idea) are Mommsen 209 and 235–238; Grosse 32 f., 45, and 57–59; W. Seston, *Historia* 4 (1955) 284 and 294; idem, *Relazioni del X Congr. int. di scienze storiche* 2 (1955) 431–433; J. Moreau, *Scripta minora* (1964) 43–49; giving sole credit to Constantine is van Berchem 99 f., 108, and passim, carefully argued but vulnerable. Most recently, Hoffmann 1.2 f., 132 f., 170, 181, 186–188, 200, 224, 227, 245, 261, and passim persuasively portrays Constantine as real establisher of a fully and firmly organized *comitatenses.* In particular, some of the points from the opposing view can be met with his discussion on pp. 231 f. For his estimate of the size of the mobile army,

excluding Africa, in mid-fourth cent., at 110-120,000, see p. 304. My very brief remarks in the text draw principally on the cited pages in Hoffmann.

22 On *clibanarii,* see Hoffmann 1.266 f. and 270-275; O. Gamber, *Jb. kunsthist. Sammlungen in Wien* 64 (1968) 12-23; J. Eadie, *JRS* 57 (1967) 169-172; MacMullen, *Art Bull.* 46 (1964) 439 f. These troops improved on the third-cent. *cataphractarii.* They are first attested in use by Constantine in 312.

23 Hoffmann 1.182 f.; E. W. Marsden, *Greek and Roman Artillery* (1969) 192 and 195-198.

24 Aside from Hadrian, who put his mind to war as to everything else and to whom Apollodorus addressed a treatise on the subject—see SHA *Had.* 10.7 and E. Sander, *Hist. Zeitschr.* 149 (1934) 457-460—the series begins with the Severi: note Arrius Menander's *De re milit.,* perhaps not only on military law, cf. J. Crook, *Consilium Principis* (1955) 139 n.3; and Sextus Iulius Africanus' *Taktikos, RE* s.v. Sext. Iul. Africanus (Kroll, 1917) 116 f., and J.-R. Vieillefond, *Les "Cestes" de Julius Africanus* . . . (1970) 62, 149 f., 152-159, and 171. In the fourth cent., besides the anon. *De rebus bell.* and Vegetius, note, on Julian, Lydus, *De mag.* 1.47, and on Valentinian, Amm. 30.9.4 and *Epit. de Caes.* 45.6, texts showing interests in military inventions.

25 Van Berchem 51 f. and 55, and *DE* s.v. Limes (G. Forni, 1959-1962) 1163; ibid., 1216, H.-J. Kellner, *Germania* 31 (1953) 176 f., and H. von Petrikovits, *JRS* 61 (1971) 178; D. Tudor, *Historia* 14 (1965) 380; B. H. Warmington, *The North African Provinces from Diocletian* . . . (1954) 21, 30, and 70 f.; M. Rachet, *Rome et les Berbères* (1970) 258; but cf. J. Boube, *Bull. d'arch. marocaine* 4 (1960) 379.

26 G. Gomolka, *Klio* 50 (1968) 173 f., 208, 210, 225, 232, and 244, Iatrus in Moesia in Tetrarchic and fourth-cent. layers; Petrikovits 195; and MacMullen, *Soldier and Civilian* 126-128.

27 MacMullen, *Soldier and Civilian* 147; R. Fellmann, *Historia* 4 (1955) 209 f.; van Berchem 27.

28 E.g. Toulouse, above, chap. 5, n.69; A. Blanchet, *Buletinul Societatii numismatice Romane* 18 (1923) 3-7, fortifications

in the Balkans from Marcus up to Gordian; *CIL* 2.4202
(second cent.?), in Tarraco; Nicaea, in A. M. Schneider and
W. Karnapp, *Die Stadtmauer von Iznik* (1938) 42. Note,
too, Marcus Aurelius' directive that cities must gain imperial
permission to put up walls, *Dig.* 50.10.6.

29   *CIL* 5.3329; 11.6308–9; on soldiers' help, see *CIL* 3.8031;
13.5203; H.-G. Pflaum, *Syria* 21 (1952) 307 and 321; Mac-
Mullen, *Soldier and Civilian* 36 f.; on mixed state and local
financing, see *CIL* 8.22766, an African *castellum;* on pillaged
stones and whole structures incorporated into walls, see H. I.
Bell et al., *The Abinnaeus Archive* . . . (1962) 16 and 21,
describing a fortress-granary in Egypt, and western castles
like Deutz, Neumagen, and Kreuznach, in E. Anthes, *BRGK*
10 (1917) 104, 106, and 115, and C. Jullian, *Hist. de la Gaule
romaine* (1926) 7.114. For pillage etc. in city walls, see A.
Blanchet, *Les enceintes romaines de la Gaule* (1907) 278 f.
and 314; Petrikovits 199; Schneider and Karnapp 36; P.
Marconi, *Verona Romana* (1937) 20 f.; MacMullen, *Soldier
and Civilian* 129; and above, chap. 5, n.4.

30   Zos. 2.31; *Philostorgius Kirchengeschichte,* ed. J. Bidez,
p. 73; Amm. 14.11.13, in Thrace; 16.2.1 and 16.4.1, in Gaul;
P. Lon. 1245, BGU 316, and P. Beatty Panop. 1.132, in
Egypt; for architectural evidence, see van Berchem 17, 29,
and 31 f., and C. Watzinger and K. Wulzinger, *Damaskus*
. . . (1924) 39 and 55–57; for inscriptions, D. Tudor, *Germania* 25 (1941) 240, on Romula; E. Will, *Rev. du Nord* 36
(1954) 143 f., on Amiens; *IRT* 907, on Ghadames; *CIL*
3.1633, 19, on Mehadia; G. Deschamps and G. Cousin, *BCH*
12 (1888) 102, in Caria shortly before 311; and van Berchem
104, on Aquileia; *Not. Dig. Or.* 28.14 and 16, etc.; and Mac-
Mullen, *Soldier and Civilian* 131. After the 350s, evidence becomes less relevant for our purposes, though more plentiful.

31   Amm. 18.9.3, the garrison installed; and 20.11.5, Ursulus' remarks on its failures.

32   R. O. Fink, *Roman Military Records on Papyrus* (1971)
381 f. = P. Dura 55 (218–220), *derelictis castris . . . disciplina . . . ut ex disciplina agant,* etc., Fink's restorations,
p. 382, being very free.

33   Petrikovits 192; M. Biro, *Acta archaeologica* 26 (1974) 33,

43 f., and 49; B. Saria, *Omagiu lui C. Daicoviciu* (1960) 497 f., association with military gravestones; B. Thomas, *Röm. Villen in Pannonien* (1964) 49, 60, 76, 114, 131 f. (legionary brick stamps), 153 f., 181 (military brick stamps), 207 (ditto), 226 (ditto), 243, 257 f. (ditto), 262 f. (ditto), 293 f. (ditto), 304 (ditto), 308 (ditto), 347, and 362; and MacMullen, *Soldier and Civilian* 147–149.

34 Paneg. vet. 4(8).9.4; *CT* 7.20.3 (320; 326). On the *laeti* and *gentiles* as a militia, much has been written, e.g. recently E. Demougeot, *Beiträge zur alten Geschichte . . . Festschr. für F. Altheim* (1970) 101 f. and 107 f.; W. Seston, *Historia* 4 (1955) 291; and above, n.7.

35 For tribal-occupied *castella* in Mauretania, see P.-A. Février, *Cah. de Tunisie* 15 (1967) 60–63; further east, Rachet 223 f. and van Berchem 21, 43–48, and 86, assuming that *limitanei* are active farmers; still further east, in Tripolitania, A. Di Vita, *Libya antiqua* 1 (1964) 72, 82–84 (denying the term *limitanei* to the occupants of the buildings), and 97, and P. Trousset, *Recherches sur le Limes Tripolitanus* (1974) 38 (seeing *limitanei* from the mid-third cent. on) and passim.

36 I would now carry further my doubts about formally enrolled members of the army doing any farming (cf. *Soldier and Civilian* 17 f.); but I do not think certainty is possible. For a compact statement of the arguments against farmer-soldiers, see Jones 650 f., against various other scholars, e.g. A. Piganiol, *L'empire chrétien*[2] (1972) 365, and Rachet, van Berchem, and Trousset in the preceding note. Terminology in itself—*ripenses* first in 325, *CT* 7.20.4, *militia limitanea* in 363, *CT* 12.1.56, *castellani* etc. later still—proves nothing on either side.

CHAPTER 9

1 Augustine, with similar passages, in MacMullen, *RIDA* 10 (1963) 224; above, chaps. 4, n.71; 5, n.16, and 7, n.48.

2 Above, chap. 1, n.38.

3 MacMullen, *Soldier and Civilian . . .* (1963) 171 f. and 179 f.; idem, *Art Bull.* 46 (1964) 448–450.

4   D. Vital, *Origins of Zionism* (1975) 288, an English observer
    in Constantinople in 1896, and p. 289, a French observer
    slightly later.

5   Above, chap. 7, n.6.

6   H. Henne, *Mitt. Papyrussammlung Oesterr. Nationalbiblio-
    thek* 5, 2 (1956) 64. The rise of great estates in Egypt is cer-
    tainly attested in the fourth cent. but should not be exagger-
    ated. One must balance the warnings of H. Braunert, *Die
    Binnenwanderung* . . . (1964) 312 f., and I. F. Fikhman,
    Jb. Oesterr. Byzantinistik 22 (1973) 17, against the views of
    G. Mickwitz, *Geld u. Wirtschaft im röm. Reich* . . . (1932)
    142, C. J. Kraemer and N. Lewis, *TAPA* 68 (1937) 366 f.,
    and J. Lallemand, *L'administration civile de l'Egypte* . . .
    (1964) 227 f.

7   P. Thead. 17 = A. S. Hunt and C. C. Edgar, *Select Papyri*
    2 (1956) 300 f. On the private armies of rural magnates, see
    CT 15.15.1 (364) and MacMullen, *Soldier and Civilian* 139 f.
    They are evidently at work in seizing other people's estates
    in Africa, Italy, and Spain, in *CT* 9.10.1 (317?) to 3 (319);
    9.1.1 (316; 317); and *CJ* 11.59.10 (398).

8   In Palestine, see D. Sperber, *Dine Israel* (Tel Aviv Univ.) 4
    (1973) xxiv; idem, *Israel Law Rev.* 8 (1973) 266; in Pan-
    nonia, E. B. Thomas, *Röm. Villen in Pannonien* (1964)
    389 f., and A. Mocsy, *Pannonia and Upper Moesia* . . .
    (1974) 236 and 239; in Gaul, A. Grenier, *Habitations gaul-
    oises . . . dans la cité des Médiomatrices* (1906) 180 f.;
    idem, *Manuel d'archéologie gallo-romaine* 2 (1934) 864 and
    936; in Italy, L. Cracco Ruggini, *Economia e società nell'Italia
    annonaria* (1961) 24 f. And *CT* 12.1.50.2 (362) applies gen-
    erally throughout the empire.

9   Emphasized but not studied: there seems to be no good treat-
    ment of rural autarky in the Principate, though surely the
    materials, mostly archaeological, exist for some advance in
    our knowledge. See, as random little items on manufacturing
    in cottages and villas, R. Lantier, *CRAI* 1947, 130; M. Amand
    and J. Willems, *Chron. arch. du pays de Liège* 54 (1963) 3–
    19; *Dig.* 14.4.1.1, 33.7.12.12; and *Bab. Talmud, Baba Kamma*
    10.9 and 119a. Similarly for the Dominate, e.g. Pallad. 1.6.2.

On the prominence of rent payable in kind in fourth-cent. Egypt, see Mickwitz 121–123, 127, 137, and 143, and more generally on "the preeminence enjoyed by rural property in the hierarchy of types of wealth," C. Dupont, *La réglementation économique dans les constitutions de Constantin* (1963) 22.

10 On magnates' juridical role, see Nemesianus in the second half of the third cent., *Ecl.* 1.52 f., *tu ruricolum discernere lites assueras;* with similar evidence in MacMullen, *Roman Social Relations* (1974) 39 f. On their dictating religion, see Aug., *Ep.* 58 and 66.1 f.; on private jails, *CT* 9.11.1 (388); on exploitation, Joh. Chrys., *Hom. in Matth.* 61.3 (*PG* 58.591 f.); on use of the terms *dominus* (δεσπότης), see G. Diosdi, *JJP* 14 (1962) 61 f.; I. Hahn, *Klio* 50 (1968) 262; and L. Flam-Zuckerman, *Historia* 21 (1972) 117.

11 *CT* 11.7.4 (327) and many later laws, e.g. 11.7.12; E. Wipszycka, *Eos* 50 (1966) 355.

12 *Symm., Rel.* 31.1 f., an extreme but interesting case.

13 *CJ* 2.13(14).1 (293), reviving a law of Claudius II against the *potentiorum domorum opes;* cf. P. Lon. 408 (346); and scofflaws in *CT* 1.16.4 (328); 9.38.10 (400; 405); A. Schulten, *JOAI* 9 (1906) 49; P. Petit, *Libanius et la vie municipale* . . . (1955) 34 nn.1 f., 40 n.1, and 151 f. n.11; MacMullen, *JRS* 54 (1964) 50–53; and above, chap. 4, nn.33 f. and 60; 5, n.4; and on venality of the courts up through our period, see chap. 4, nn.65–69; at a later date, Amm. 15.2.9; Synes., *Ep.* 2 (R. Hercher, *Epistolographi graeci,* p. 638); Symm., *Ep.* 9.116; Aug., *Sermo* 302.11; and many laws in the *CT.*

14 *CT* 13.10.1 (313); 11.16.3 (324; 325); and many later laws— but also earlier ones, *Dig.* 50.4.11.1 and 50.7.5.5; for Basil exerting his influence to get his taxes lowered, see M. Forlin Patrucco, *Athenaeum* 51 (1973) 300; and for a good illustration of how a man's tax load is increased by "those very powerful men of these parts, and violent, too," in the early fourth cent., see N. Lewis and A. A. Schiller in *Daube Noster. Essays . . . for D. Daube* (1974) 189 (datable, 191 n.9).

15 For senators as *potentes,* target of legislation, see e.g. *CT* 9.1.1 (317) and *CJ* 2.13(14).1.2.

16 Phrases strung together from Firm. Matern., *Math.* 3.4.30; 3.5.14 f. and 21; 3.6.1 and 9 f.; 3.7.21; and 3.10.7. On *pleni gratia,* see e.g. the letters in P. Ryl. 623 (317–324), and p. 104 f. of vol. IV of the Rylands papyri. On *patrocinium* more generally, see e.g. MacMullen, *HSCP* 68 (1964) 308–310 and 316 n.43, and esp. L. Harmand, *Le patronat sur les collectivités publiques* (1957) 447 and 421–466 passim.

17 SB 7673—the standard formula, see e.g. P. Oslo 111.

18 P. Cair. Isidor. 126.

19 *IG* 14.2300 (401), someone from a village (suggesting a peasant by origin) of Apamea, now in north Italy; similar cases in G. Brusin, *Aquileia nostra* 24–25 (1953–1954) 60, Syrian villagers in Aquileia and Trier; a settler in Pannonia from the territory (not the city) of Laodicea, *CIL* 3.4220; and MacMullen, *JRS* 54 (1964) 51.

20 Chap. 4, n.69.

INDEX

DATE DUE

GAYLORD			PRINTED IN U.S.A.